FONT

FONT

classic typefaces for
contemporary graphic design

TAMYE RIGGS
with James Grieshaber

RotoVision

A RotoVision Book

Published and distributed by RotoVision SA
Route Suisse 9
CH-1295 Mies
Switzerland

RotoVision SA
Sales and Editorial Office
Sheridan House, 114 Western Road
Hove BN3 1DD, UK

Tel: +44 (0)1273 72 72 68
Fax: +44 (0)1273 72 72 69
www.rotovision.com

10 9 8 7 6 5 4 3 2 1

ISBN: 978-2-88893-151-5

Art Director for RotoVision: Tony Seddon
Design: James Grieshaber
Typeset in Avenir Next LT Pro and Sabon Next LT Pro

Reprographics in Singapore by ProVision Pte.
Tel: +65 6334 7720
Fax: +65 6334 7721

Printing and binding in Singapore by Star Standard Industries (Pte) Ltd.

CONTENTS

1

2

3

INTRODUCTION

When RotoVision approached me about writing this book, they positioned it as both a tribute to historic type design and a typographic reference. The general idea was to highlight each included typeface with specimen showings and informational text, and to provide a few examples of the type in use, along with some typographic reference tools.

I was immediately taken with the idea. I could see tremendous potential for such a type book. Let me preface this by saying that I'm a big fan of living type designers and I support their efforts as much as possible. But while plenty of graphic designers employ new typefaces in their projects, there is still a tremendous amount of stunning work being produced using type that originated in the twentieth century and much earlier.

I started checking in with some of my favorite graphic designers and exploring portfolios on the web. It became evident rather quickly that RotoVision's initial list of fonts would have to be adjusted to some degree. A few of the proposed script and display types weren't seen in use enough to warrant inclusion, even though they were historically important. To my dismay, the script section shrank tremendously—designers use a lot of scripts, but primarily newer arrivals that can't yet be considered classics.

After careful consideration, and no small amount of debate with a few fellow type fanatics, I decided to include several typefaces from the latter part of the twentieth century in the book. While purists might argue that typefaces from the 1980s and 1990s such as Meta and Cezanne are not "historical" enough and have no place alongside Baskerville and Helvetica, it begs the question, "When does a typeface become a classic?" This is not as easy to define as one might think. I'll take the liberty of equating typefaces with automobiles. Some automotive enthusiasts consider James Bond's first Aston Martin DB5, from *Goldfinger* (1964), a classic, while others point to the 1955 Ford Thunderbird convertible as a better example. At the extreme ends of the spectrum, the Ford Model T, which first came to market in 1908, is undeniably a classic, but so is the highly combustible 1973 Pinto from the same manufacturer (by regulatory standards, anyway). In fact, it seems that every few years a new vehicle is deemed an "instant classic" by someone in a position to make such judgments.

Meta became incredibly popular upon its public release in 1991, as did Cezanne, which, although it was released in 1996, is based on the handwriting of a French Impressionist painter who left this world in 1906.

Car buffs are keen to describe the objects of their affections with terms like historic, collectible, and antique—all of which can be applied to typefaces. It seems logical to call Monotype's Bembo historic, since it was modeled on letterforms from 1495. But this design was first revived for metal in 1929, while the legalese in the Bembo Book roman OpenType font includes copyright notices for the years 1990 and 2005 (the font file itself was created in 2006). Blackoak and Rosewood are certainly antique, as well as highly collectible, albeit in their original nineteenth-century wood forms. But they weren't actually digitized until the early 1990s. Trajan could be called ancient—although it was developed as a digital typeface in 1989, it was derived from the inscription on Trajan's Column in Rome (a monument that was completed in AD 113). Helvetica and Univers have been significantly updated and expanded since they first came into being in the 1950s—are they not still classic models, even in their retooled forms?

How, then, did we determine which fonts would be featured in a book about "classic" fonts? Ultimately, this book is a collection of typefaces that hallmark important eras in typographic and printing history. We consider all of these types to be classics in their own right, as do the typographers around the world who use them.

There are 46 "base" typeface sections, many shown in multiple styles and weights. If a design has become available in multiple versions and from multiple sources over the years, we've tried to list at least one of those alternatives. We limited the alternate listings to those with very similar names—for example, there are dozens of Garamond-inspired fonts on the market under a variety of names, but we focused our listings on those bearing the Garamond name to try to avoid confusion. (Exploring some of the typographic references listed in the back will yield many related treasures.)

As you look through this book, you'll notice that some typefaces have more pages devoted to "type in use" than others. After reviewing thousands of creative projects for possible inclusion, we realized this weighting was necessary. We felt it was critical to offer the truest snapshot of what contemporary designers are using in their work. What is included is ultimately not the preference of the authors—the content evolved organically from a thorough exploration of typography in the design world.

—*Tamye Riggs*

ACKNOWLEDGMENTS

This book would not have been possible without the support and contributions of many valued friends and colleagues.

I want to thank my partner on this project and many others, James Grieshaber from Typeco. Not only did he design this book, but he contributed thoughtful ideas and took part in countless discussions about its content. He was a pleasure to work with, and his participation was essential to the success of this project.

I owe thanks to many other wonderful people:

Tony Seddon and Lindy Dunlop from RotoVision, for their patience and guidance throughout this entire project.

Karen Cheng, for suggesting to RotoVision that I was the right person to write this book.

Tiffany Wardle de Sousa, for her ideas, enthusiasm, and assistance with research.

Allan Haley and Deborah Gonet from Monotype Imaging, Otmar Hoefer from Linotype, Richard Kegler from P22, and Stephen Coles from FontShop and Typographica. Their support of the type community is unflagging, and their early commitment and "can-do" attitudes helped this project come to fruition.

Friends from other participating foundries who contributed wholeheartedly: Veronika Elsner, Wolfgang Hartmann, Harvey Hunt, Hans van Leeuwen, David Lemon, Jim Lyles, Harry Parker, Thomas Phinney, and Peter Rosenfeld.

Gregory Ruffa, for shedding more light on the shrouded mysteries of wood type.

I wish to acknowledge the volunteer Board of Directors of The Society of Typographic Aficionados (sota) and everyone involved in TypeCon, an event that keeps me deeply involved with the type community on an ongoing basis. I am blessed to work with such an amazing group of people who are as passionate about type as I am. Daily, they inspire me to continue learning and helping others to learn about type and typography.

Most of all, I wish to thank my family, who were so patient over the months I have been engrossed in this project. My mother, Barbara Peerson, fielded countless phone calls and offered continual support and encouragement. My son, Jonathan Charles Jones, is a constant source of inspiration in all things and is also turning out to be a fine young apprentice.

HOW TO USE THIS BOOK

1 Typeface Name This denotes the generic name of a typeface design featured in each section. Some typefaces have evolved over the years so that many variations by multiple designers and foundries take the name of the original design/designer. For example, multiple versions of Bodoni and Baskerville have been developed since the original types were cast in metal. But a typeface like FF Meta, which originated in the digital era, has so far been developed only under the direction of its original creator, and has only been published by the originating foundry.

2 Typeface Sample This area shows common Latin alpha-numerics and some punctuation and diacritics from a base weight of the principal type design featured in this section. In a text design, this sample will usually be shown in a roman or regular style. Characters that are particularly helpful in identifying a featured typeface are highlighted in red.

3 Other Styles This section shows some of the additional weights and style variants that are available for a given type family, over and above its base weight/style.

4 Other Notable Cuts Multiple versions of a type design are shown, when available, to illustrate the similarities and differences that might have been applied to a historic type design. The additional versions of a featured typeface might be from the same foundry and/or designer as the original, or be a completely different interpretation or revival.

5 Text Sample This section illustrates how the base weight of a typeface design looks at different text sizes.

CLARENDON

slab serif • bracketed serifs

9/10pt
HOW RAZORBACK-JUMPING FROGS CAN LEVEL SIX piqued gymnasts! Jackdaws love my big sphinx of quartz. Jaded zombies acted quaintly but kept driving their oxen forward. The quick brown fox jumps over a lazy dog. The public was amazed to view the quickness and dexterity of the juggler. A mad boxer shot a quick, gloved jab to the jaw of his dizzy opponent. The five boxing wizards jump

10/12pt
HOW RAZORBACK-JUMPING FROGS CAN LEVEL six piqued gymnasts! Jackdaws love my big sphinx of quartz. Jaded zombies acted quaintly but kept driving their oxen forward. The quick brown fox jumps over a lazy dog. The public was amazed to view the quickness and dexterity of the juggler. A

12/14pt
HOW RAZORBACK-JUMPING FROGS CAN level six piqued gymnasts! Jackdaws love my big sphinx of quartz. Jaded zombies acted quaintly but kept driving their oxen

Clarendon Roman
abcdefghijklmnopqrstuvwxyz12345678
ABCDEFGHIJKLMNOPQRSTUVWXYZ

Clarendon Heavy
abcdefghijklmnopqrstuvwxyz1234567
ABCDEFGHIJKLMNOPQRSTUVWXYZ

Clarendon Bold
abcdefghijklmnopqrstuvwxyz1234567
ABCDEFGHIJKLMNOPQRSTUVWXYZ

Clarendon Black
abcdefghijklmnopqrstuvwxyz1234567
ABCDEFGHIJKLMNOPQRSTUVWXYZ

Clarendon Condensed
abcdefghijklmnopqrstuvwxyz1234567890
ABCDEFGHIJKLMNOPQRSTUVWXYZ

Other notable cuts:
Clarendon LT [Linotype]

Clarendon Light [Bitstream]
abcdefghijklmnopqrstuvwxyz
ABCDEFGHIJKLMNOPQ
RSTUVWXYZ1234567890
[àóüßç](.,:;?!$€£&-*){ÀÓÜÇ}

52

Old Style

Originating from the Renaissance and fifteenth-century Venetian printers, Old Style types were based on pen-drawn forms. Garalde, Aldine, and Venetian are groups in the Old Style class. Also called Old Face. Examples include Goudy (above) and Sabon.

Transitional

A class of Serif types first introduced in the late eighteenth century by John Baskerville, Transitional styles (also called Réale or Realist) are the major class between Old Style and Modern faces. Examples include Baskerville (above) and Perpetua.

Modern/Didone

Moderns retain some of the characteristics of engraving. These high-contrast letterforms date from the late eighteenth to early nineteenth centuries and feature vertical stresses and straight serifs. Examples include Bodoni (above) and Walbaum.

Slab Serif/Egyptian

A style with slab or square serifs and nearly uniform strokes. Forms are low-contrast and usually mechanistic. Slab designs may have unbracketed (see Rockwell, above) or bracketed serifs (see Clarendon).

Major changes to the face of typography came with the Industrial Revolution. For more than three centuries, typography and printing had been firmly tied to book publishing and its refined aesthetics. In the early 1800s, the printing industry veered off in a new direction. New print media appealing to the masses—newspapers, magazines, and all forms of advertising—were emerging as a dominant force, calling for a new style of type design compatible with mass production and consumer tastes. Print journalism necessitated types that were both readable and boldly eye-catching. Slab Serifs, also known as Egyptian typefaces, quickly became the flavor of the day.

A more evolved form of Egyptian was Clarendon, designed by Robert Besley for London's Fann Street Foundry in 1845. It was intended as a bold display companion to text faces for commercial printing. This design, named for the Clarendon Press in Oxford, had the strong presence of the typical Egyptian, but was more refined, with greater contrast between thick and thin strokes and its trademark bracketed serifs. Its instant success spurred multiple foundries to issue their own variants, and an entire sub-classification of Slab Serifs was named after the typeface. Clarendon's popularity continued, and Edouard Hoffmann and Hermann Eidenbenz at Haas revived the typeface in 1953. A variety of Clarendons have been issued since then, with added weights and styles making this design suitable for both text and display applications.

If you like …

Clarendon

… you could also consider:

Bookman
Century
Courier
Rockwell
ROSEWOOD

Near left:
POSTER
Client New Dance Horizons
Studio Bradbury Branding and Design
Principal Typeface Clarendon

Far left:
PACKAGING
Client CasCioppo Brothers
Studio Turnstyle
Designer Madeleine Eiche
Principal Typefaces Trade Gothic, Clarendon Bold, Century Gothic, and Helvetica Neue

53

6 Classification These labels denote the major classifications, sub-classifications, and other major typographic categories that are traditionally used to describe a featured typeface design (see descriptions below).

7 Diagram This area shows character earmarks that are often found in a particular typeface classification and/or sub-class.

8 Historical Notes This section describes the development of featured typefaces. Information can include notes on the era the type was developed, details about its designer and/or foundry, applications, why it is significant to the history of typography, and other important facts.

9 Cross-reference This section lists other typefaces in this book that are harmonious in terms of style, classification, or feel. For example, the cross-reference for a Geometric Sans Serif like Futura will include other Geometric types, as well as typefaces in other classifications that would be well suited to similar applications.

10 Graphic Samples Each featured typeface is shown in use in contemporary design. Some typefaces are used strictly for text purposes, while other examples show type in use more as a primary graphic element in a piece of design. Some samples also show the typeface as inspiration for an illustration or a starting point for a new custom type design. The popularity of a given type design can be measured proportionately by how many in-use examples are displayed in this book.

Grotesque

This class of Sans Serif typefaces is also referred to as Gothic. Forms have some contrast and may have quirky characteristics. Examples include Akzidenz-Grotesk and Bureau Grotesque (above).

Geometric

A class of Sans Serif influenced by the Bauhaus movement. Forms are low contrast and mechanistic. Examples include Futura (above) and Eurostile.

Humanist

A class of Sans Serif types based on Humanist Roman faces, bearing characteristics of hand-drawn forms. Examples include Frutiger and Gill Sans (above).

Neo-Grotesque

This class of Sans Serif typefaces is based on the nineteenth-century Grotesque model, but its members are more modern. Forms are low-contrast and neutral. Examples include Helvetica (above) and Univers.

TYPOGRAPHIC TIMELINE

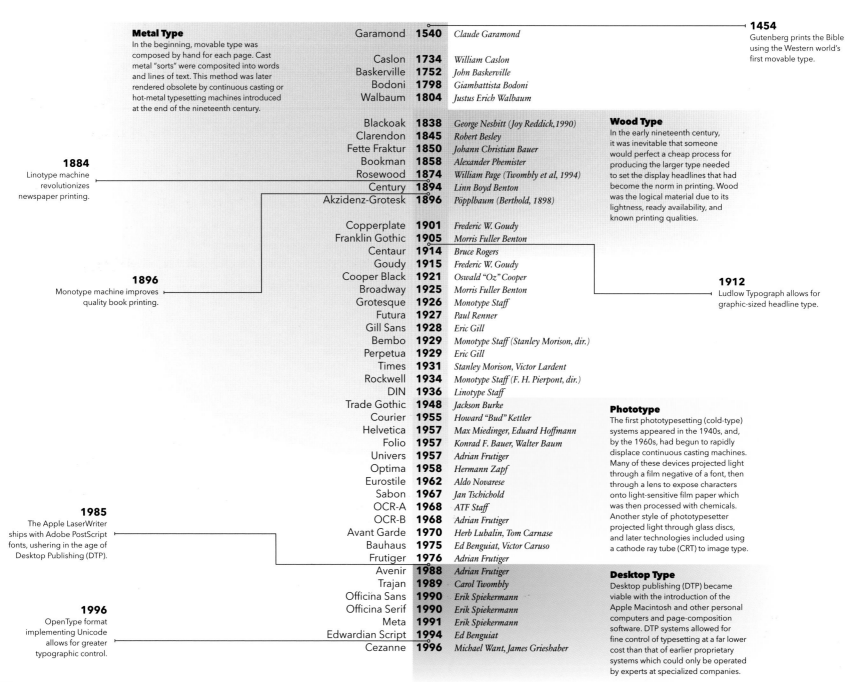

Metal Type
In the beginning, movable type was composed by hand for each page. Cast metal "sorts" were composited into words and lines of text. This method was later rendered obsolete by continuous casting or hot-metal typesetting machines introduced at the end of the nineteenth century.

Garamond **1540** *Claude Garamond*

Caslon **1734** *William Caslon*
Baskerville **1752** *John Baskerville*
Bodoni **1798** *Giambattista Bodoni*
Walbaum **1804** *Justus Erich Walbaum*

1454
Gutenberg prints the Bible using the Western world's first movable type.

Blackoak **1838** *George Nesbitt (Joy Reddick,1990)*
Clarendon **1845** *Robert Besley*
Fette Fraktur **1850** *Johann Christian Bauer*
Bookman **1858** *Alexander Phemister*
Rosewood **1874** *William Page (Twombly et al, 1994)*
Century **1894** *Linn Boyd Benton*
Akzidenz-Grotesk **1896** *Pöpplbaum (Berthold, 1898)*

Wood Type
In the early nineteenth century, it was inevitable that someone would perfect a cheap process for producing the larger type needed to set the display headlines that had become the norm in printing. Wood was the logical material due to its lightness, ready availability, and known printing qualities.

1884
Linotype machine revolutionizes newspaper printing.

Copperplate **1901** *Frederic W. Goudy*
Franklin Gothic **1905** *Morris Fuller Benton*
Centaur **1914** *Bruce Rogers*
Goudy **1915** *Frederic W. Goudy*
Cooper Black **1921** *Oswald "Oz" Cooper*
Broadway **1925** *Morris Fuller Benton*
Grotesque **1926** *Monotype Staff*
Futura **1927** *Paul Renner*
Gill Sans **1928** *Eric Gill*
Bembo **1929** *Monotype Staff (Stanley Morison, dir.)*
Perpetua **1929** *Eric Gill*
Times **1931** *Stanley Morison, Victor Lardent*
Rockwell **1934** *Monotype Staff (F. H. Pierpont, dir.)*
DIN **1936** *Linotype Staff*

1896
Monotype machine improves quality book printing.

1912
Ludlow Typograph allows for graphic-sized headline type.

Trade Gothic **1948** *Jackson Burke*
Courier **1955** *Howard "Bud" Kettler*
Helvetica **1957** *Max Miedinger, Eduard Hoffmann*
Folio **1957** *Konrad F. Bauer, Walter Baum*
Univers **1957** *Adrian Frutiger*
Optima **1958** *Hermann Zapf*
Eurostile **1962** *Aldo Novarese*
Sabon **1967** *Jan Tschichold*
OCR-A **1968** *ATF Staff*
OCR-B **1968** *Adrian Frutiger*
Avant Garde **1970** *Herb Lubalin, Tom Carnase*
Bauhaus **1975** *Ed Benguiat, Victor Caruso*
Frutiger **1976** *Adrian Frutiger*

Phototype
The first phototypesetting (cold-type) systems appeared in the 1940s, and, by the 1960s, had begun to rapidly displace continuous casting machines. Many of these devices projected light through a film negative of a font, then through a lens to expose characters onto light-sensitive film paper which was then processed with chemicals. Another style of phototypesetter projected light through glass discs, and later technologies included using a cathode ray tube (CRT) to image type.

1985
The Apple LaserWriter ships with Adobe PostScript fonts, ushering in the age of Desktop Publishing (DTP).

Avenir **1988** *Adrian Frutiger*
Trajan **1989** *Carol Twombly*
Officina Sans **1990** *Erik Spiekermann*
Officina Serif **1990** *Erik Spiekermann*
Meta **1991** *Erik Spiekermann*
Edwardian Script **1994** *Ed Benguiat*
Cezanne **1996** *Michael Want, James Grieshaber*

Desktop Type
Desktop publishing (DTP) became viable with the introduction of the Apple Macintosh and other personal computers and page-composition software. DTP systems allowed for fine control of typesetting at a far lower cost than that of earlier proprietary systems which could only be operated by experts at specialized companies.

1996
OpenType format implementing Unicode allows for greater typographic control.

VISUAL FONT INDEX

ABCDEFGHIJI

This text is set in Berthold Walbaum Book Bold

KLMSERIFNOF

BASKERVILLE

transitional serif • legible

od

9/10pt

HOW RAZORBACK-JUMPING FROGS CAN LEVEL SIX piqued gymnasts! Jackdaws love my big sphinx of quartz. Jaded zombies acted quaintly but kept driving their oxen forward. The quick brown fox jumps over a lazy dog. The public was amazed to view the quickness and dexterity of the juggler. A mad boxer shot a quick, gloved jab to the jaw of his dizzy opponent. The five boxing wizards jump quickly. How razorback-jumping frogs can level six piqued

10/12pt

HOW RAZORBACK-JUMPING FROGS CAN LEVEL SIX piqued gymnasts! Jackdaws love my big sphinx of quartz. Jaded zombies acted quaintly but kept driving their oxen forward. The quick brown fox jumps over a lazy dog. The public was amazed to view the quickness and dexterity of the juggler. A mad boxer shot a quick, gloved jab to the jaw of his dizzy opponent. The

12/14pt

HOW RAZORBACK-JUMPING FROGS CAN level six piqued gymnasts! Jackdaws love my big sphinx of quartz. Jaded zombies acted quaintly but kept driving their oxen forward. The quick brown fox

Baskerville Italic

abcdefghijklmnopqrstuvwxyz1234567890
ABCDEFGHIJKLMNOPQRSTUVWXYZ

Baskerville Bold

abcdefghijklmnopqrstuvwxyz12345678
ABCDEFGHIJKLMNOPQRSTUVWXYZ

Baskerville Bold Italic

abcdefghijklmnopqrstuvwxyz12345678
ABCDEFGHIJKLMNOPQRSTUVWXYZ

Other notable cuts:

Baskerville Oldface [URW++]
Baskerville BT [Bitstream]
ITC New Baskerville [ITC]
Baskerville Classico [Linotype]

Baskerville [Monotype Imaging]

abcdefghijklmnopqrstuvwxyz
ABCDEFGHIJKLMNOPQ
RSTUVWXYZ1234567890
[àóüßç](.,:;?!$€£&-*){ÀÓÜÇ}

A legend of the printing and lettering arts, John Baskerville (1706–1775) was somewhat overshadowed during his lifetime by his more renowned contemporary William Caslon I. Baskerville is now considered one of the two transformative figures of British printing and typefounding history.

After working as a headstone engraver in Birmingham, UK, Baskerville raised the capital to set up a printing business, hiring John Handy as his punchcutter. With the goal of creating a typographically perfect book, Baskerville was responsible for innovations in press construction, printing ink, and papermaking, and experimented with improving legibility.

His seminal namesake typefaces were the result of his desire to improve upon Caslon's Old Style types. He began designing the Baskerville faces circa 1752, giving careful attention to drawing consistent and refined letterforms that retained the elegance and spirit of the hand. Baskerville's types were popular throughout the remainder of the eighteenth century, when they fell out of favor with the advent of Modern designs like Bodoni.

In 1917, American typographer Bruce Rogers revived Baskerville, using it in work for the Harvard University Press. The Baskerville types soon became fashionable again. In 1923, Stanley Morison created a version for British Monotype as part of its program of historical revivals. George W. Jones' revival for Linotype appeared in 1929, and soon every major foundry had its own version of Baskerville. A variety of Baskerville-inspired designs have been developed in the digital era and are frequently seen in quality book typography and similar projects where readability and refinement are the focus.

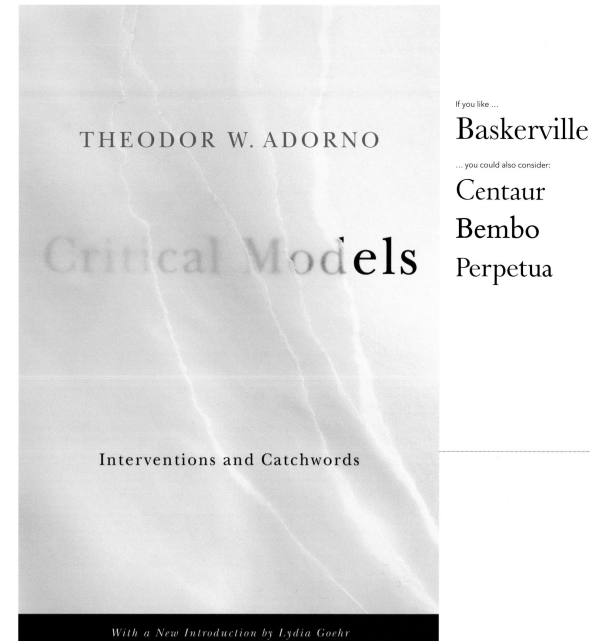

BOOK COVER
Publisher Columbia University Press, New York
Studio Salamander Hill Design
Designer David Drummond
Principal Typeface ITC Baskerville

If you like …

Baskerville

… you could also consider:

Centaur

Bembo

Perpetua

PACKAGING
Client Mastronardi Produce
Studio Crave, Inc.
Designers Russ Martin and David Edmundson
Principal Typeface Baskerville

New packaging system developed for Sunset Gourmet fresh produce line.

PRINTS
Studio Ginger Monkey
Designer Ginger Monkey/Tom Lane
Principal Typeface Baskerville

Inspiring Words series of limited-edition prints.

Con Gioia
EARLY MUSIC ENSEMBLE

presents

THE MUSICAL WORLD
OF JANE AUSTEN

*Songs & Sonatas from Her Own Collection
with Readings from Her Novels*

renowned soprano

JULIANNE BAIRD

*with
fortepianist,* PREETHI de SILVA
and ALFRED CRAMER, *violinist
and readings from Austen's novels by
British actress* MICHELLE ARTHUR

Songs by Handel, Gluck,
Arne, Dibdin, Storace *et al.*
Instrumental music by
Haydn *and*
Maria Hester Park
        née Reynolds

Sunday
FEBRUARY 4, 2007
5:00 P.M.
The NEIGHBORHOOD CHURCH
301 North Orange Grove Blvd.
Pasadena, CA 91103

General admission: $25
Seniors, SCEMS, EMA: $20
Friends of Con Gioia: $18
Students (with ID) and children: $15
Prepaid reservations (to be held at the door)
accepted until February 2.
Please send checks to
Con Gioia, 1020 Kent Drive
Claremont, CA 91711
www.congioia.org

MAILER
Client Con Gioia
Studio still room
Designer Jessica Fleischmann
Principal Typefaces Baskerville and ITC Edwardian Script

Promotional piece for Con Gioia's World of Jane Austen concert.

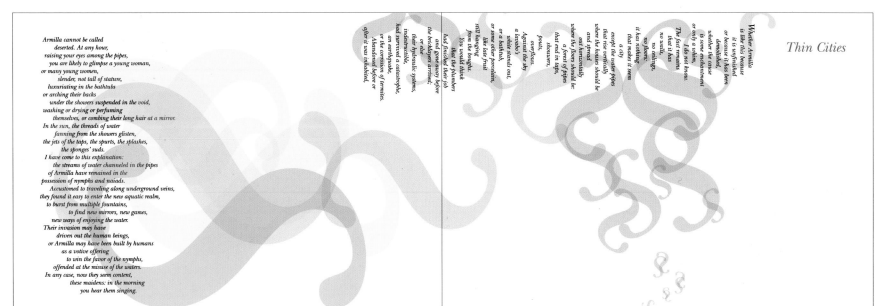

Armilla cannot be called
deserted. At any hour,
raising your eyes among the pipes,
you are likely to glimpse a young woman,
or many young women,
slender, not tall of stature,
luxuriating in the bathtubs
or arching their backs
under the showers suspended in the void,
washing or drying or perfuming
themselves, or combing their long hair at a mirror.
In the sun, the threads of water
fanning from the showers glisten,
the jets of the taps, the spurts, the splashes,
the sponges' suds.
I have come to this explanation:
the streams of water channeled in the pipes
of Armilla have remained in the
possession of nymphs and naiads.
Accustomed to traveling along underground veins,
they found it easy to enter the new aquatic realm,
to burst from multiple fountains,
to find new mirrors, new games,
new ways of enjoying the water.
Their invasion may have
driven out the human beings,
or Armilla may have been built by humans
as a votive offering
to win the favor of the nymphs,
offended at the misuse of the waters.
In any case, now they seem content,
these maidens: in the morning
you hear them singing.

Whether Armilla
is like this because
it is unfinished
or because it has been
demolished,
whether the cause
is some enchantment
or only a whim,
I do not know.
The fact remains
that it has
no walls,
no floors,
no ceilings,
that makes it seem
it has nothing
a city
except the water pipes
that rise vertically
where the houses should be
and spread
out horizontally
where the floors should be:
a forest of pipes
that end in taps,
showers,
spouts,
overflows.
Against the sky
a lavabo's
white stands out,
or a bathtub,
or some other porcelain,
like late fruit
still hanging
from the boughs.
You would think
that the plumbers
had finished their job
and gone away before
the bricklayers arrived;
or else
their hydraulic systems,
indestructible,
had survived a catastrophe,
an earthquake,
or the corrosion of termites.
Abandoned before or
after it was inhabited,

Thin Cities

Both images this page:

BOOK
Designer Natalia Tomaszewska
Principal Typefaces Baskerville and Univers

*Handmade book with experimental typography
based on the book* Invisible Cities *by Italo Calvino.*

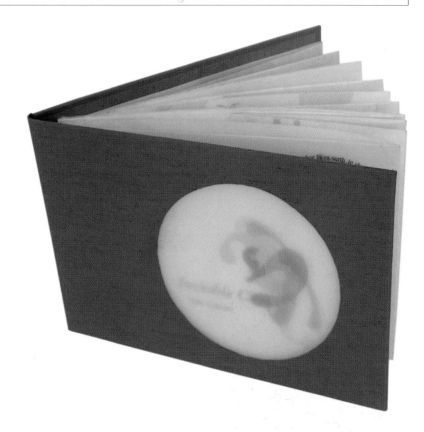

ERIC HELLEINER

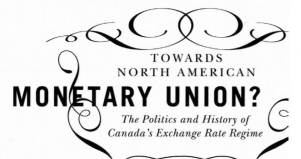

TOWARDS
NORTH AMERICAN
MONETARY UNION?
*The Politics and History of
Canada's Exchange Rate Regime*

MATTHEW KNEALE

Whitbread Award-winning author of *English Passengers*

Smal Crimes

in an Age

of Abundance

Stories

"Electrifies. . . . A firecracker in broad daylight, an out-of-nowhere bombshell sure
to throw some sparks in the literary world. . . . Kneale's characters are wholly
believable, his plots flawless. . . . [He is an] extraordinary author."
—*The San Diego Union-Tribune*

Near left:
BOOK COVER
Publisher Random House, New York
Studio Salamander Hill Design
Designer David Drummond
Principal Typeface ITC New Baskerville

Far left:
BOOK COVER
Publisher McGill-Queen's University Press, Montreal
Studio Salamander Hill Design
Designer David Drummond
Principal Typefaces Trade Gothic and
   ITC New Baskerville

LOGO
Client Cassis Catering
Studio Typeco
Designer James Grieshaber
Principal Typeface Baskerville Classico

BEMBO

garalde • legible

od

9/10pt

HOW RAZORBACK-JUMPING FROGS CAN LEVEL SIX PIQUED gymnasts! Jackdaws love my big sphinx of quartz. Jaded zombies acted quaintly but kept driving their oxen forward. The quick brown fox jumps over a lazy dog. The public was amazed to view the quickness and dexterity of the juggler. A mad boxer shot a quick, gloved jab to the jaw of his dizzy opponent. The five boxing wizards jump quickly.

10/12pt

HOW RAZORBACK-JUMPING FROGS CAN LEVEL SIX piqued gymnasts! Jackdaws love my big sphinx of quartz. Jaded zombies acted quaintly but kept driving their oxen forward. The quick brown fox jumps over a lazy dog. The public was amazed to view the quickness and dexterity of the juggler. A mad boxer shot a quick, gloved jab to the jaw of his dizzy opponent. The five boxing

12/14pt

HOW RAZORBACK-JUMPING FROGS CAN level six piqued gymnasts! Jackdaws love my big sphinx of quartz. Jaded zombies acted quaintly but kept driving their oxen forward. The quick brown fox jumps over a lazy dog. The public was amazed to view the quickness

Bembo Book Italic

abcdefghijklmnopqrstuvwxyz1234567890
ABCDEFGHIJKLMNOPQRSTUVWXYZ

Bembo Book Bold

abcdefghijklmnopqrstuvwxyz1234567890
ABCDEFGHIJKLMNOPQRSTUVWXYZ

Bembo Book Bold Italic

abcdefghijklmnopqrstuvwxyz1234567890
ABCDEFGHIJKLMNOPQRSTUVWXYZ

Other notable cuts:

BEMBO TITLING [Monotype Imaging]

Bembo Infant [Monotype Imaging]

Bembo [Monotype Imaging]

Bembo Book [Monotype Imaging]

abcdefghijklmnopqrstuvwxyz
ABCDEFGHIJKLMNOPQ
RSTUVWXYZ1234567890
[àóüßç](.,:;?!$€£&-*){ÀÓÜÇ}

Bembo was modeled on a Roman design by Venetian punchcutter Francesco Griffo in 1495. This typeface was created for Aldus Manutius' printing of *De Aetna*, a text by Italian Cardinal Pietro Bembo, and was also used to great effect in *Hypnerotomachia Poliphili*, considered one of the most beautiful books of the fifteenth century. Parisian publisher Claude Garamond took inspiration from this face in his own type-design endeavors—the original Garamond types display the influence of Griffo's handiwork. Griffo's types, the Garamonds, and other Old Style faces were in widespread use in Europe for two centuries.

In 1929, Monotype Corporation resurrected Griffo's work as part of its historic revivals program. Under the supervision of Stanley Morison, a Roman based on Griffo's punches was carefully drawn to capture the spirit of the original (dubbed Bembo in honor of the famed pontiff). As Griffo had not cut italics, Bembo's italic variants were derived from the work of Venetian writing master Giovanni Tagliente (1524).

LOGO
Clients Friends of Vista House and Oregon State Parks Trust
Studio Jeff Fisher LogoMotives
Designer Jeff Fisher
Creative Director Sue Fisher
Principal Typefaces Bembo and Copperplate

VISTA HOUSE
EST. 1918
RESTORE THE JEWEL AT CROWN POINT

LEARNING TO LOOK

A VISUAL

RESPONSE TO

MAVIS GALLANT'S

FICTION

LESLEY D. CLEMENT

BOOK COVER
Publisher McGill-Queen's University Press, Montreal
Studio Salamander Hill Design
Designer David Drummond
Principal Typefaces Bembo and Futura

If you like …

Bembo

… you could also consider:

Baskerville
Centaur
Garamond
Goudy
Sabon

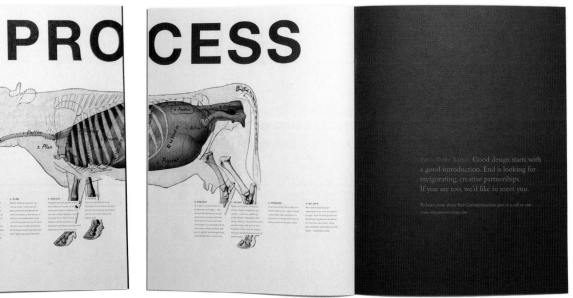

PROCESS

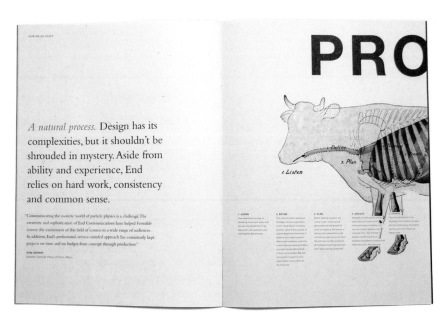

A natural process. Design has its complexities, but it shouldn't be shrouded in mystery. Aside from ability and experience, End relies on hard work, consistency and common sense.

"Communicating the esoteric world of particle physics is a challenge. The creativity and sophistication of End Communications have helped Fermilab convey the excitement of this field of science to a wide range of audiences. In addition, End's professional, service-minded approach has consistently kept projects on time and on budget from concept through production."

Andy Jackson
Director, Fermilab Office of Public Affairs

Let's shake hands. Good design starts with a good introduction. End is looking for invigorating, creative partnerships. If you are too, we'd like to meet you.

To learn more about End Communications, give us a call or visit www.endcommunications.com.

PROSPECTUS
Studio End Communications
Principal Typefaces Helvetica Neue and Bembo

PROMOTION
Client Norwegian Chamber Orchestra
Studio Neue Design Studio
Designers Benjamin Stenmarck and Øystein Haugseth
Principal Typefaces Sloop, Bembo, and Perpetua

Promotion for the orchestra's performance of Dido & Aeneas. *The opera was part of the Hard Barokk concept (a new approach to classical music, fusing baroque with rap) and was shown at the Oslo Winternight Festival. Commission included all promotional material, illustrations, identities, and backdrops. Neue also developed the identity for Hard Barokk, featuring a heavily modified/illustrated version of Bembo at its center.*

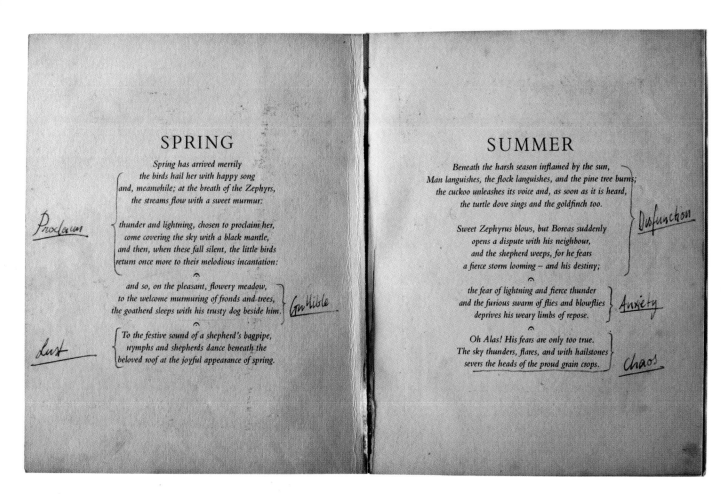

SPRING

Spring has arrived merrily
the birds hail her with happy song
and, meanwhile; at the breath of the Zephyrs,
the streams flow with a sweet murmur:

thunder and lightning, chosen to proclaim her,
come covering the sky with a black mantle,
and then, when these fall silent, the little birds
return once more to their melodious incantation:

and so, on the pleasant, flowery meadow,
to the welcome murmuring of fronds and trees,
the goatherd sleeps with his trusty dog beside him.

To the festive sound of a shepherd's bagpipe,
nymphs and shepherds dance beneath the
beloved roof at the joyful appearance of spring.

Proclaim

Gullible

Lust

SUMMER

Beneath the harsh season inflamed by the sun,
Man languishes, the flock languishes, and the pine tree burns;
the cuckoo unleashes its voice and, as soon as it is heard,
the turtle dove sings and the goldfinch too.

Sweet Zephyrus blows, but Boreas suddenly
opens a dispute with his neighbour,
and the shepherd weeps, for he fears
a fierce storm looming – and his destiny;

the fear of lightning and fierce thunder
and the furious swarm of flies and blowflies
deprives his weary limbs of repose.

Oh Alas! His fears are only too true.
The sky thunders, flares, and with hailstones
severs the heads of the proud grain crops.

Dysfunction

Anxiety

Chaos

MUSIC PACKAGING
Studio Neue Design Studio
Designer Benjamin Stenmarck
Principal Typeface Bembo

This student project was created to pay homage to The Four Seasons *by Vivaldi. The CD cover was designed as a booklet featuring 12 illustrations based on the artist's interpretation of the music.*

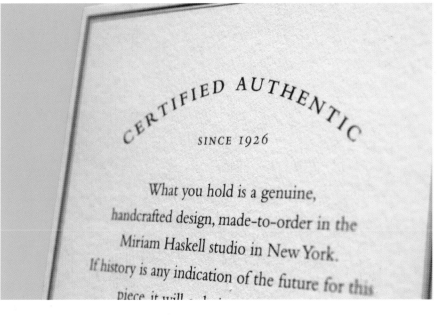

CERTIFIED AUTHENTIC

SINCE 1926

What you hold is a genuine,
handcrafted design, made-to-order in the
Miriam Haskell studio in New York.
If history is any indication of the future for this
piece, it will...

COLLATERAL
Client Miriam Haskell
Studio Think Studio
Designers John Clifford and Herb Thornby
Copywriter Mary-Catherine Jones
Principal Typeface Bembo

BODONI

od

9/10pt

HOW RAZORBACK-JUMPING FROGS CAN LEVEL SIX PIQUED gymnasts! Jackdaws love my big sphinx of quartz. Jaded zombies acted quaintly but kept driving their oxen forward. The quick brown fox jumps over a lazy dog. The public was amazed to view the quickness and dexterity of the juggler. A mad boxer shot a quick, gloved jab to the jaw of his dizzy opponent. The five boxing wizards jump quickly.

10/12pt

HOW RAZORBACK-JUMPING FROGS CAN LEVEL SIX piqued gymnasts! Jackdaws love my big sphinx of quartz. Jaded zombies acted quaintly but kept driving their oxen forward. The quick brown fox jumps over a lazy dog. The public was amazed to view the quickness and dexterity of the juggler. A mad boxer shot a quick, gloved jab to the jaw of his dizzy opponent. The five box

12/14pt

HOW RAZORBACK-JUMPING FROGS CAN LEVEL six piqued gymnasts! Jackdaws love my big sphinx of quartz. Jaded zombies acted quaintly but kept driving their oxen forward. The quick brown fox jumps over a lazy dog. The public was amazed to view the quickness

Bodoni Book Italic

abcdefghijklmnopqrstuvwxyz1234567890
ABCDEFGHIJKLMNOPQRSTUVWXYZ

Bodoni Bold

abcdefghijklmnopqrstuvwxyz123456789
ABCDEFGHIJKLMNOPQRSTUVWXYZ

Bodoni Bold Italic

abcdefghijklmnopqrstuvwxyz123456789
ABCDEFGHIJKLMNOPQRSTUVWXYZ

Other notable cuts:

Bodoni Poster [Adobe]

Bauer Bodoni [Linotype]

ITC Bodoni Six [ITC]

ITC Bodoni Seventy-Two [ITC]

Bodoni Book [Adobe]

abcdefghijklmnopqrstuvwxyz

ABCDEFGHIJKLMNOPQ

RSTUVWXYZ1234567890

[àóüßç](.,:;?!$€£&-*){ÀÓÜÇ}

At the end of the eighteenth century, in Parma, Italy, Giambattista Bodoni developed a series of typefaces to exemplify his ideal of contemporary typographic beauty and evolve the work of his idol John Baskerville. Bodoni types are known for their high-contrast, slightly condensed vertical forms. Part of the Modern/Didone class, Bodoni types were more geometrically inspired than their predecessors, with delicate strokes evoking characteristics of copperplate engraving methods.

Noted more for their beauty than their readability, Modern types changed the face of typography. In the early twentieth century, Morris Fuller Benton began a Bodoni revival with his version for American Type Founders (ATF). Since then, many designers and foundries have released versions of Bodoni and other Modern types, with varying degrees of relation to the original concepts.

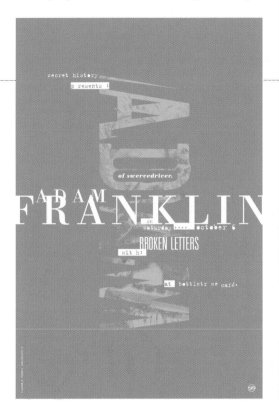

If you like …

Bodoni

… you could also consider:

Baskerville
Caslon
Walbaum

POSTER
Client Bottletree
Studio TEN
Designer Roy Burns
Principal Typefaces Bodoni, Univers, and FF Trixie

POSTER
Client Sasquatch! Music Festival
Studio strawberryluna
Designers strawberryluna and Craig Seder
Principal Typeface Berthold Bodoni Old Face

BOOK COVER
Client Mostafa Majidi
Studio Words Are Pictures
Designer Craig Ward
Principal Typeface Bodoni (modified)

POSTER
Client RAR florists
Studio Studio AND
Designer Jean-Benoît Lévy
Photographer Adriano Biondo
Principal Typeface Bauer Bodoni

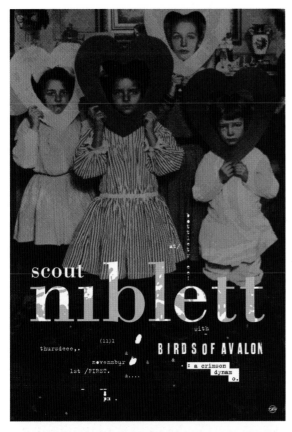

Above left:

POSTER
Client Bottletree
Studio TEN
Designer Roy Burns
Principal Typefaces Bodoni, found wood type, and FF Trixie

CORPORATE IDENTITY
Client Kombinatrotweiss
Studio desres design studio
Art Director/Typographer Michaela Kessler
Principal Typeface Bauer Bodoni

Kombinatrotweiss represents photographers, illustrators, and digital artists. The wide variety of artists represented is indicated by printing with black ink on a range of different-colored papers.

BOOK COVER
Publisher University of Washington Press, Seattle and London
Designer Ashley Saleeba
Principal Typeface Bodoni

POSTER
Client Bottletree
Studio TEN
Designer Roy Burns
Principal Typefaces Bodoni Poster,
Forelle, Univers, and FF Trixie

POSTER
Client We Are Busy Bodies
Studio Doublenaut
Designer Matt McCracken
Principal Typefaces Bodoni Poster and Futura

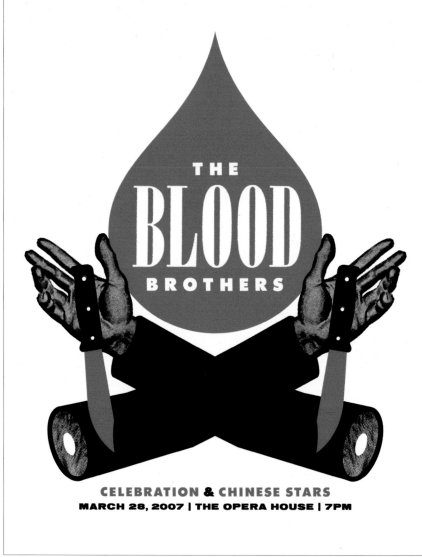

ILLUSTRATION
Publication *Metropolis* magazine
Art Director/Illustrator Lisa Maione
Creative Director Criswell Lappin
Principal Typeface Based on Bodoni

i can't
come to [yo u.]
He **doesn**'t have the sense
to feel the bird's PAIN:
and the wings can't fly.

I know a thousand roads,
a thousand places,
but without a heart
there is *nowhere*

to go .

H o w c an
a pain in the chest be so *softened?*
The darts of death are
nearer than your hands:
THERE'S
SO MUCH
LOST WANT *and* ABSENCE, i tremble.
Our love is a small bird tied by a child,
the bird *sips* the lake of death
and the boy goes on with his game.
[*you* cant come to me,

ILLUSTRATION
Studio Neue Design Studio
Designers Øystein Haugseth
Principal Typeface Bauer Bodoni

*Experimental typographic treatments of a collection
of 16 Arabic love poems entitled* Majnun Laila.

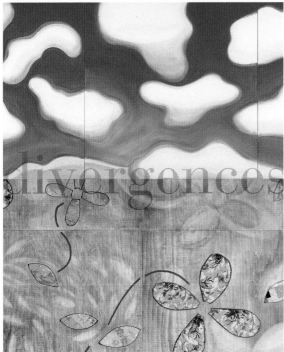

CATALOG COVER
Client MacKenzie Art Gallery
Studio Bradbury Branding and Design
Principal Typeface Bodoni

STORE ENVIRONMENT
Client Pinkberry, Inc.
Studio Ferroconcrete
Designer/Creative Director Yolanda Santosa
Designers Sunjoo Park and Wendy Thai
Copywriter Luellen Renn
Principal Typeface Bodoni

*Pinkberry's holiday wall features a typographic
Christmas carol.*

POSTCARD
Studio From Keetra
Designer Keetra Dean Dixon
Principal Typeface Bodoni Poster

From the artist's Cordial Invitations series.

GARDEN
TOUR 08

September 7th 2008 | $10 PNA members, $15 General Public - available online and at the PNA
Phinney Neighborhood Association | 11am - 4pm | 6532 Phinney Ave North | 206.783.2244 | phinneycenter.org

ILLUSTRATION
Publication *Grafik* magazine
Designer Sarah King
Principal Typeface Bodoni (hand rendered)

*Customized fruit featuring hand lettering
based on Bodoni.*

POSTER
Client Phinney Neighborhood Association
Studio Modern Dog Design Co.
Designer Robynne Raye
Principal Typeface ITC Bodoni

BOOKMAN

od

9/10pt

HOW RAZORBACK-JUMPING FROGS CAN LEVEL SIX piqued gymnasts! Jackdaws love my big sphinx of quartz. Jaded zombies acted quaintly but kept driving their oxen forward. The quick brown fox jumps over a lazy dog. The public was amazed to view the quickness and dexterity of the juggler. A mad boxer shot a quick, gloved jab to the

10/12pt

HOW RAZORBACK-JUMPING FROGS CAN LEVEL six piqued gymnasts! Jackdaws love my big sphinx of quartz. Jaded zombies acted quaintly but kept driving their oxen forward. The quick brown fox jumps over a lazy dog. The public was amazed to view the quickness and dexterity of the juggler. A

12/14pt

HOW RAZORBACK-JUMPING FROGS CAN level six piqued gymnasts! Jackdaws love my big sphinx of quartz. Jaded zombies acted quaintly but kept driving their oxen forward. The quick brown fox jumps over a

ITC Bookman Light Italic

abcdefghijklmnopqrstuvwxyz123456789
ABCDEFGHIJKLMNOPQRSTUVWXYZ

ITC Bookman Bold

abcdefghijklmnopqrstuvwxyz123456
ABCDEFGHIJKLMNOPQRSTUVWXYZ

ITC Bookman Bold Italic

abcdefghijklmnopqrstuvwxyz12345
ABCDEFGHIJKLMNOPQRSTUVWXYZ

ITC Bookman Swashes

ßeffikm̩n̩o̩pqrtvwyfifl
&123456789AABBCD
EFGHIJKKLMNOPR
RSTThUVVWWXYZ

ITC Bookman Light [ITC]

abcdefghijklmnopqrstuvwxyz
ABCDEFGHIJKLMNOPQRS
TUVWXYZ1234567890
[àóüßç](.,:;?!$€£&-*){ÀÓÜÇ}

32

The Bookman types are based on forms originated in the 1850s by Alexander Phemister for the Miller and Richard foundry in Scotland. His Old Style Antique was designed as an alternative to Caslon. Phemister's design improved on Caslon's quirkier traits, incorporating straighter serifs and shorter ascenders and descenders. Several other foundries released their own versions under different names, including Bruce Type Foundry with its 1901 edition Bartlett Oldstyle. When American Type Founders (ATF) acquired Bruce shortly thereafter, they changed the name to Bookman Oldstyle.

Linotype's Chauncey H. Griffith created a revival in 1936, but the most famous Bookman is the version by Ed Benguiat. His ITC Bookman, issued in 1975, pays homage to the original Phemister type, but was drawn with a larger x-height and includes four weights with companion cursive italics. The master lettering artist also incorporated the bold swash characters that became so closely associated with 1970s/1980s typography, and which have experienced a recent resurgence in popularity.

Yo La Tengo

KUSF 30th Anniversary Benefit
with CITAY and DJ IRWIN | AUGUST 3, 2007 | BIMBO'S 365 CLUB

If you like …

Bookman

… you could also consider:

Caslon

Century

Clarendon

Cooper Black

LOGO
Client Kiss Cheesecake
Studio Emblem
Designer Jeanine Donofrio
Principal Typeface ITC Bookman

POSTER
Client KUSF
Studio The Small Stakes
Designer Jason Munn
Principal Typeface Bookman

kiss
CHEESECAKE

POSTER

School École supérieure art et design de Saint-Étienne
Designer Aurore Chassé
Principal Typefaces Futura Maxi and
Bookman Old Style

*Posters created to promote a conference session
by artist Olivier Soulerin.*

POSTER

Client Capitol Records
Studio The Small Stakes
Designer Jason Munn
Principal Typeface Bookman

*Design commissioned to promote the
release of Ben Harper's* Lifeline *album.*

LOGO
Client Gluten Free for Good
Studio Michael Renaud Design
Designer/Illustrator Michael Renaud
Principal Typeface ITC Bookman (hand rendered)

EDITORIAL DESIGN AND ILLUSTRATION
Author Simon Renaud
Studio atelier aquarium
Designers Simon Renaud and Jérémie Nuel
Photographer Véronique Pêcheux
Principal Typeface ITC Bookman

CASLON

od

9/10pt

HOW RAZORBACK-JUMPING FROGS CAN LEVEL SIX PIQUED gymnasts! Jackdaws love my big sphinx of quartz. Jaded zombies acted quaintly but kept driving their oxen forward. The quick brown fox jumps over a lazy dog. The public was amazed to view the quickness and dexterity of the juggler. A mad boxer shot a quick, gloved jab to the jaw of his dizzy opponent. The five

10/12pt

HOW RAZORBACK-JUMPING FROGS CAN LEVEL SIX piqued gymnasts! Jackdaws love my big sphinx of quartz. Jaded zombies acted quaintly but kept driving their oxen forward. The quick brown fox jumps over a lazy dog. The public was amazed to view the quickness and dexterity of the juggler. A mad boxer shot a quick, gloved jab to the

12/14pt

HOW RAZORBACK-JUMPING FROGS CAN level six piqued gymnasts! Jackdaws love my big sphinx of quartz. Jaded zombies acted quaintly but kept driving their oxen forward. The quick brown fox jumps over a lazy dog. The public

ITC Caslon 224 Book Italic

abcdefghijklmnopqrstuvwxyz123456789
ABCDEFGHIJKLMNOPQRSTUVWXYZ

ITC Caslon 224 Bold

abcdefghijklmnopqrstuvwxyz12345678
ABCDEFGHIJKLMNOPQRSTUVWXYZ

ITC Caslon 224 Bold Italic

abcdefghijklmnopqrstuvwxyz1234567
ABCDEFGHIJKLMNOPQRSTUVWXYZ

Other notable cuts:

Adobe Caslon [Adobe]

Caslon 540 [Linotype]

Berthold Caslon Book [Berthold]

LTC Caslon [P22/Lanston Type Company]

ITC Caslon 224 Book [ITC]

abcdefghijklmnopqrstuvwxyz
ABCDEFGHIJKLMNOPQRS
TUVWXYZ1234567890
[àóüßç](.,:;?!$€£&-*){ÀÓÜÇ}

William Caslon I was one of the most important figures in British typographic history. A punchcutter and typefounder, he released his first typefaces circa 1722. At the time, Dutch Old Style types were in heavy use in the UK. While Caslon based his own types on the seventeenth-century Dutch model, his faces quickly became highly regarded because of their spark of personality, solid yet delicate styling, and variety of design.

Caslon cut a number of non-Latin types (including Greek, Arabic, and Hebrew) and also designed elegant swashed characters and ornaments to complement his text forms. Caslon types were immensely popular in Europe and colonial America—Benjamin Franklin used them almost exclusively, and the *Declaration of Independence* and many other historic documents were set in Caslon. Due to its success, countless variants of Caslon have been produced over the centuries, some bearing little resemblance to the original model. Some Caslons do not include a bold weight, as it was uncommon to use bold weights in eighteenth-century typesetting. Some digital revivals of Caslon and other historical types feature roughened edges. This is a nod to the decayed appearance of much early American printing, thought to be caused by the oxidation of metal type during lengthy exposure to seawater when transported from the UK.

If you like …

Caslon

… you could also consider:

Baskerville
Bookman
Goudy
Perpetua
Times

FLYER
Client Sankeys
Studio Yolo
Designer Martin Fewell
Principal Typefaces ITC Caslon 224 and Carousel

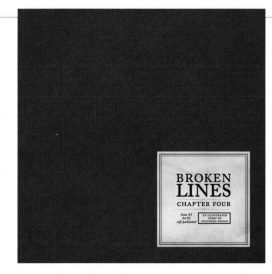

BOOK COVER
Studio Standard Design
Designer Tom Pappalardo
Principal Typeface Adobe Caslon

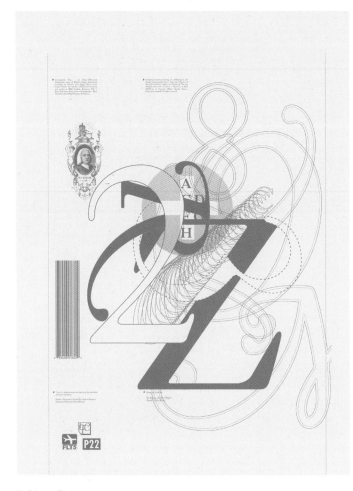

Both images this page:

CD PACKAGING AND POSTER
Client P22/Lanston Type Company
Studio P22
Designers Richard Kegler and Colin Kahn
Letterpress Printer Bruce Licher,
　Independent Project Press
Principal Typeface LTC Caslon

*P22 is known for combining contemporary music
and historical and artistic fonts into unique packages.
For this project, the P22 record label teamed with
FLT5 records to combine music from the William
Caslon Experience with a special "remixed" font
based on the Lanston Caslon family. Each "discfolio"
package is numbered and includes a fold-out,
broadside liner notes sheet that doubles as a type-
specimen poster.*

DON'T POLLUTE

ffi interviews

ek thongprasert
glenn martens
yu fukumoto
yoeri van yper
andrea cammarosano

DVD SLEEVE AND LABEL
Client Flanders Fashion Institute
Studio Kiggen
Designer Bart Kiggen
Principal Typeface ITC Caslon 224

BOOK SPREAD
Publisher CDA Press, San Francisco
Studio Chen Design Associates
Designer Max Spector
Creative Director/Art Director Joshua C. Chen
Principal Typeface Caslon 540

Peace: 100 Ideas (*Joshua C. Chen and Dr. David Krieger*) pairs text set in a variety of typefaces with original illustrations and photographs intended to promote peace. The book was expanded into a line of T-shirts and a traveling exhibition, with a portion of sales proceeds going to benefit wagingpeace.org.

crk-
us

POSTER
Client The M's
Studio Michael Renaud Design
Designer/Illustrator/Printer Michael Renaud
Principal Typefaces Adobe Caslon (hand
    rendered), Isla, and Verlag

*In this screenprinted gig poster, Adobe Caslon Bold
was used as a strict model for the sea monster and
the drops in the water.*

Above and opposite page:
POSTER
Client Design Academy Eindhoven
Designers Germans Ermičs and Søren Wibroe
Principal Typeface Adobe Caslon

*Poster designed to promote a student shop set up at
the Academy during Dutch Design Week in 2008.*

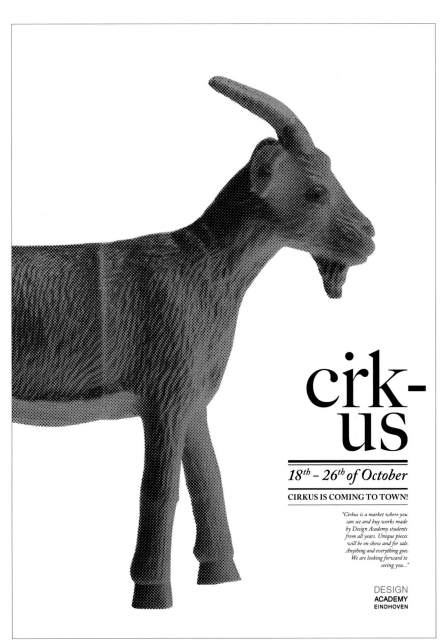

crk-us

18th – 26th of October

CIRKUS IS COMING TO TOWN!

"Cirkus is a market where you can see and buy works made by Design Academy students from all years. Unique pieces will be on show and for sale. Anything and everything goes. We are looking forward to seeing you…"

DESIGN
ACADEMY
EINDHOVEN

—Season's Greetings
from Kiggen

www.kiggen.be
info@kiggen.be

GREETING CARD
Studio Kiggen
Designer Bart Kiggen
Principal Typefaces Caslon 540, Kada, and
Gotham Rounded

CENTAUR

early old style serif • venetian • italian

od

9/10pt

HOW RAZORBACK-JUMPING FROGS CAN LEVEL SIX PIQUED
gymnasts! Jackdaws love my big sphinx of quartz. Jaded zombies acted quaintly
but kept driving their oxen forward. The quick brown fox jumps over a lazy
dog. The public was amazed to view the quickness and dexterity of the juggler.
A mad boxer shot a quick, gloved jab to the jaw of his dizzy opponent. The
five boxing wizards jump quickly.

10/12pt

HOW RAZORBACK-JUMPING FROGS CAN LEVEL SIX
piqued gymnasts! Jackdaws love my big sphinx of quartz. Jaded
zombies acted quaintly but kept driving their oxen forward. The quick
brown fox jumps over a lazy dog. The public was amazed to view the
quickness and dexterity of the juggler. A mad boxer shot a quick,
gloved jab to the jaw of his dizzy opponent. The five boxing wizards

12/14pt

HOW RAZORBACK-JUMPING FROGS CAN LEVEL
six piqued gymnasts! Jackdaws love my big sphinx of
quartz. Jaded zombies acted quaintly but kept driving their
oxen forward. The quick brown fox jumps over a lazy dog.
The public was amazed to view the quickness and dexterity

Centaur Italic

abcdefghijklmnopqrstuvwxyz1234567890
ABCDEFGHIJKLMNOPQRSTUVWXYZ
ABCDEFGHIJKLMNOPQRSTUVWXYZ
ABCDEFGHIJKLMN
OPQRSTUVWXYZ

Centaur Bold

abcdefghijklmnopqrstuvwxyz1234567890
ABCDEFGHIJKLMNOPQRSTUVWXY
ABCDEFGHIJKLMNOPQRSTUVWXYZ

Centaur Bold Italic

abcdefghijklmnopqrstuvwxyz1234567890
ABCDEFGHIJKLMNOPQRSTUVWXYZ
ABCDEFGHIJKLMNOPQRSTUVWXYZ

Centaur [Monotype Imaging]

abcdefghijklmnopqrstuvwxyz

ABCDEFGHIJKLMNOPQ

RSTUVWXYZ1234567890

[àóüßç](.,:;?!$€£&-*){ÀÓÜÇ}

American Bruce Rogers (1870–1957) was one of the finest typographers and book designers of the twentieth century. In addition to using type impeccably, Rogers also designed several typefaces for his book projects. Notable among these is Centaur, one of the best-known renditions of the fifteenth-century Roman type cut by French typographer Nicolas Jenson.

Rogers designed Centaur as an exclusive typeface for the Metropolitan Museum of Art in 1914. He had drawn another Jenson-modeled face, Montaigne, in 1902, but was never completely happy with the cut. With Centaur, Rogers undertook to emphasize the printed quality of Jenson's original forms. Working with enlarged photos of Jenson's type, he drew over the letters with a flat pen. After refinements were made with a brush and white paint, the best letters were used as patterns and cut by Robert Wiebking. Centaur was named in honor of the first book Rogers designed using the type—*The Centaur* by Maurice de Guérin, published by Montague Press in 1915.

Fine printers requested that the typeface be made available to the trade. Rogers agreed, and London's Lanston Monotype released the commercial version of Centaur in 1929. As Jenson's original type did not include a companion italic, Centaur was first developed as a roman only. Monotype added an italic by Frederic Warde, which was based on the work of sixteenth-century printer and calligrapher Ludovico degli Arrighi da Vicenza. The Centaur font family was expanded for the digital era with the addition of swash capitals in the italic by Monotype's Patricia Saunders and Robin Nicholas. The swash forms were inspired by three characters drawn by Frederic Warde which had never before been used as the basis for a typeface.

If you like …

Centaur

… you could also consider:

Bembo
Garamond
Goudy

BOOK COVER
Publisher Editora Nova Fronteira, Rio de Janeiro
Designer Ana Sofia Mariz
Principal Typefaces Centaur and Vera Sans

LOGO
Client The Society of Typographic Aficionados
Studio Typeco
Designer James Grieshaber
Principal Typeface Centaur

INTERACTIVE ART PROJECT

Studios Silo Design Inc. with JRVisuals
Designer Terje Vist

Illustrations by visitors to www.typeisart.com. Artwork is constructed on the fly by combining parts of Centaur glyphs. Creators are known by screen names they choose at sign-up.

1. Kryston
2. Dean Toby
3. Micael
4. Yoy
5. Willoughby Jackson
6. Matt-o
7. King Tommy
8. Paul "the n00b"

1

4

7

2

5

3

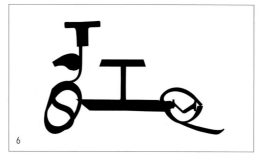

6

8

INTERNATIONAL

HOUSE OF FONTS

LOGO
Client P22 Type Foundry
Studio P22
Designer James Grieshaber
Principal Typeface Centaur

*Identity for a new font distribution
channel under the P22 umbrella.*

PARTS OF A CHARACTER

Arm	Ascender	Bar	Bowl	Counter	Descender	Ear	Hairline	Serif	Shoulder	Spine	Spur	Stem	Stress	Stroke	Swash	Tail	Terminal	x-Height

PRINT

Studio Silo Design Inc.
Designer Susanne Cerha
Principal Typeface Centaur

*Limited-edition educational print explaining
the parts of the characters in the Latin alphabet.
The main art element was constructed from
components of Centaur letterforms.*

©2008 SUSANNE CERHA | WWW.SILO-DESIGN.COM | NEW YORK

CENTURY

od

9/10pt

HOW RAZORBACK-JUMPING FROGS CAN LEVEL SIX piqued gymnasts! Jackdaws love my big sphinx of quartz. Jaded zombies acted quaintly but kept driving their oxen forward. The quick brown fox jumps over a lazy dog. The public was amazed to view the quickness and dexterity of the juggler. A mad boxer shot a quick, gloved jab to the jaw of his

10/12pt

HOW RAZORBACK-JUMPING FROGS CAN LEVEL six piqued gymnasts! Jackdaws love my big sphinx of quartz. Jaded zombies acted quaintly but kept driving their oxen forward. The quick brown fox jumps over a lazy dog. The public was amazed to view the quickness and dexterity of the juggler. A mad boxer shot a quick,

12/14pt

HOW RAZORBACK-JUMPING FROGS CAN level six piqued gymnasts! Jackdaws love my big sphinx of quartz. Jaded zombies acted quaintly but kept driving their oxen forward. The quick brown fox jumps over a lazy dog.

Century Schoolbook Italic

abcdefghijklmnopqrstuvwxyz123456789
ABCDEFGHIJKLMNOPQRSTUVWXY

Century Schoolbook Bold

abcdefghijklmnopqrstuvwxyz12345
ABCDEFGHIJKLMNOPQRSTUVW

Century Schoolbook Bold Italic

abcdefghijklmnopqrstuvwxyz123456
ABCDEFGHIJKLMNOPQRSTUVWX

Other notable cuts:

Century Old Style [Monotype Imaging]
ITC Century [ITC]
Century Expanded [Monotype Imaging]

Century Schoolbook [Monotype Imaging]

abcdefghijklmnopqrstuvwxyz
ABCDEFGHIJKLMNOPQ
RSTUVWXYZ1234567890
[àóüßç](.,:;?!$€£&-*){ÀÓÜÇ}

Under a commission by Theodore Low De Vinne, publisher of *The Century Magazine,* American type designer Linn Boyd Benton commenced work on a custom typeface for the publication in 1890. Completed in 1894, this new type, Century Roman, was typical of the neorenaissance movement in typography that was prevalent at the time. Its large x-height and slightly condensed appearance made Century a workhorse—sturdy and eminently readable. A number of typefaces modeled on this Benton design were developed in the early twentieth century, most branded with the Century name for marketing purposes. L. B. Benton's son, Morris Fuller Benton, produced several variants for American Type Founders (ATF). Competing foundries Linotype, Intertype, and Monotype cast their own versions.

One notable example is Century Schoolbook (1924), which is familiar to many North Americans because it was the typeface they learned to read with. In developing this face, M. F. Benton relied on research which showed that young readers recognized letterforms with contrasting weight and very open counters more quickly than other letterforms. For this rendition of Century, M. F. Benton increased the x-height, stroke width, and overall letterspacing. Although the original ATF Century Schoolbook did not include italics, later revivals by Linotype and ITC added cursive forms.

Procurement Headaches?

costs out of control?

too many suppliers?

logistics nightmares?

LET US HELP.

ANCILLARE

Global Procurement Strategies

If you like …

Century

… you could also consider:

Bookman
Caslon
Clarendon

THE RED OAKS
SCHOOL

LOGO
Client The Red Oaks School
Studio Lippincott
Designers Brendán Murphy, Jenifer Lecker, and Julia McGreevy
Creative Director Brendán Murphy
Principal Typeface Century Schoolbook

BROCHURE
Client Caridan Marketing Labs
Studio Emblem
Designer Jeanine Donofrio
Principal Typeface Century Schoolbook

EXHIBITION DESIGN
Client Reuters
Studio StudioMakgill
Principal Typeface Century 725 BT

Design for Bearing Witness, a photography exhibition documenting five years of news reporting on the war in Iraq.

presented by

The Society of Typographic Aficionados

in association with

Minnesota Center
for Book Arts

Hamilton Wood Type
and Printing Museum

Minneapolis College
of Art and Design

University of Minnesota
Design Institute

Walker Art Center

S{o}T A   The fifth annual TypeCon is presented by The Society of Typographic Aficionados.

TYPECON 2003   JULY 17–20, 2003
MINNEAPOLIS, MINNESOTA USA
www.typecon2003.com

counter culture

TYPECON 2003

counter culture

LOGO AND POSTER/SELF-MAILER
Client The Society of Typographic Aficionados
Studio Mark Simonson Studio
Designer Mark Simonson
Principal Typefaces Century Expanded,
Hellenic Wide, Alternate Gothic,
Trade Gothic, Metallophile Sp8

*Identity design and collateral for the
TypeCon2003: Counter Culture conference.*

WEBSITE
Studio missbeck
Designer Marianne Beck
Principal Typeface ITC Century

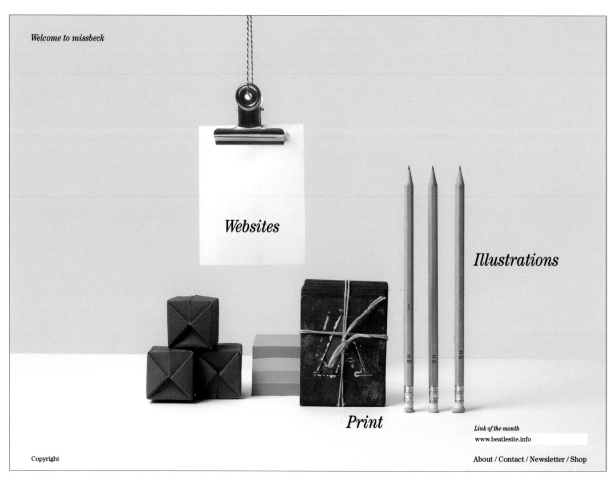

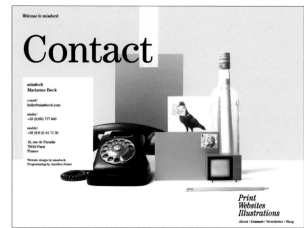

WEBSITE
Client Caroline Breton
Studio atelier aquarium
Designers Simon Renaud and Jérémie Nuel
Photographers Véronique Pêcheux,
Cléia Schaeffer, and François Coquerel
Principal Typeface ITC Century

CLARENDON

slab serif • bracketed serifs

od

9/10pt

HOW RAZORBACK-JUMPING FROGS CAN LEVEL SIX piqued gymnasts! Jackdaws love my big sphinx of quartz. Jaded zombies acted quaintly but kept driving their oxen forward. The quick brown fox jumps over a lazy dog. The public was amazed to view the quickness and dexterity of the juggler. A mad boxer shot a quick, gloved jab to the jaw of his dizzy opponent. The five boxing wizards jump

10/12pt

HOW RAZORBACK-JUMPING FROGS CAN LEVEL six piqued gymnasts! Jackdaws love my big sphinx of quartz. Jaded zombies acted quaintly but kept driving their oxen forward. The quick brown fox jumps over a lazy dog. The public was amazed to view the quickness and dexterity of the juggler. A

12/14pt

HOW RAZORBACK-JUMPING FROGS CAN level six piqued gymnasts! Jackdaws love my big sphinx of quartz. Jaded zombies acted quaintly but kept driving their oxen

Clarendon Roman

abcdefghijklmnopqrstuvwxyz12345678
ABCDEFGHIJKLMNOPQRSTUVWXYZ

Clarendon Heavy

abcdefghijklmnopqrstuvwxyz1234567
ABCDEFGHIJKLMNOPQRSTUVWXYZ

Clarendon Bold

abcdefghijklmnopqrstuvwxyz1234567
ABCDEFGHIJKLMNOPQRSTUVWXYZ

Clarendon Black

abcdefghijklmnopqrstuvwxyz1234567
ABCDEFGHIJKLMNOPQRSTUVWXYZ

Clarendon Condensed

abcdefghijklmnopqrstuvwxyz1234567890
ABCDEFGHIJKLMNOPQRSTUVWXYZ

Other notable cuts:

Clarendon LT [Linotype]

Clarendon Light [Bitstream]

abcdefghijklmnopqrstuvwxyz
ABCDEFGHIJKLMNOPQ
RSTUVWXYZ1234567890
[àóüßç](.,:;?!$€£&-*){ÀÓÜÇ}

Major changes to the face of typography came with the Industrial Revolution. For more than three centuries, typography and printing had been firmly tied to book publishing and its refined aesthetics. In the early 1800s, the printing industry veered off in a new direction. New print media appealing to the masses—newspapers, magazines, and all forms of advertising—were emerging as a dominant force, calling for a new style of type design compatible with mass production and consumer tastes. Print journalism necessitated types that were both readable and boldly eye-catching. Slab Serifs, also known as Egyptian typefaces, quickly became the flavor of the day.

A more evolved form of Egyptian was Clarendon, designed by Robert Besley for London's Fann Street Foundry in 1845. It was intended as a bold display companion to text faces for commercial printing. This design, named for the Clarendon Press in Oxford, had the strong presence of the typical Egyptian, but was more refined, with greater contrast between thick and thin strokes and its trademark bracketed serifs. Its instant success spurred multiple foundries to issue their own variants, and an entire sub-classification of Slab Serifs was named after the typeface. Clarendon's popularity continued, and Edouard Hoffmann and Hermann Eidenbenz at Haas revived the typeface in 1953. A variety of Clarendons have been issued since then, with added weights and styles making this design suitable for both text and display applications.

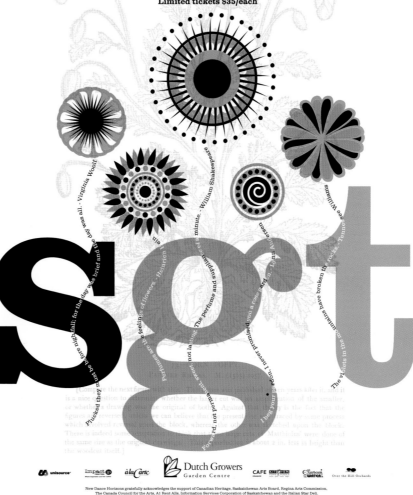

Near left:

POSTER
Client New Dance Horizons
Studio Bradbury Branding and Design
Principal Typeface Clarendon

Far left:

PACKAGING
Client CasCioppo Brothers
Studio Turnstyle
Designer Madeleine Eiche
Principal Typefaces Trade Gothic, Clarendon Bold, Century Gothic, and Helvetica Neue

If you like …

Clarendon

… you could also consider:

Bookman
Century
Courier
Rockwell
ROSEWOOD

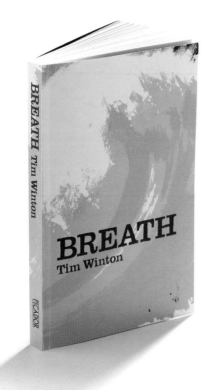

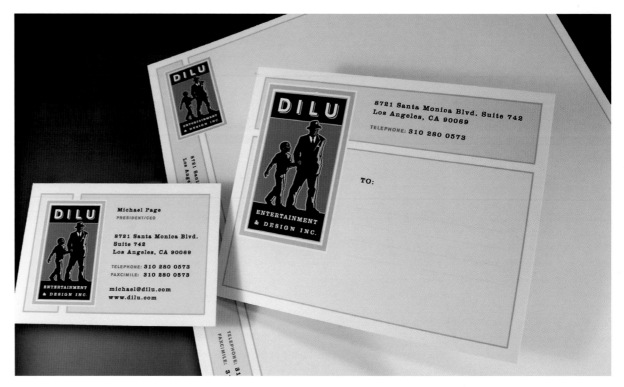

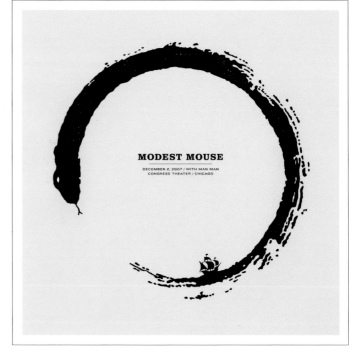

BOOK COVER
Client Pan Macmillan
Studio Jawa and Midwich
Designers Simon Dovar and Nils Davey
Principal Typeface Clarendon (hand rendered)

STATIONERY SYSTEM
Client DILU
Studio Evenson Design Group
Designer Mark Sojka
Creative Director Stan Evenson
Principal Typeface Clarendon

POSTER
Client Modest Mouse
Studio The Small Stakes
Designer Jason Munn
Principal Typeface Clarendon

POSTER
Client Bottletree
Studio TEN
Designer Roy Burns
Principal Typefaces Clarendon and FF Trixie

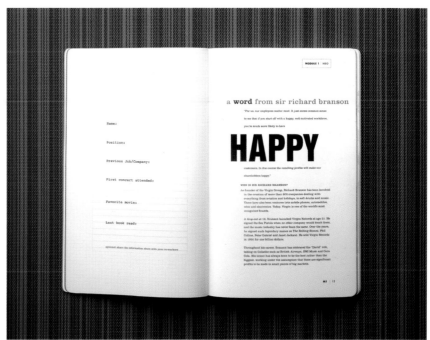

BOOK SPREAD
Client Virgin Entertainment
Studio konnectDesign
Designers David Whitcraft and Caroline Plasencia
Creative Director Karen Knecht
Principal Typefaces Clarendon, Mrs Eaves,
Helvetica Inserat, and Futura

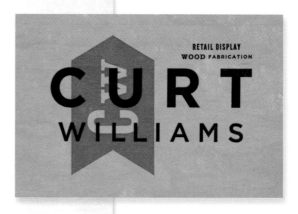

STATIONERY SYSTEM
Client Curt Williams Wood Fabrication
Studio Seedoubleyou Design
Designer Chuck Williams
Principal Typefaces Gotham, Clarendon,
  Agency Gothic, and Alternate Gothic

MUSIC PACKAGING
Client 4AD Records
Studio v23
Designer Timothy O'Donnell
Art Director Vaughan Oliver
Photographer Dominic Davies
Principal Typeface Clarendon

BOOK COVER AND SPREAD
Client IPSCO Inc.
Studio Bradbury Branding and Design
Principal Typefaces Clarendon and Copperplate

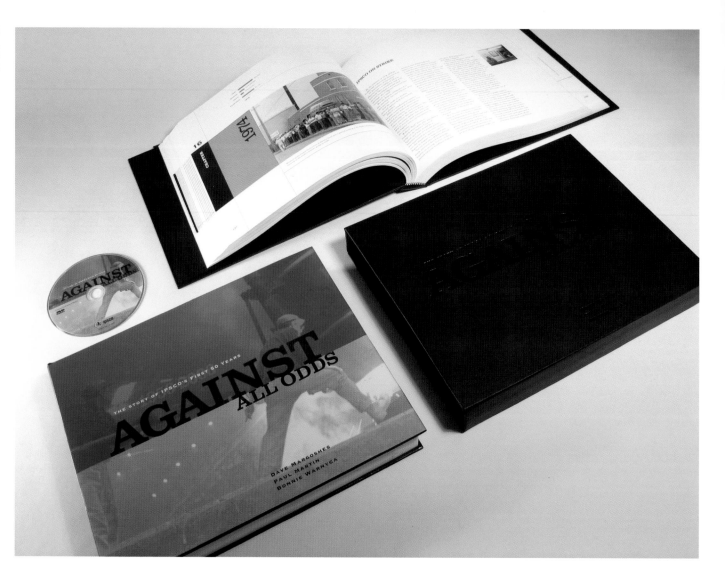

IDENTITY
Client Plain English Media
Art Director/Designer Brent Barson
Principal Typeface Clarendon

POSTER
Client Olga Koumoundouros
Designer Jessica Fleischmann
Principal Typeface Clarendon

Screenprinted poster created for a CalArts (California Institute of the Arts) graduate student's art exhibit/performance. The poster is printed on tent fabric, as a tent suspended in a canyon figured prominently in the show.

COPPERPLATE

glyphic • engraved • small caps

ON

9/10pt

HOW RAZORBACK-JUMPING FROGS CAN LEVEL SIX PIQUED GYMNASTS! JACKDAWS LOVE MY BIG SPHINX OF QUARTZ. JADED ZOMBIES ACTED QUAINTLY BUT KEPT DRIVING THEIR OXEN FORWARD. THE QUICK BROWN FOX JUMPS OVER A LAZY DOG. THE PUBLIC WAS AMAZED TO VIEW THE QUICKNESS AND DEXTERITY OF THE JUGGLER. A MAD BOXER SHOT A QUICK, GLOVED JAB TO THE JAW OF HIS DIZZY OPPONENT. THE FIVE BOXING WIZARDS JUMP

10/12pt

HOW RAZORBACK-JUMPING FROGS CAN LEVEL SIX PIQUED GYMNASTS! JACKDAWS LOVE MY BIG SPHINX OF QUARTZ. JADED ZOMBIES ACTED QUAINTLY BUT KEPT DRIVING THEIR OXEN FORWARD. THE QUICK BROWN FOX JUMPS OVER A LAZY DOG. THE PUBLIC WAS AMAZED TO VIEW THE QUICKNESS AND DEXTERITY OF THE JUGGLER. A MAD

12/14pt

HOW RAZORBACK-JUMPING FROGS CAN LEVEL SIX PIQUED GYMNASTS! JACKDAWS LOVE MY BIG SPHINX OF QUARTZ. JADED ZOMBIES ACTED QUAINTLY BUT KEPT DRIVING THEIR OXEN FOR

Copperplate Gothic 29BC

ABCDEFGHIJKLMNOPQRSTUVWXYZ1234567890
ABCDEFGHIJKLMNOPQRSTUVWXYZ

Copperplate Gothic 30AB

ABCDEFGHIJKLMNOPQRSTUVWXYZ1234567890
ABCDEFGHIJKLMNOPQRSTUVWXYZ

Copperplate Gothic 30BC

ABCDEFGHIJKLMNOPQRSTUVWXYZ1234567890
ABCDEFGHIJKLMNOPQRSTUVWXYZ

Copperplate Gothic 31AB

ABCDEFGHIJKLMNOPQRSTUVWXYZ123
ABCDEFGHIJKLMNOPQRSTUVWXY

Copperplate Gothic 31BC

ABCDEFGHIJKLMNOPQRSTUVWXYZ1234567890
ABCDEFGHIJKLMNOPQRSTUVWXYZ

Copperplate Gothic 32AB

ABCDEFGHIJKLMNOPQRSTUVWXYZ123
ABCDEFGHIJKLMNOPQRSTUVWXY

Copperplate Gothic 29AB [Monotype Imaging]

ABCDEFGHIJKLMNOPQRSTUVWXYZ
ABCDEFGHIJKLMNOPQRSTUV
WXYZ1234567890
[ÀÓÜSSÇ](.,:;?!$€£&-*){ÀÓÜÇ}

Legendary typographer Frederic W. Goudy designed the original Copperplate Gothic in 1901 for American Type Founders (ATF), while Clarence C. Marder later drew additional weights. Although called a Gothic (a term more often associated with Sans Serif types), this face actually features tiny glyphic serifs. This bit of detailing gives the edges an appearance akin to that of letters engraved in copperplate with a burin (a hardened steel tool used for delicate cutting).

Copperplate Gothic has no lowercase, instead featuring a harmonious set of capitals and small capitals. Despite having no lowercase, the faces are highly legible at small sizes because of their width and open counters. The full type family includes nine weights and styles. The fonts are systematically named, the first part a numbering system (29–33) relating to the width and weight of a given face, and the second part (AB–BC) indicative of the height of its caps and small caps.

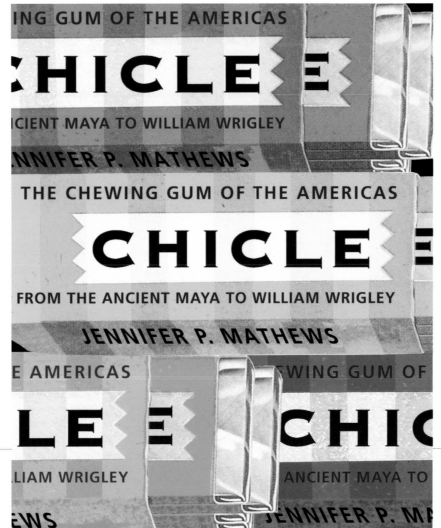

LOGO AND OUTDOOR SIGNAGE
Client Gallery C
Studio Evenson Design Group
Designer Mark Sojka
Creative Director Stan Evenson
Principal Typeface Copperplate Gothic 32BC

BOOK COVER
Publisher The University of Arizona Press, Tucson
Studio Salamander Hill Design
Designer David Drummond
Principal Typefaces Copperplate Gothic
and Frutiger

If you like …

COPPERPLATE

… you could also consider:

AVENIR
EUROSTILE
OPTIMA
TRAJAN

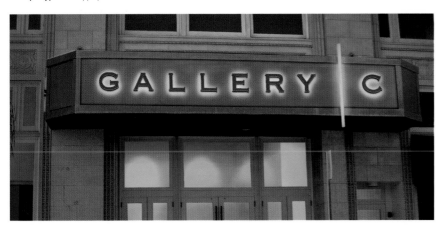

COURIER

slab serif • typewriter • monospaced

9/10pt

HOW RAZORBACK-JUMPING FROGS CAN LEVEL SIX piqued gymnasts! Jackdaws love my big sphinx of quartz. Jaded zombies acted quaintly but kept driving their oxen forward. The quick brown fox jumps over a lazy dog. The public was amazed to view the quickness and dexterity of the juggler.

10/12pt

HOW RAZORBACK-JUMPING FROGS CAN LEVEL SIX piqued gymnasts! Jackdaws love my big sphinx of quartz. Jaded zombies acted quaintly but kept driving their oxen forward. The quick brown fox jumps over a lazy dog. The public was amazed to view

12/14pt

HOW RAZORBACK-JUMPING FROGS CAN level six piqued gymnasts! Jackdaws love my big sphinx of quartz. Jaded zombies acted quaintly but kept driving their oxen forward. The

Courier Italic

abcdefghijklmnopqrstuvwxyz1234
ABCDEFGHIJKLMNOPQRSTUVWXYZ

Courier Bold

abcdefghijklmnopqrstuvwxyz1234
ABCDEFGHIJKLMNOPQRSTUVWXYZ

Courier Bold Italic

abcdefghijklmnopqrstuvwxyz1234
ABCDEFGHIJKLMNOPQRSTUVWXYZ

Other notable cuts:

Courier New [Monotype Imaging]
Courier [Adobe]

Courier [Linotype]

abcdefghijklmnopqrstuvwxyz
ABCDEFGHIJKLMNOPQRSTUVWXYZ
1234567890
[àóüßç] (.,:;?!$€£&-*) {ÀÓÜÇ}

Courier was designed by Howard "Bud" Kettler in 1955. This monospaced Slab Serif was meant to resemble output from a strike-on typewriter, where all characters are given the same amount of space regardless of their width. Courier was commissioned by IBM for use in its typewriters, but the company failed to obtain the legal rights to exclusive use of the design. Courier became the standard font used throughout the typewriter industry for decades. Adrian Frutiger later redrew the typeface for the IBM Selectric Composer series of electric typewriters.

In the digital era, Courier became widely used in texts where columns of characters required consistent alignment. Variants of Courier are among the default fonts found in many computer operating systems, and are bundled with major software applications. Some forms of Courier feature soft, rounded terminals, while others have blunt, squared-off stroke ends.

If you like …

Courier

… you could also consider:

Century
Clarendon
O C R – B
Officina Serif

BOOK COVER
Publishers Chronicle Books, San Francisco and
Thames & Hudson, London
Studio MacFadden & Thorpe
Designer Brett MacFadden
Illustrator Alena Akhmadullina
Principal Typeface Courier New

POSTER
Client Vroni Jäggi Solothurn
Studio Studio AND
Designer Jean-Benoît Lévy
Photo Montage Artist Jean-Pascal Imsand
Principal Typeface Courier (modified)

GARAMOND

old style serif • garalde

od

old style serif • garalde

9/10pt

HOW RAZORBACK-JUMPING FROGS CAN LEVEL SIX PIQUED gymnasts! Jackdaws love my big sphinx of quartz. Jaded zombies acted quaintly but kept driving their oxen forward. The quick brown fox jumps over a lazy dog. The public was amazed to view the quickness and dexterity of the juggler. A mad boxer shot a quick, gloved jab to the jaw of his dizzy opponent. The five boxing wizards jump quickly. How razorback-jumping

10/12pt

HOW RAZORBACK-JUMPING FROGS CAN LEVEL SIX piqued gymnasts! Jackdaws love my big sphinx of quartz. Jaded zombies acted quaintly but kept driving their oxen forward. The quick brown fox jumps over a lazy dog. The public was amazed to view the quickness and dexterity of the juggler. A mad boxer shot a quick, gloved jab to the jaw of his dizzy opponent. The five boxing

12/14pt

HOW RAZORBACK-JUMPING FROGS CAN level six piqued gymnasts! Jackdaws love my big sphinx of quartz. Jaded zombies acted quaintly but kept driving their oxen forward. The quick brown fox jumps over a lazy dog. The public was amazed to view the quickness

Garamond Premier Italic

abcdefghijklmnopqrstuvwxyz1234567890
ABCDEFGHIJKLMNOPQRSTUVWXYZ

Garamond Premier Bold

abcdefghijklmnopqrstuvwxyz1234567890
ABCDEFGHIJKLMNOPQRSTUVWXYZ

Garamond Premier Bold Italic

abcdefghijklmnopqrstuvwxyz1234567890
ABCDEFGHIJKLMNOPQRSTUVWXYZ

Other notable cuts:

Adobe Garamond [Adobe]

Garamond Classico [Linotype]

Garamond 3 [Linotype]

ITC Garamond [ITC]

Garamond Premier [Adobe]

abcdefghijklmnopqrstuvwxyz
ABCDEFGHIJKLMNOPQ
RSTUVWXYZ1234567890
[àóüßç](.,:;?!$€£&-*){ÀÓÜÇ}

The Garamond types are a class of Old Style Serif faces named for sixteenth-century punchcutter and typefounder Claude Garamond (Paris, 1480–1561). These particular Old Styles are also known as the subclass Garalde. Garamond's first type was used in 1530 for a book by Erasmus: *Paraphrasis in Elegantiarum Libros Laurentii Vallae*. This face was based on the Venetian Old Style type—cut by Francesco Griffo—that Aldus Manutius used to print Cardinal Bembo's *De Aetna* in 1495. Garamond's star rose in the 1540s, when he designed a Greek typeface (Grec du Roi), under commission by French king Francis I, for use in a series of books by Robert Estienne. Garamond's Roman faces were later adopted by the French court for its printing, and subsequently influenced typography throughout France and Western Europe. Much of Garamond's lowercase was based on the handwriting of Angelo Vergecio, librarian to Francis I. The companion italics in contemporary Garamonds are based mainly on the italics of Garamond's assistant, Robert Granjon.

Although some types bearing the name Garamond were directly inspired by the Parisian typographer's designs, others are more closely related to the work of French printer Jean Jannon. In 1621, Jannon released a specimen of types displaying characteristics similar to those of Garamond's designs. In later years, some of Jannon's work was mistakenly attributed to Garamond. By the time the error was discovered, the Garamond name was already firmly tied to the Jannon style as well as those designs actually created by Garamond. Notable among today's Garamonds are Adobe Garamond, Adobe's first historical type revival (1989); and Garamond Premier, Robert Slimbach's vibrant and technologically advanced interpretation of the original Garamond types housed in the Plantin-Moretus Museum in Antwerp, Belgium.

Both images this page:
GREETING CARD
Studio TYPORETUM
Designer/Printer Justin Knopp
Principal Typeface Monotype Garamond (metal)

This letterpress piece, bearing an Archimedes quotation, was hand typeset in Monotype Garamond Roman and Italic at 48 point, 60 point, and 72 point. The type used was cast on a Monotype machine at the Cambridge University Press in the UK.

Give me but one FIRM SPOT on which to stand, & I WILL move the EARTH.

If you like …

Garamond

… you could also consider:

Bembo
Centaur
Goudy
Sabon

All images this page:

EDITORIAL DESIGN

Client *Delvaux* magazine
Studio Kiggen for Flink
Designers Bart Kiggen and Bodo Peeters
Principal Typeface Garamond Premier

Toile de Cuir revisited

The Delvaux Autumn/Winter 2008/09 collection, and more specifically the Dolce Vita family, is available in a modern and original material, Toile de Cuir.

This woven material, invented and developed by Charles Schambourg in the 1960s, has been used decoratively by the world's greatest architects and was first used in leather goods by Solange Schwennicke at the beginning of the 1980s. Today, Toile de Cuir is one of the most luxurious materials that Delvaux uses.

master aesthetician
permanent cosmetic technician

HEATHER BROCK

801 631 3404
heatherbrockaesthetics@yahoo.com

your next appointment

_____

date

_____

time

master aesthetician
permanent cosmetic technician

HEATHER BROCK

801 631 3404
heatherbrockaesthetics@yahoo.com

your next appointment

_____

date

_____

time

JOAN TEMPLETON

MUNCH'S IBSEN

A PAINTER'S VISIONS OF A PLAYWRIGHT

BOOK COVER
Publisher University of Washington Press,
Seattle and London
Designer Ashley Saleeba
Principal Typeface Adobe Garamond

BUSINESS CARDS
Client Heather Cowley Brock
Studio HADDEN 3
Designers Anthony Hadden and Wendy Hadden
Principal Typefaces Adobe Garamond and Helvetica Neue

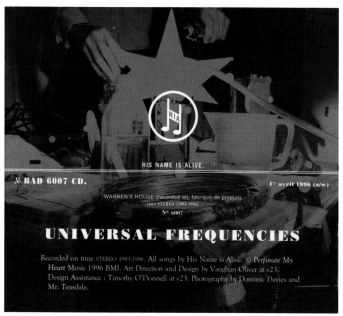

MUSIC PACKAGING
Client 4AD Records
Studio v23
Designer Timothy O'Donnell
Art Director Vaughan Oliver
Photographer Dominic Davies
Principal Typefaces Bodoni Poster, Adobe
  Garamond, News Gothic, and Helvetica

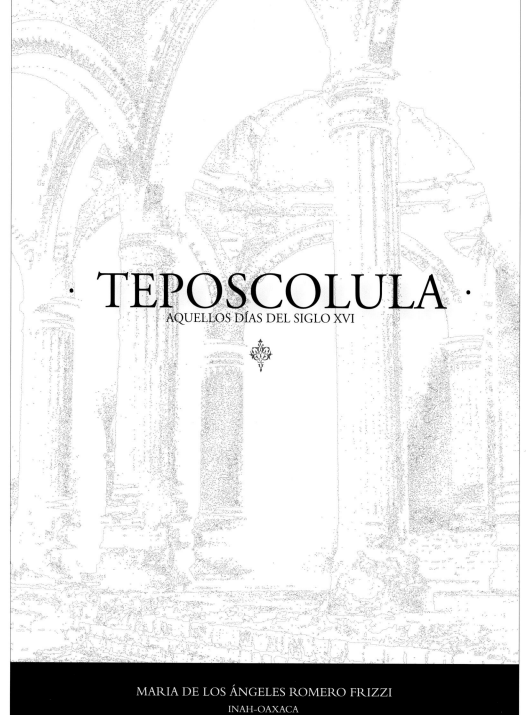

BOOK COVER
Client Culturas Populares
Studio huizar 1984
Designer José Ignacio Zárate Huizar
Principal Typeface Adobe Garamond

BOOK
Client Law Society of Saskatchewan
Studio Bradbury Branding and Design
Principal Typeface Garamond

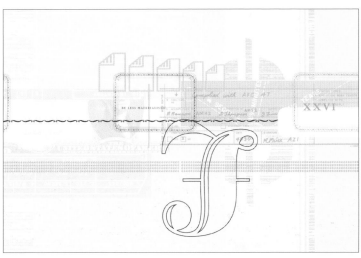

BOOK SPREAD
Publisher CDA Press, San Francisco
Studio Chen Design Associates
Designer Max Spector
Creative Director/Art Director Joshua C. Chen
Principal Typefaces Garamond No. 3 and DIN

Illustration from Peace: 100 Ideas.

All images this page:
FOUNDATION REPORT
Client Stiftung Nord/LB · Öffentliche
(in cooperation with HBK Braunschweig)
Designers Florian Hardwig and Tobias Tank
Illustrators Stefan Gunnesch,
Jonas Laugs, and Johanna Seipelt
Principal Typeface Garamond Premier

The Joseph & Marie Grant Spring Concert
DePaul Symphony Orchestra

Wednesday, May 21, 2008
8:00pm (Doors open at 7:15pm)

Orchestra Hall at Symphony Center
220 South Michigan Avenue, Chicago

DEPAUL UNIVERSITY
SCHOOL OF MUSIC
Office of the Dean
804 West Belden
Chicago, Illinois 60614

SPRING CONCERT & GALA AT SYMPHONY CENTER

The Joseph & Marie Grant Spring Concert & Gala
DePaul Symphony Orchestra

WEDNESDAY, MAY 21, 2008
ORCHESTRA HALL AT SYMPHONY CENTER

Reserve your complimentary tickets online:
music.depaul.edu
All seats are general admission. You may also
request tickets by calling (773) 325-7260.

DEPAUL UNIVERSITY SCHOOL OF MUSIC
SPRING CONCERT & GALA

Office of Advancement
Attn: Ms. Elizabeth J. Soete
1 East Jackson Boulevard
Chicago, Illinois 60604-2287

IDENTITY AND COLLATERAL
Client DePaul University School of Music
Studio End Communications
Principal Typeface Adobe Garamond

Se·man·tix

LOGO
Client Semantix
Studio Evenson Design Group
Designer Mark Sojka
Creative Director Stan Evenson
Principal Typeface Adobe Garamond

GOUDY

od

9/10pt

HOW RAZORBACK-JUMPING FROGS CAN LEVEL SIX PIQUED gymnasts! Jackdaws love my big sphinx of quartz. Jaded zombies acted quaintly but kept driving their oxen forward. The quick brown fox jumps over a lazy dog. The public was amazed to view the quickness and dexterity of the juggler. A mad boxer shot a quick, gloved jab to the jaw of his dizzy opponent. The five boxing wizards jump quickly. How razorback

10/12pt

HOW RAZORBACK-JUMPING FROGS CAN LEVEL SIX piqued gymnasts! Jackdaws love my big sphinx of quartz. Jaded zombies acted quaintly but kept driving their oxen forward. The quick brown fox jumps over a lazy dog. The public was amazed to view the quickness and dexterity of the juggler. A mad boxer shot a quick, gloved jab to the jaw of his dizzy opponent. The five

12/14pt

HOW RAZORBACK-JUMPING FROGS CAN level six piqued gymnasts! Jackdaws love my big sphinx of quartz. Jaded zombies acted quaintly but kept driving their oxen forward. The quick brown fox jumps over a lazy dog. The public was amazed to view

Goudy Old Style Italic

abcdefghijklmnopqrstuvwxyz1234567890
ABCDEFGHIJKLMNOPQRSTUVWXYZ

Goudy Old Style Bold

abcdefghijklmnopqrstuvwxyz1234567890
ABCDEFGHIJKLMNOPQRSTUVWXYZ

Other notable cuts:

Goudy Catalogue [Monotype Imaging]

Goudy Modern [Monotype Imaging]

Goudy Heavyface [Lanston Type Corp]

Goudy Old Style [Adobe]

abcdefghijklmnopqrstuvwxyz
ABCDEFGHIJKLMNOPQ
RSTUVWXYZ1234567890
[àóüßç](.,:;?!$€£&-*){ÀÓÜÇ}

American typographer and book designer Frederic W. Goudy (1865–1947) worked with American Type Founders (ATF) and served as art director for Lanston Monotype from 1920–1947. Goudy drew a number of distinct designs bearing his name (it was common practice at that time to name types after their creators). The most successful of these was Goudy Old Style. Released in 1915 by ATF, the design was inspired by the Froben capitals probably cut in the sixteenth century by Peter Schöffer the Younger, son of Johannes Gutenberg's apprentice. Although generally classified as a Garalde, some characteristics of this typeface display a Venetian influence.

The original Goudy Old Style consisted only of a roman and an italic. Due to the extreme popularity of Cooper Black (1921), Lanston requested heavy versions of Goudy Old Style. Goudy responded with Goudy Heavyface and Heavyface Italic, which were released in 1925. Several more weights were added to Goudy's types in subsequent years.

BUSINESS CARD
Client Vivendi Development
Studio Helena Seo Design
Creative Director/Designer Helena Seo
Printer Simon Printing, Inc.
Principal Typefaces Goudy Old Style and Trade Gothic

BOOK COVER
Publisher Chronicle Books, San Francisco
Studio MacFadden & Thorpe
Designer Brett MacFadden
Principal Typefaces Goudy Heavyface and ITC Avant Garde Gothic (modified)

If you like …

Goudy

… you could also consider:

Bembo
Sabon
Cooper Black

OFFICINA SERIF

transitional serif • legible

nd

9/10pt

HOW RAZORBACK-JUMPING FROGS CAN LEVEL SIX PIQUED GYMNASTS! Jackdaws love my big sphinx of quartz. Jaded zombies acted quaintly but kept driving their oxen forward. The quick brown fox jumps over a lazy dog. The public was amazed to view the quickness and dexterity of the juggler. A mad boxer shot a quick, gloved jab to the jaw of his dizzy opponent. The five boxing wizards jump quickly. How razorback-

10/12pt

HOW RAZORBACK-JUMPING FROGS CAN LEVEL SIX PIQUED gymnasts! Jackdaws love my big sphinx of quartz. Jaded zombies acted quaintly but kept driving their oxen forward. The quick brown fox jumps over a lazy dog. The public was amazed to view the quickness and dexterity of the juggler. A mad boxer shot a quick, gloved jab to the jaw of his dizzy opponent. The

12/14pt

HOW RAZORBACK-JUMPING FROGS CAN LEVEL SIX piqued gymnasts! Jackdaws love my big sphinx of quartz. Jaded zombies acted quaintly but kept driving their oxen forward. The quick brown fox jumps over a lazy dog. The public was amazed to

ITC Officina Serif Book Italic

abcdefghijklmnopqrstuvwxyz1234567890
ABCDEFGHIJKLMNOPQRSTUVWXYZ

ITC Officina Serif Bold

abcdefghijklmnopqrstuvwxyz1234567890
ABCDEFGHIJKLMNOPQRSTUVWXYZ

ITC Officina Serif Bold Italic

abcdefghijklmnopqrstuvwxyz1234567890
ABCDEFGHIJKLMNOPQRSTUVWXYZ

ITC Officina Serif Black

abcdefghijklmnopqrstuvwxyz123456789
ABCDEFGHIJKLMNOPQRSTUVWXYZ

ITC Officina Serif Black Italic

abcdefghijklmnopqrstuvwxyz123456789
ABCDEFGHIJKLMNOPQRSTUVWXYZ

ITC Officina Serif Book [ITC]

abcdefghijklmnopqrstuvwxyz
ABCDEFGHIJKLMNOPQRSTU
VWXYZ1234567890
[àóüßç](.,:;?!$€£&-*){ÀÓÜÇ}

ITC Officina Serif was developed by German design powerhouse Erik Spiekermann and released in 1990, along with the matching Officina Sans. Originally just two weights with italics, this pair was intended for business applications requiring extreme legibility under less than optimal conditions. The serif variants in particular display traits of traditional typewriter text, but greatly modified to suit technological advancements. Upon its release, designers worldwide took notice and the ITC Officina suite became an instant modern classic. Noting its widespread use by trendsetters in a variety of projects, Spiekermann collaborated with Ole Schäfer to add the extra weights and small caps necessary to make the typeface suitable for magazines, books, and advertising.

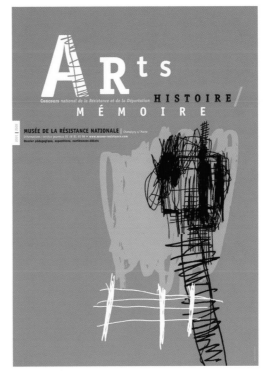

POSTER
Client Musée de la Résistance Nationale
Designer Olivier Umecker
Principal Typefaces ITC Officina Serif
and ITC Officina Sans

If you like …

Officina Serif

… you could also consider:

Clarendon

Courier

Meta

ART EXHIBITION BROCHURE
Client Moose Jaw Museum & Art Gallery
Studio Bradbury Branding and Design
Principal Typeface ITC Officina Serif

PERPETUA

od

9/10pt

HOW RAZORBACK-JUMPING FROGS CAN LEVEL SIX PIQUED GYM-nasts! Jackdaws love my big sphinx of quartz. Jaded zombies acted quaintly but kept driving their oxen forward. The quick brown fox jumps over a lazy dog. The public was amazed to view the quickness and dexterity of the juggler. A mad boxer shot a quick, gloved jab to the jaw of his dizzy opponent. The five boxing wizards jump quickly. How razorback-jumping frogs can level six piqued

10/12pt

HOW RAZORBACK-JUMPING FROGS CAN LEVEL SIX PIQUED gymnasts! Jackdaws love my big sphinx of quartz. Jaded zombies acted quaintly but kept driving their oxen forward. The quick brown fox jumps over a lazy dog. The public was amazed to view the quickness and dex-terity of the juggler. A mad boxer shot a quick, gloved jab to the jaw of his dizzy opponent. The five boxing wizards jump quickly. How razor-

12/14pt

HOW RAZORBACK-JUMPING FROGS CAN LEVEL SIX piqued gymnasts! Jackdaws love my big sphinx of quartz. Jaded zombies acted quaintly but kept driving their oxen forward. The quick brown fox jumps over a lazy dog. The public was amazed to view the quickness and dexterity of

Perpetua Italic

abcdefghijklmnopqrstuvwxyz1234567890
ABCDEFGHIJKLMNOPQRSTUVWXYZ

Perpetua Bold

abcdefghijklmnopqrstuvwxyz1234567
ABCDEFGHIJKLMNOPQRSTUVWXY

Perpetua Bold Italic

abcdefghijklmnopqrstuvwxyz1234567890
ABCDEFGHIJKLMNOPQRSTUVWXYZ

Perpetua Titling Light

ABCDEFGHIJKLMNOPQRSTUVWX

Perpetua Titling Regular

ABCDEFGHIJKLMNOPQRSTUVW

Perpetua Titling Bold

ABCDEFGHIJKLMNOPQRSTUV

Perpetua [Monotype Imaging]

abcdefghijklmnopqrstuvwxyz
ABCDEFGHIJKLMNOPQ
RSTUVWXYZ1234567890
[àóüßç](.,:;?!$€£&-*){ÀÓÜÇ}

Perpetua is the creation of Eric Gill (1882–1940), the noted British sculptor, typeface designer, stonecutter, and printmaker. Stanley Morison, typographical advisor to Monotype in the UK, was looking for a new typeface for the foundry. At his request, Gill began work on Perpetua in 1925. He gave his large-scale drawings to Parisian punchcutter Charles Malin to cut from, and the roman was issued in 1929. Perpetua's first italic companion, Felicity, was not used. Instead, Gill drew another, more sloped version, which was released as Perpetua Italic. The types first appeared in a limited edition of the book *The Passion of Perpetua and Felicity*, which inspired the naming of the new designs.

Although Perpetua was designed later than the historical period of Transitional type (the pinnacle being John Baskerville's work in the latter half of the eighteenth century), Perpetua is classed as such due to earmarks like its high degree of stroke contrast and bracketed serifs. Perpetua stands out among the Transitionals due to the personality of Gill's hand—the types bear all the refinement and charm of letterforms the artist cut in stone.

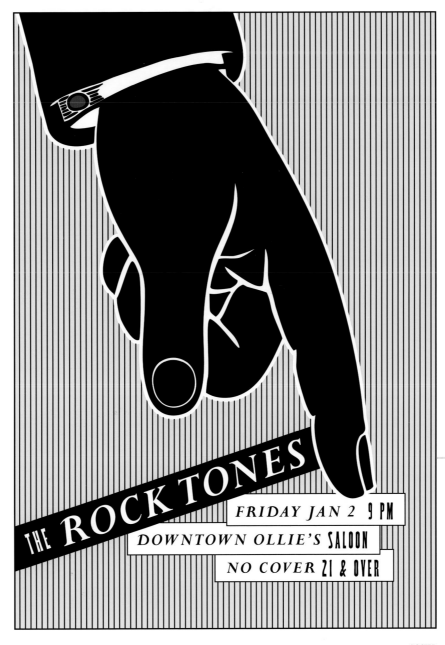

MARCEAU
ANTIQUE GALLERY

If you like …

Perpetua

… you could also consider:

Bembo

Centaur

Times

POSTER
Client The Rock Tones
Designer Mara Garcia
Principal Typefaces Perpetua and P22 Woodtype

LOGO
Client Marceau Antique Gallery
Studio Typeco
Designer James Grieshaber
Principal Typeface Perpetua Titling

All images this page:

BOOK
Designer/Illustrator Alisha Fund
Book Binder Wert Bookbinding
Photographer Beth Wong
Principal Typefaces Perpetua and Gill Sans

Created for Carolina de Bartolo's online Type Systems course at San Francisco's Academy of Art University, The Story of Germ Life *describes how bacteria thrive despite human efforts to control them. As an expression of the microscopic nature of bacteria, all type is set in 8 points or smaller throughout the book. The textures of punctuation marks represent the various kinds of bacteria that are shaped like periods, commas, colons, vertical slashes, and tildes.*

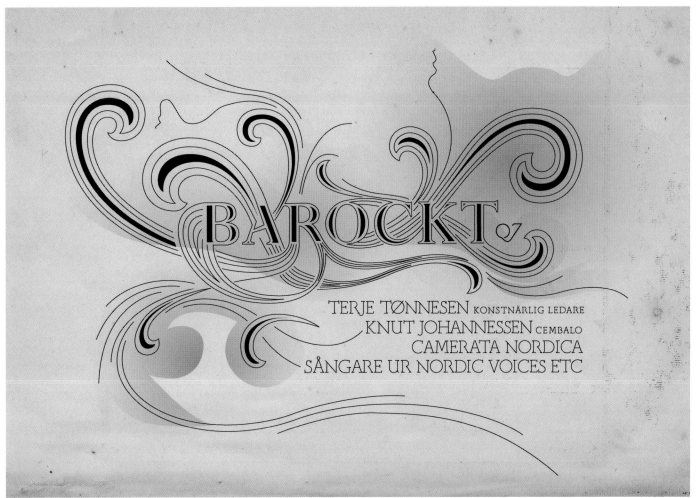

IDENTITY AND PROMOTIONAL MATERIALS
Clients Länsmusiken and Kalmar Läns Musikstiftelse
Studio Neue Design Studio
Designers Benjamin Stenmarck and Øystein Haugseth
Principal Typefaces Gill Sans and Perpetua (modified)

Identity design, poster, and promotional material for Barockt 07, a classical music festival in Sweden. The logo features a heavily modified and illustrated version of Perpetua.

IDENTITY
Client Ape&Bjorn
Studio Neue Design Studio
Designers Benjamin Stenmarck and Øystein Haugseth
Principal Typefaces Perpetua (modified), FF Kievit, and Burgues Script

Profile for a movie production company. The project included identity, illustrations, stationery, business cards, mailerheads, folders, CD/DVD packaging, and presentation materials. The logotype is a heavily modified version of Perpetua.

ROCKWELL

nd

9/10pt

HOW RAZORBACK-JUMPING FROGS CAN LEVEL SIX PIQUED gymnasts! Jackdaws love my big sphinx of quartz. Jaded zombies acted quaintly but kept driving their oxen forward. The quick brown fox jumps over a lazy dog. The public was amazed to view the quickness and dexterity of the juggler. A mad boxer shot a quick, gloved jab to the jaw of his dizzy opponent. The five boxing

10/12pt

HOW RAZORBACK-JUMPING FROGS CAN LEVEL SIX piqued gymnasts! Jackdaws love my big sphinx of quartz. Jaded zombies acted quaintly but kept driving their oxen forward. The quick brown fox jumps over a lazy dog. The public was amazed to view the quickness and dexterity of the juggler. A mad boxer shot a quick, gloved jab to the jaw

12/14pt

HOW RAZORBACK-JUMPING FROGS CAN level six piqued gymnasts! Jackdaws love my big sphinx of quartz. Jaded zombies acted quaintly but kept driving their oxen forward. The quick brown fox jumps over a lazy dog. The public was

Rockwell Light Italic
abcdefghijklmnopqrstuvwxyz1234567890
ABCDEFGHIJKLMNOPQRSTUVWXYZ

Rockwell Regular
abcdefghijklmnopqrstuvwxyz1234567890
ABCDEFGHIJKLMNOPQRSTUVWXYZ

Rockwell Italic
abcdefghijklmnopqrstuvwxyz1234567890
ABCDEFGHIJKLMNOPQRSTUVWXYZ

Rockwell Bold
abcdefghijklmnopqrstuvwxyz123456789
ABCDEFGHIJKLMNOPQRSTUVWXYZ

Rockwell Bold Italic
abcdefghijklmnopqrstuvwxyz1234567890
ABCDEFGHIJKLMNOPQRSTUVWXYZ

Rockwell Extra Bold
abcdefghijklmnopqrstuvwxyz
ABCDEFGHIJKLMNOPQRSTUVW

Rockwell Light [Monotype Imaging]

abcdefghijklmnopqrstuvwxyz

ABCDEFGHIJKLMNOPQ

RSTUVWXYZ1234567890

[àóüßç](.,:;?!$€£&-*){ÀÓÜÇ}

Rockwell was derived from the first geometric Slab Serif (Egyptian), Litho Antique (originally produced by the Inland Typefoundry of St. Louis, USA, in 1910). Morris Fuller Benton cut several new weights for an American Type Founders (ATF) revival of the design in the 1920s. The Monotype Corporation produced its own version, called Rockwell, in 1933/1934, with that foundry's in-house design team working under the direction of Frank Hinman Pierpont. Its precisely drawn forms feature very round counters paired with squared-off (unbracketed) serifs, and a monoline stroke weight. Rockwell was intended as a competitor to the German Stempel foundry's Memphis type, which was also influenced by Litho Antique. Due to an error in marketing, Rockwell was sometimes incorrectly referred to as Stymie Bold, and the two similar designs are still confused today.

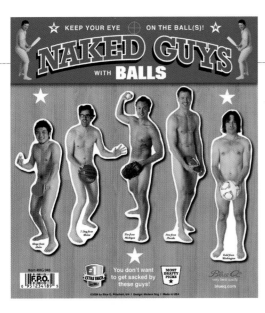

MAGNETS AND PACKAGING
Client Blue Q
Studio Modern Dog Design Co.
Designer Michael Strassburger
Photographer Ron Carraher
Principal Typefaces Rockwell and Helvetica

CD PACKAGING
Client Difusiones Cristianas
Studio huizar 1984
Designer José Ignacio Zárate Huizar
Principal Typeface Rockwell

If you like …

Rockwell

… you could also consider:

Blackoak

Clarendon

Courier

Officina Serif

SABON

od

9/10pt

HOW RAZORBACK-JUMPING FROGS CAN LEVEL SIX PIQUED gymnasts! Jackdaws love my big sphinx of quartz. Jaded zombies acted quaintly but kept driving their oxen forward. The quick brown fox jumps over a lazy dog. The public was amazed to view the quickness and dexterity of the juggler. A mad boxer shot a quick, gloved jab to the jaw of his dizzy opponent. The five boxing wizards

10/12pt

HOW RAZORBACK-JUMPING FROGS CAN LEVEL SIX piqued gymnasts! Jackdaws love my big sphinx of quartz. Jaded zombies acted quaintly but kept driving their oxen forward. The quick brown fox jumps over a lazy dog. The public was amazed to view the quickness and dexterity of the juggler. A mad boxer shot a quick, gloved jab to the jaw of his

12/14pt

HOW RAZORBACK-JUMPING FROGS CAN level six piqued gymnasts! Jackdaws love my big sphinx of quartz. Jaded zombies acted quaintly but kept driving their oxen forward. The quick brown fox jumps over a lazy dog. The public was amazed

Sabon Next Italic

abcdefghijklmnopqrstuvwxyz1234567890
ABCDEFGHIJKLMNOPQRSTUVWXYZ
ABCDEFGHIJKLMNOPQRSTUVWXYZ

Sabon Next Bold

abcdefghijklmnopqrstuvwxyz1234567890
ABCDEFGHIJKLMNOPQRSTUVWXYZ
ABCDEFGHIJKLMNOPQRSTUVWXYZ

Sabon Next Bold Italic

abcdefghijklmnopqrstuvwxyz1234567890
ABCDEFGHIJKLMNOPQRSTUVWXYZ
ABCDEFGHIJKLMNOPQRSTUVWXYZ

Other notable cuts:

Sabon [Monotype Imaging]

Sabon Next Regular [Linotype]

abcdefghijklmnopqrstuvwxyz
ABCDEFGHIJKLMNOPQ
RSTUVWXYZ1234567890
[àóüßç](.,:;?!$€£&-*){ÀÓÜÇ}

Sabon is an Old Style typeface descended from the forms originated by French type designer Claude Garamond. This Garalde design was developed to meet the needs of a group of German printers seeking a typeface that would remain identical in form when produced by three different metal-casting technologies. Jan Tschichold commenced work on Sabon in 1964; it was jointly released by Stempel, Linotype, and Monotype in 1967.

Sabon's roman is based on a Garamond specimen printed by Frankfurt printer Konrad F. Berner in the sixteenth century. Berner was married to the widow of a fellow printer, Jacques Sabon, and Tschichold's new face was named in his honor. The italic is based on the work of Robert Granjon, Garamond's assistant. Bradbury Thompson was one of the first to use Sabon, for setting the text of the Washburn College Bible in 1973. The text was set by hand using the thought-unit method of typography—Thompson broke each line at its spoken syntactical break.

Parisian type designer Jean-François Porchéz developed a contemporary version for Linotype in 2002. Called Sabon Next, it is based both on the work of Tschichold and on his own study of original Garamond models.

POSTER
Art Director/Designer Michael Braley
Principal Typefaces Helvetica and Sabon

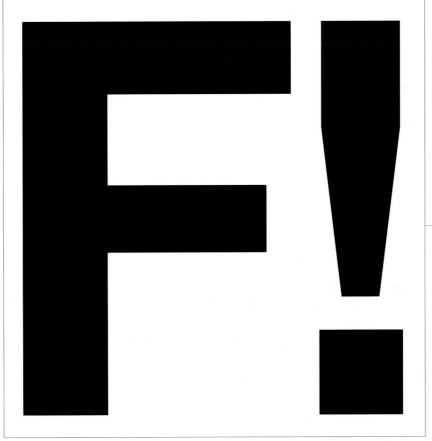

F___! So, now what?

Michael Braley
Temple University
Tyler School of Art
Friday, March 4, 2005
Penrose Room 108 1:30 p.m.
Elkins Park, Pennsylvania

If you like …

Sabon

… you could also consider:

Bembo
Garamond
Goudy

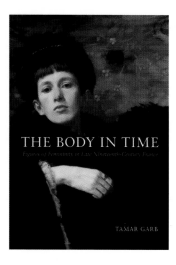

THE BODY IN TIME

Figures of Femininity in Late Nineteenth-Century France

TAMAR GARB

PORTRAITURE & THE NEW WOMAN

TWO WOMEN ARTISTS ARE STAGED IN A MOMENT OF SUSPENDED labor. Their occupation, as much as their appearance, defines them. The one, palette in one hand, laden brushes in the other, is dressed plainly and comfortably in her working attire (fig. 19). Her belted apron and dark daywear constitute a sensible and appropriate costume for working at the easel, while her unadorned head and plain hairgrip offer no distraction from the intensity of her gaze and the intelligence of her expression. Framed by a plain brown drape, which provides a sober backdrop to the alert figure, the erect body seems perched on its hard wooden chair, ready to rise or turn back to the easel and continue with its work. This is a self-portrait by the Polish painter Anna Bilinska-Bohdanowiczowa, who lived in Paris, and in it, the artist seems to assert her professional identity and character, her individuality.

The portrait *Rosa Bonheur,* painted some ten years later by Bonheur's companion, Anna Elizabeth Klumpke, is equally forthright in its assertion of professional and personal particularity (fig. 20). The renowned animal

39

scumbled facticity of his works, leaving his mark on his opaque and densely worked canvases without smoothing over or erasing his touch.

Degas created highly individuated compositions by constructing particularized, unorthodox viewpoints and angles of vision. Neither neutral observer nor fictive disembodied spectator, Degas inscribed his own singular perspective on the events of his time by adopting a view from the sidelines, throwing into disorder the orchestrated frontality of the conventional auditorium vantage point. In a pastel like *Dancers at the Old Opera House* (1877), for example, Degas fabricated a putative position from which to look and depict, ostensibly placing himself above the stage and looking down from the wings (fig. 5). In a work such as *Ballet Scene from Meyerbeer's Opera "Robert le Diable"* (1876), he seems to occupy the lower perspective of the musicians in the orchestra pit (fig. 6). In each case, the singularity and veracity of viewpoint was part of the realist fiction to which he was committed. Although Degas was neither seated below the stage with his friends in the orchestra nor suspended above the stage on a platform in the wings when actually executing his pastels and paintings, his works nevertheless presuppose just such a viewpoint. The fiction serves to endorse the illusion of presence and presentness that Realism entails. Realist time is always the present, and its rhetorical alibi is the putative presence of the artist as witness.[6]

Research into the conditions of production of works like these, however, reveals the artifice that was at their source. *Dancers at the Old Opera House,* for example, was executed some years after the ballet had ceased to be held at the old theatre in the rue Le Peletier, which the image evidently depicts. Executed in pastel over monotype, the work could not predate Degas' invention of monotype in 1876. And yet the architectural detail of cornices, pilasters, and the decoration of the "loges" (the private viewing boxes that are clearly depicted) confirm the work's setting as the stage and auditorium of the building that had been destroyed by fire in 1873.[7] Placed high above the stage, behind the shadowy pilaster that forms the boundary between the space of the performers and that of the orchestra and audience, Degas invents for himself a privileged bird's-eye view which allows him to picture fragments of all components of this social scene: the legs and the chorus of dancers together with a sketchy rendering of their hands, heads, and torsos; the dark mass of the orchestra punctuated by flesh tones that stand for hands and faces; and the animated presence of the audience ensconced, across the way, in their private boxes, a flurry of gesture, movement, and agitated paintwork. United on the plane of the picture, the participants of the social scene are signified by touch and texture, smudged, smeared, and stroked onto the paper's surface.

14 TEMPORALITY & THE DANCER

All images this page:

BOOK COVER AND INTERIOR
Publisher University of Washington Press,
  Seattle and London
Designer Ashley Saleeba
Principal Typeface Sabon

"Lewis Mumford describes the city as the point of maximum concentration for the power and culture of a community, a place where the diffused rays of many separate beams of life fall into focus, and where we witness the form and symbol of integrated social relationships."

"if you go out with a magnifying glass and hunt carefully, you may find somewhere a point no bigger than the head of a pin which, if you look at it slightly enlarged, reveals within itself the roofs, the antennas, the skylights,

the gardens, the pools,

the streamers across the streets,

the kiosks in the squeares,

the horse-racing track.

That point does not remain there: a year later you will find it

the size of half a lemon, then as large as a mush-room, then a

soup plate. And then it becomes a full-size city, enclosed within

the earlier city: a new city that forces its way ahead in the earlier

city and presses its way toward the outside."

"The city's streets were streets where they went to work every day, with no link any more to the dreamed chase. Which, for that matter, had long been forgotten. New men arrived from other lands, having had a dream like theirs, and, they recognized something from the streets of the dream, and they changed the positions of arcades and stairways to resemble more closely the path of the pursued woman and so, at the spot where she had vanished, there would remain no avenue of escape. The first to arrive could not understand what drew these people to, this ugly city, this trap. The clean and dirty, the order and chaos, the heaven and hell of the city exist side by side."

"For what kind of dreams lie beneath the spatial

schizophrenia of our contemporary cities?

What visions are nurtured in the gaps between

the vacated opulence of the shopping precinct

and the crowded dereliction of the streets?"

"They saw a woman running

at night through an unknown city;"

"she was seen from behind, with long hair, and she was naked. They dreamed of pursuing her. As they twisted and turned, each of them lost her. After the dream, they set out in search of that city; they never found it, but they found one another; they decided to build a city like the one in the dream. In laying out the streets, each followed the course of his pursuit; at the spot where they had lost the fugitive's trail, they arranged spaces and walls differently from the dream, so she would be unable to escape again. This was where they settled, waiting for that scene to be repeated one night. None of them, asleep or awake, ever saw the woman again."

All images this page:

BOOK
Designer Natalia Tomaszewska
Principal Typefaces Basquiat and Sabon

Urban Landscapes *is a personal project of Tomaszewska's depicting Dudley Square in Boston. Her objective was to capture the essence of the place through type and image to illustrate the area's mix of tradition and modern living.*

TIMES

od

9/10pt

HOW RAZORBACK-JUMPING FROGS CAN LEVEL SIX piqued gymnasts! Jackdaws love my big sphinx of quartz. Jaded zombies acted quaintly but kept driving their oxen forward. The quick brown fox jumps over a lazy dog. The public was amazed to view the quickness and dexterity of the juggler. A mad boxer shot a quick, gloved jab to the jaw of his dizzy opponent. The five boxing

10/12pt

HOW RAZORBACK-JUMPING FROGS CAN LEVEL six piqued gymnasts! Jackdaws love my big sphinx of quartz. Jaded zombies acted quaintly but kept driving their oxen forward. The quick brown fox jumps over a lazy dog. The public was amazed to view the quickness and dexterity of the juggler. A mad boxer shot a quick, gloved jab to the jaw of

12/14pt

HOW RAZORBACK-JUMPING FROGS CAN level six piqued gymnasts! Jackdaws love my big sphinx of quartz. Jaded zombies acted quaintly but kept driving their oxen forward. The quick brown fox jumps over a lazy dog. The public was

Times New Roman Italic

abcdefghijklmnopqrstuvwxyz1234567890
ABCDEFGHIJKLMNOPQRSTUVWXYZ

Times New Roman Bold

abcdefghijklmnopqrstuvwxyz1234567890
ABCDEFGHIJKLMNOPQRSTUVWXYZ

Times New Roman Bold Italic

abcdefghijklmnopqrstuvwxyz1234567890
ABCDEFGHIJKLMNOPQRSTUVWXYZ

Other notable cuts:

Times Ten [Linotype]
Times Roman [Linotype]
Times NR Seven [Monotype Imaging]
Times Small Text [Monotype Imaging]

Times New Roman [Monotype Imaging]

abcdefghijklmnopqrstuvwxyz
ABCDEFGHIJKLMNOPQ
RSTUVWXYZ1234567890
[àóüßç](.,:;?!\$€£&-*){ÀÓÜÇ}

Times New Roman was designed in 1931
by Stanley Morison and Victor Lardent for
the UK foundry Monotype. The typeface was
commissioned by *The Times* after Morison wrote
an outspoken article vehemently criticizing
the paper for its poor printing and outdated
typography. Morison used the Plantin Old Style
Garalde as a model for the new design, making
careful revisions to improve legibility and add
economy of space. Lardent, an artist in the
advertising department of *The Times,* drew the
typeface under Morison's supervision. Times Old
Roman was the type formerly used by *The Times,*
so the new design was dubbed Times New Roman.
The custom face debuted in the October 3, 1932
issue of the paper, and was released for commercial
use after a year of exclusivity.

The Times used Times New Roman for 40 years.
Continued advances in technology and production
processes, and a change in format from broadsheet
to tabloid, have necessitated changing typefaces
a number of times since 1972, but the font updates
were all developed from Times New Roman.
There are myriad typefaces issued by multiple
foundries that bear some form of the name Times,
and some version of Times is a staple in computer
operating systems. Although Times New Roman
is no longer used by *The Times,* it remains one
of the most common typefaces worldwide and
is frequently used in book publishing and by
other newspapers.

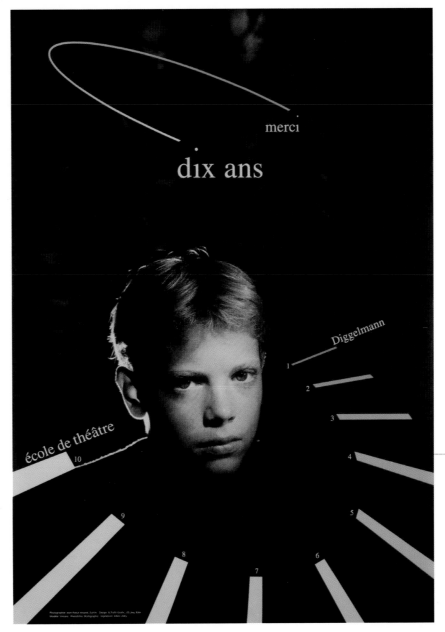

If you like …

Times

… you could also consider:

Baskerville
Caslon
Perpetua

POSTER
Client École de Théâtre Diggelman Lausanne
Studio Studio AND
Designer Jean-Benoît Lévy
Photographer Jean-Pascal Imsand
Principal Typeface Times New Roman

LOGO
Client Scripps Health
Studio Lippincott
Creative Director Brendán Murphy
Principal Typeface Times New Roman

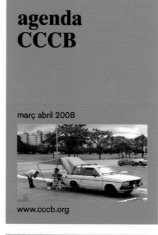

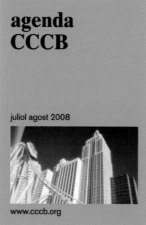
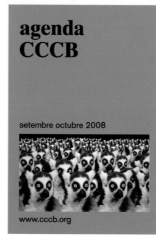

AGENDA
Client Contemporary Culture Center of Barcelona (CCCB)
Studio toormix
Principal Typefaces Times Ten and Akzidenz-Grotesk

POSTER
Client Higher Ground Music
Studio JDK Design
Designer Peter Sunna
Principal Typeface Times Modern

WALBAUM

didone • modern

od

9/10pt

HOW RAZORBACK-JUMPING FROGS CAN LEVEL SIX piqued gymnasts! Jackdaws love my big sphinx of quartz. Jaded zombies acted quaintly but kept driving their oxen forward. The quick brown fox jumps over a lazy dog. The public was amazed to view the quickness and dexterity of the juggler. A mad boxer shot a quick, gloved jab to the jaw of his

10/12pt

HOW RAZORBACK-JUMPING FROGS CAN LEVEL six piqued gymnasts! Jackdaws love my big sphinx of quartz. Jaded zombies acted quaintly but kept driving their oxen forward. The quick brown fox jumps over a lazy dog. The public was amazed to view the quickness and dexterity of the juggler. A mad boxer shot a quick,

12/14pt

HOW RAZORBACK-JUMPING FROGS CAN level six piqued gymnasts! Jackdaws love my big sphinx of quartz. Jaded zombies acted quaintly but kept driving their oxen forward. The quick brown fox jumps over a lazy dog.

Berthold Walbaum Book Italic

abcdefghijklmnopqrstuvwxyz1234567890
ABCDEFGHIJKLMNOPQRSTUVWXYZ

Berthold Walbaum Book Medium

abcdefghijklmnopqrstuvwxyz1234567890
ABCDEFGHIJKLMNOPQRSTUVWXYZ

Berthold Walbaum Book Medium Italic

abcdefghijklmnopqrstuvwxyz123456789
ABCDEFGHIJKLMNOPQRSTUVWXYZ

Berthold Walbaum Book Bold

abcdefghijklmnopqrstuvwxyz12345678
ABCDEFGHIJKLMNOPQRSTUVWXYZ

Other notable cuts:

Monotype Walbaum [Monotype]
Walbaum Com [Linotype]

Berthold Walbaum Book [Berthold]

abcdefghijklmnopqrstuvwxyz
ABCDEFGHIJKLMNOPQ
RSTUVWXYZ1234567890
[àóüßç](.,:;?!$€£&-*){ÀÓÜÇ}

Walbaum is based on the types of Justus Erich Walbaum (1768–1839), a punchcutter and typefounder who set up shop in Weimar, Germany, circa 1798. Walbaum was heavily influenced by the Modern/Didone typefaces from France, including those cut by Firmin Didot. His namesake type, cut in 1804, is distinguished from other Moderns by its larger x-height and wider capitals. There are several versions of Walbaum in digital form, including two from Berthold that were developed by Günter Gerhard Lange and released in 1976. Berthold Walbaum Book is based on the 16-point size of the original type and is more high-contrast than the foundry's "standard" version, which is based on the 8- and 10-point sizes, and is more appropriate for smaller text. Monotype Walbaum is also based on the smaller cuts, and is delicately styled in its lighter weights.

BROCHURE
Client Musée d'Orsay
Studio Nicolas Portnoï designer graphique
Photographer © Patrice Schmidt/Musée d'Orsay
Principal Typeface Berthold Walbaum Book

Musée d'Orsay project coordination: Nadia Leriche and
Frédérique de Redon (graphic studio), and Yann Le Touher (patronage).

If you like …

Walbaum

… you could also consider:

Baskerville
Bodoni
Caslon

TYPE SPECIMEN
Designer Sam Mallett
Principal Typeface Monotype Walbaum

ABCDEFGHIJK

This text is set in Avenir Next LT Pro Heavy

LMSANSSERIFM

AKZIDENZ-GROTESK

grotesque • legible

aC

9/10pt

HOW RAZORBACK-JUMPING FROGS CAN LEVEL SIX piqued gymnasts! Jackdaws love my big sphinx of quartz. Jaded zombies acted quaintly but kept driving their oxen forward. The quick brown fox jumps over a lazy dog. The public was amazed to view the quickness and dexterity of the juggler. A mad boxer shot a quick, gloved jab to the jaw of his dizzy opponent. The five boxing

10/12pt

HOW RAZORBACK-JUMPING FROGS CAN LEVEL SIX piqued gymnasts! Jackdaws love my big sphinx of quartz. Jaded zombies acted quaintly but kept driving their oxen forward. The quick brown fox jumps over a lazy dog. The public was amazed to view the quickness and dexterity of the juggler. A mad boxer shot a quick, gloved jab to the jaw

12/14pt

HOW RAZORBACK-JUMPING FROGS CAN level six piqued gymnasts! Jackdaws love my big sphinx of quartz. Jaded zombies acted quaintly but kept driving their oxen forward. The quick brown fox jumps over a lazy dog. The public was amazed

Akzidenz-Grotesk Italic

abcdefghijklmnopqrstuvwxyz1234567890
ABCDEFGHIJKLMNOPQRSTUVWXYZ

Akzidenz-Grotesk Bold

abcdefghijklmnopqrstuvwxyz1234567890
ABCDEFGHIJKLMNOPQRSTUVWXYZ

Akzidenz-Grotesk Bold Italic

abcdefghijklmnopqrstuvwxyz1234567890
ABCDEFGHIJKLMNOPQRSTUVWXYZ

Akzidenz-Grotesk Super

abcdefghijklmnopqrstuvwxyz12345678
ABCDEFGHIJKLMNOPQRSTUVWXYZ

Akzidenz-Grotesk Condensed

abcdefghijklmnopqrstuvwxyz1234567890
ABCDEFGHIJKLMNOPQRSTUVWXYZ

Akzidenz-Grotesk Extended

abcdefghijklmnopqrstuvwxyz12345
ABCDEFGHIJKLMNOPQRSTUVW

Akzidenz-Grotesk [Berthold]

abcdefghijklmnopqrstuvwxyz
ABCDEFGHIJKLMNOPQ
RSTUVWXYZ1234567890
[àóüßç](.,:;?!$€£&-*){ÀÓÜÇ}

Akzidenz-Grotesk was first issued by Berlin's H. Berthold AG typefoundry in 1898. (Akzidenz means "trade printing, printing of a limited number of copies" in German.) One of the best-known Sans, and one that has influenced many designs since its release, the first weight of this realist type was fairly light and intended for display use. Akzidenz-Grotesk was made up of a variety of designs from multiple sources, which explains why some of its letterforms have a certain quirkiness, with unexpected differences seen in characters across weights and styles.

Upon its release, Akzidenz-Grotesk became incredibly popular, inciting other foundries to create their own versions. Although the modernist movement of the 1920s made geometric Sans like Futura more fashionable, the Grotesque style ruled much of the twentieth century. The contemporary Akzidenz-Grotesk dates from the 1950s, when Günter Gerhard Lange enlarged the family for Berthold, making it more useful for text work while retaining the character of the original forms.

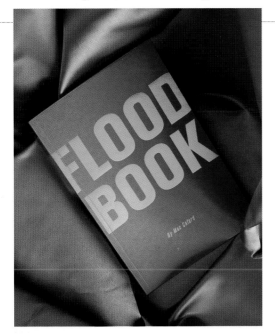

If you like …

Akzidenz-Grotesk

… you could also consider:

Folio
Franklin Gothic
Grotesque
Helvetica
Trade Gothic

T-SHIRT ART
Client Alexisonfire
Studio Doublenaut
Designer Andrew McCracken
Principal Typeface Akzidenz-Grotesk

BOOK COVER
Publisher Psychic Swamp Books, New Orleans
Studio Nancy Sharon Collins, Stationer
Designer Nancy Sharon Collins
Principal Typeface Akzidenz-Grotesk

POSTER
Client Polaris Music Prize
Studio Doublenaut
Designer Matt McCracken
Principal Typeface Akzidenz-Grotesk

All images right, top to bottom:
BOOK
Publisher Balcony Press, Glendale
Studio DISTINC
Designers Jean-Marc Durviaux and John Wiese
Principal Typefaces Akzidenz-Grotesk and
Bureau Grotesque

Both images above:
CD COVER
Client Smalltown Superjazzz
Designer Rune Mortensen
Photographer Ken Vandermark
Principal Typeface Akzidenz-Grotesk

POSTER
Client The Shins
Studio The Small Stakes
Designer Jason Munn
Principal Typeface Akzidenz-Grotesk

ALBUM COVER
Client Troubled Hubble
Studio End Communications
Principal Typeface Akzidenz-Grotesk

IDENTITY SYSTEM
Client John DeMerritt Bookbinding
Studio konnectDesign
Designer Sarah Rainwater
Creative Director Karen Knecht
Principal Typeface Akzidenz-Grotesk

VIEWBOOK
Client Wheeling Jesuit University
Studio 160over90
Designer Adam Garcia
Chief Creative Director Darryl Cilli
Creative Director Stephen Penning
Copywriter Brendan Quinn
Principal Typefaces Akzidenz-Grotesk,
Apex New, and Clarendon

EXHIBITION CATALOG COVER
Client Centre Culturel de la Caixa de Terrassa
Studio Müller-Lancé Diseño Gráfico
Designers Joachim Müller-Lancé with Katrin Meyer
Printer Font Diestre
Principal Typeface Akzidenz-Grotesk

Designed in collaboration with the exhibition firm
Croquis Disseny d'Espais in Barcelona.

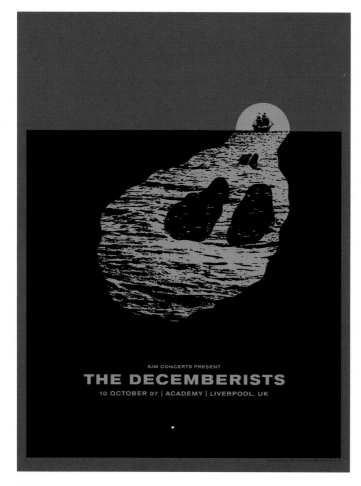

POSTER
Client The Decemberists
Studio The Small Stakes
Designer Jason Munn
Principal Typeface Akzidenz-Grotesk

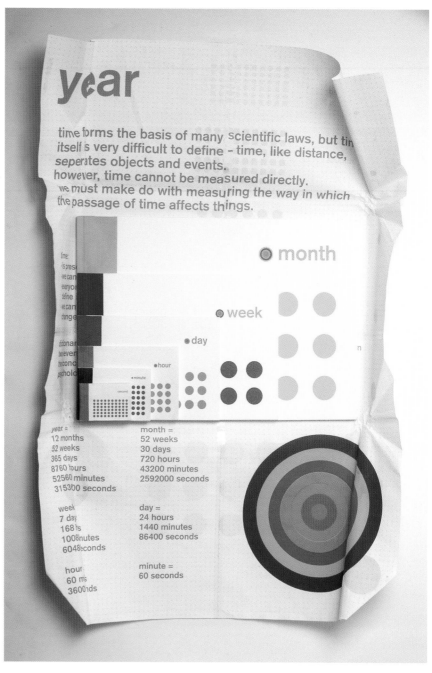

BOOKS AND POSTER
Studio missbeck
Designer Marianne Beck
Principal Typeface Akzidenz-Grotesk

Beachdown
Festival
—

Devil's Dyke
Brighton
22—25 August
2008
—

Acts include

De La Soul
Gogol Bordello
The Magic
Numbers
Nouvelle Vague
José González
Roisin Murphy
Amp Fiddler
Reverend &
the Makers
The Maccabees
Azymuth
Terry Callier
Sia
Alabama 3
Horace Andy &
the Dub Asante
—

Fun Loving
Criminals
Roy Ayers &
Bah Samba
Light Speed
Champion
Bonobo
Mr Scruff
The Heavy
The Brakes
Jah Wobble
Freak Power
The Young
Knives
Los Albertos
The Infadels
Gloria Cycles
—

The Men They
Couldn't Hang
Imperial Leisure
Wayne
Hemingway
(DJ Set)
Hercules &
Love Affair
Peggy Sue &
the Pirates
—

Plus more acts
to be confirmed
—

Brighton stage:
The Splendour
Shona Foster
Transformer
12 Stone Toddler
Acoustic Dregs
Doll & The Kicks
Heels Catch Fire
Drookit Dogs
The Hat
Hardkandy
The Miserable Rich
Damn Dirty Humans
Black Grass
Carnival Collective
Baby Charles
My Federation

Brighton club nights
Stick it On
Roots Garden
Bust the Box
Born Bad
Jazz Bop
—
Full DJ line-up
to be announced
—

4 days of music and entertainment with sea views,
the best in organic food
and cocktails prepared by
award-winning mixologists
—

Tickets available from
beachdownfestival.com
and normal Brighton outlets
including The Dorset,
Minky, Resident, Amnesty
bookshop, Rounder,
Tickled, Damage and where
you see posters displayed
—

£85 plus booking fee
including free camping
all weekend
—

beachdownfestival.com

CONFERENCE IDENTITY
Client National Membership
Committee on Psychoanalysis
Studio End Communications
Principal Typeface Akzidenz-Grotesk

POSTER
Client Future Festivals
Studio StudioMakgill
Principal Typefaces Akzidenz-Grotesk
and Century 725 BT

AVANT GARDE

9/10pt

HOW RAZORBACK-JUMPING FROGS CAN LEVEL SIX PIQUED GYM-nasts! Jackdaws love my big sphinx of quartz. Jaded zombies acted quaintly but kept driving their oxen forward. The quick brown fox jumps over a lazy dog. The public was amazed to view the quickness and dexterity of the juggler. A mad boxer shot a quick, gloved jab to the jaw of his dizzy opponent. The five boxing

10/12pt

HOW RAZORBACK-JUMPING FROGS CAN LEVEL SIX PIQUED gymnasts! Jackdaws love my big sphinx of quartz. Jaded zombies acted quaintly but kept driving their oxen forward. The quick brown fox jumps over a lazy dog. The public was amazed to view the quickness and dexterity of the juggler. A mad boxer shot a quick, gloved jab to the jaw of his dizzy

12/14pt

HOW RAZORBACK-JUMPING FROGS CAN LEVEL six piqued gymnasts! Jackdaws love my big sphinx of quartz. Jaded zombies acted quaintly but kept driving their oxen forward. The quick brown fox jumps over a lazy dog. The public was

ITC Avant Garde Gothic Book Italic

abcdefghijklmnopqrstuvwxyz1234567890
ABCDEFGHIJKLMNOPQRSTUVWXYZ

ITC Avant Garde Gothic Bold

abcdefghijklmnopqrstuvwxyz123456789
ABCDEFGHIJKLMNOPQRSTUVWXYZ

ITC Avant Garde Gothic Bold Italic

abcdefghijklmnopqrstuvwxyz123456789
ABCDEFGHIJKLMNOPQRSTUVWXYZ

ITC Avant Garde Gothic Book Alts (Ligatures)

SS 1 A CA EA FA GA HT KA LA M NT
PR RA ST TH UT V W A c e R LA M
ST T TU v w y © LL W w V

Other notable cuts:

ITC Avant Garde Gothic [ITC]

ITC Avant Garde Gothic Book [Elsner+Flake]

abcdefghijklmnopqrstuvwxyz

ABCDEFGHIJKLMNOPQRSTU

VWXYZ1234567890

(àóüßç)(.,:;?!$€£&-*){ÀÓÜÇ}

In the mid-1960s, New York design legend Herb Lubalin developed a unique logo for a new culture magazine titled *Avant Garde*. Lubalin's mark for the magazine was a study in geometry, with angular forms perfectly spaced to rest tightly against one another. When a full alphabet was needed for promotional materials, Lubalin and three assistants drew a complete uppercase alphabet. Tom Carnase, one of Lubalin's partners and a frequent collaborator, was brought in to the project, resulting in the creation of many additional hand-fitted character pairs, the ligatures that gave the design its completely original style.

Originally intended only for use in titling for the magazine, Avant Garde was published as a full-fledged typeface in 1970 by the International Typeface Corporation (ITC). A complete lowercase alphabet was added, with a Serif version dubbed Lubalin Graph designed by Tony DiSpigna. Another New York design giant, Ed Benguiat, drew condensed versions of Avant Garde in 1974.

ITC Avant Garde's complex design and extensive complement of ligatures proved daunting for many typographers, resulting in some of the most ugly and awkward typography of the 1970s and 1980s. When phototypesetting and PhotoTypositor headline setting gave way to digital typesetting, ITC Avant Garde was only available without its trademark ligatures, until the recent release of the extended versions by Germany's Elsner+Flake and ITC. Having fallen out of favor with designers in the 1990s, Avant Garde experienced a renaissance in the 2000s, and is currently used to great effect by designers who understand how to take advantage of its unique structure.

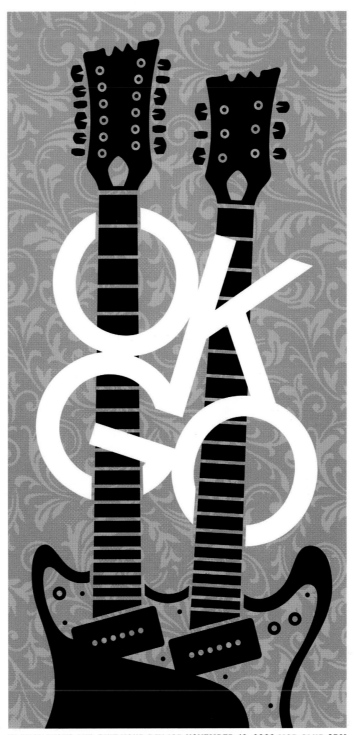

FRENCH KICKS AND QUIT YOUR DAY JOB **NOVEMBER 13, 2006** MOD CLUB **8PM**

If you like …

Avant Garde

… you could also consider:

Avenir
Bauhaus
DIN
Eurostile
Futura
Univers

Near left:

POSTER
Client Emerge Entertainment
Studio Doublenaut
Designer Matt McCracken
Principal Typeface ITC Avant Garde Gothic

Far left:

RECORD SLEEVE
Client Freerange Records
Studio Jawa and Midwich
Designer Simon Dovar and Nils Davey
Principal Typeface ITC Avant Garde Gothic
  (hand rendered)

BOOK
Client Evonik Degussa
Studio Kiggen for Flink
Designer Bart Kiggen
Photographer Koen Fasseur and
Dé Kunsthumaniora
Copywriter Frank Vandenheede
Principal Typeface ITC Avant Garde Gothic

CD COVER
Client Smalltown Superjazzz
Designer/Photographer Rune Mortensen
Principal Typeface ITC Avant Garde Gothic

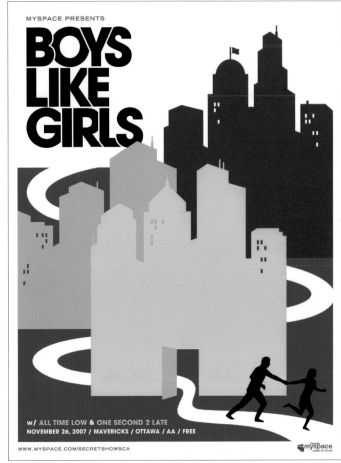

POSTER
Client MySpace Secret Shows
Studio Doublenaut
Designer Matt McCracken
Principal Typeface ITC Avant Garde Gothic

POSTER
Client Brasilcine Brazilian Film Festival
Studio Elapse
Designer Erik Jonsson
Principal Typeface ITC Avant Garde Gothic

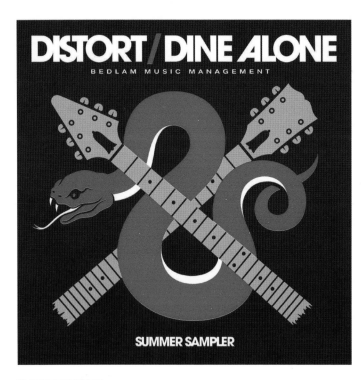

CD SAMPLER PACKAGING
Client Distort Entertainment
Studio Doublenaut
Designer Matt McCracken
Principal Typeface ITC Avant Garde Gothic

INVITATION POSTER
Client Premsela: Dutch Platform
for Design and Fashion
Studio Robin Uleman
Designers Robin Uleman, with special
thanks to Sandra Rabenou
Principal Typeface ITC Avant Garde Gothic

*This poster is part of a package of identity, collateral,
and other materials that Uleman produced for
Premsela. Additional examples from the ongoing
campaign are featured in this section
(see pages 108, 109, and 112).*

100% Chocolate Cafe.

All images this page:

IDENTITY, ENVIRONMENTAL GRAPHICS, PRODUCT DESIGN, AND PACKAGING
Client Meiji Seika Kaisha Ltd.
Interior Design Masamichi Katayama (Wonderwall)
Design Producer Koichi Ando (Ando Gallery)
Design Studio groovisions
Principal Typeface ITC Avant Garde Gothic

The design team at groovisions worked in collaboration with several creative concerns to produce branding, marketing, edible and nonedible products, and environmental design for Tokyo's 100%ChocolateCafe. ITC Avant Garde Gothic figured prominently on all items, including the text imprinted on the company's chocolate products.

IDENTITY AND STATIONERY
Client Sage Tucker-Ketcham
Designer Peter Sunna
Principal Typeface ITC Avant Garde Gothic

INVITATION POSTER
Client Premsela: Dutch Platform
for Design and Fashion
Studio Robin Uleman
Designers Robin Uleman, with special
thanks to Sandra Rabenou
Principal Typeface ITC Avant Garde Gothic

Above left:

MUSIC PACKAGING
Client Eskimo Recordings
Designer/Typographer Chris Bolton
Illustrator Vänskap
Photographer Niina Merikallio
Principal Typeface ITC Avant Garde Gothic (modified)

POSTER
Client Higher Ground Music
Studio JDK Design
Designer Peter Sunna
Principal Typeface ITC Avant Garde Gothic

IDENTITY AND STATIONERY
Client Premsela: Dutch Platform for Design and Fashion
Studio Robin Uleman
Principal Typeface ITC Avant Garde Gothic

FLYERS AND POSTER
Client 3rd Side Records
Studio missbeck
Designer Marianne Beck
Principal Typeface ITC Avant Garde Gothic

*This series of flyers was made for a party on
the boat Concorde Atlantique in Paris, with
musicians signed to 3rd Side Records acting as DJs.
Each flyer pictured one of the 3rd Side musicians/
bands or a graphic image on the front, with textual
information on the reverse. The nine individual
flyers combine to make one large poster.*

APPAREL DESIGN
Client Flatcat
Studio Kiggen
Designer Bart Kiggen
Principal Typeface ITC Avant Garde Gothic (illustrated)

29 JULY
STEL ANDI
VASILOS
HOPE / AUDIOTHERAPY

05 AUG
CHRISTIAN
CAMBAS
DEVILOCK

LA PLAYA DJ TIM
BEACH BAR
ΡΑΧΕΣ PRESS14B / BUG EYED

postentertainment [M:S] music:server

WAGNER
LOVE

CORPORATE IDENTITY AND MUSIC PACKAGING
Client EMI Music Germany
Studio desres design studio
Art Director/Typographer Michaela Kessler
Principal Typeface ITC Avant Garde Gothic
(regular and modified)

POSTER
Client Kostas Michalis
Studio sebdesign.eu
Designer Sébastien Nikolaou
Photographer DavidQ/photocase.com
Principal Typeface ITC Avant Garde Gothic

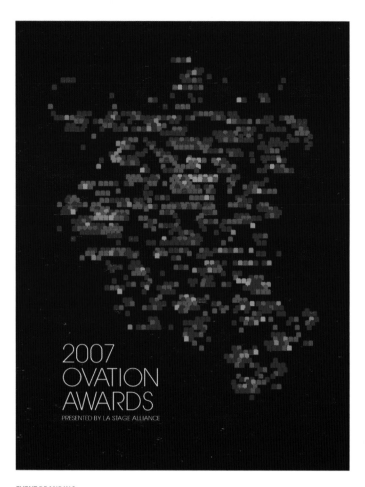

EVENT BRANDING
Client LA Stage Alliance
Studio DISTINC
Designers Jean-Marc Durviaux and Jenelle Campbell
Principal Typeface ITC Avant Garde Gothic

INVITATION FOLDER
Client Premsela: Dutch Platform
for Design and Fashion
Studio Robin Uleman
Principal Typeface ITC Avant Garde Gothic

EDITORIAL
Client SZ Real Estate
Studio DHNN (Design has No Name)
Principal Typeface ITC Avant Garde Gothic

POSTER
Studio Elapse
Designer Erik Jonsson
Principal Typeface ITC Avant Garde Gothic

AVENIR

aC

9/10pt

HOW RAZORBACK-JUMPING FROGS CAN LEVEL SIX PIQUED
gymnasts! Jackdaws love my big sphinx of quartz. Jaded zombies acted quaintly but kept driving their oxen forward. The
quick brown fox jumps over a lazy dog. The public was amazed
to view the quickness and dexterity of the juggler. A mad boxer
shot a quick, gloved jab to the jaw of his dizzy opponent. The

10/12pt

HOW RAZORBACK-JUMPING FROGS CAN LEVEL SIX
piqued gymnasts! Jackdaws love my big sphinx of
quartz. Jaded zombies acted quaintly but kept driving
their oxen forward. The quick brown fox jumps over a
lazy dog. The public was amazed to view the quickness
and dexterity of the juggler. A mad boxer shot a quick,

12/14pt

HOW RAZORBACK-JUMPING FROGS CAN
level six piqued gymnasts! Jackdaws love my
big sphinx of quartz. Jaded zombies acted
quaintly but kept driving their oxen forward.
The quick brown fox jumps over a lazy dog.

Avenir Next Italic

abcdefghijklmnopqrstuvwxyz1234567890
ABCDEFGHIJKLMNOPQRSTUVWXYZ

Avenir Next Demi

abcdefghijklmnopqrstuvwxyz1234567890
ABCDEFGHIJKLMNOPQRSTUVWXYZ

Avenir Next Demi Italic

abcdefghijklmnopqrstuvwxyz1234567890
ABCDEFGHIJKLMNOPQRSTUVWXYZ

Avenir Next Bold

abcdefghijklmnopqrstuvwxyz12345678
ABCDEFGHIJKLMNOPQRSTUVWXYZ

Avenir Next Bold Italic

abcdefghijklmnopqrstuvwxyz12345678
ABCDEFGHIJKLMNOPQRSTUVWXYZ

Avenir Next Heavy

abcdefghijklmnopqrstuvwxyz123456
ABCDEFGHIJKLMNOPQRSTUVWXYZ

Avenir Next [Linotype]

abcdefghijklmnopqrstuvwxyz

ABCDEFGHIJKLMNOPQRS

TUVWXYZ1234567890

[àóüßç](.,:;?!$€£&-*){ÀÓÜÇ}

Swiss designer Adrian Frutiger has an affinity for typefaces with human qualities. He designed Avenir in 1988, after years spent perfecting Sans types. Although a fine artist, Frutiger strove to create a typeface that was geometric and uniform in style. "Avenir is intended to be nothing more or less than a clear and clean representation of modern typographical trends," Frutiger said, "giving the designer a typeface which is strictly modern, and at the same time human, [one] that is suitably refined and elegant for use in texts of any length."

Avenir means "future" in French, hinting that it pays homage to Futura. Unlike Futura and its clinical counterparts, however, Avenir is not strictly geometric, but is sensitive to twentieth-century style. A Geometric Sans, it is eminently legible, yet retains the warmth of the human hand.

ANNUAL REPORT
Client Pacific Communications Group
Studio Evenson Design Group
Designer Dallas Duncan
Creative Directors Mark Sojka and Stan Evenson
Principal Typeface Avenir

If you like …

Avenir

… you could also consider:

Avant Garde

Frutiger

Futura

Gill Sans

Helvetica

Univers

FLYER/POSTER
Client Panic Club
Designer Stefan Weyer
Principal Typefaces Avenir, Filosofia, Charles, and LoversSquare

ENVIRONMENTAL GRAPHICS
Client eHarmony
Studio konnectDesign
Designers Joyce Pennell and David Whitcraft
Creative Director Karen Knecht
Principal Typeface Avenir

BOOK
Publisher Chronicle Books, San Francisco
Studio MacFadden & Thorpe
Designers Scott Thorpe and Brett MacFadden
Principal Typeface Avenir

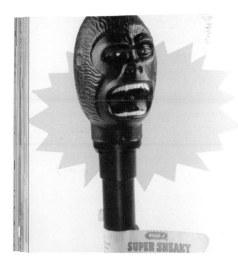

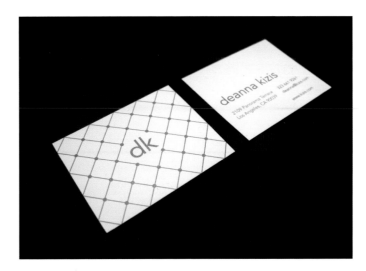

IDENTITY
Client Deanna Kizis
Studio Sarah Rainwater Design
Designer Sarah Rainwater
Principal Typeface Avenir

All images at left, this page:

BOOK
Publisher Chronicle Books, San Francisco
Studio Unflown Design
Designer Jacob Covey
Art Director Jake Gardner
Principal Typeface Avenir

Wham-O Super-Book: Celebrating 60 Years Inside the Fun Factory *is a visual history of the eccentric Wham-O toy company. The book features wildly colorful imagery full of hand lettering and custom type treatments. Unflown used Avenir as the primary text and headline typeface throughout, its warmth and clean lines unifying the contents.*

DIN

cO

9/10pt

HOW RAZORBACK-JUMPING FROGS CAN LEVEL SIX PIQUED gymnasts! Jackdaws love my big sphinx of quartz. Jaded zombies acted quaintly but kept driving their oxen forward. The quick brown fox jumps over a lazy dog. The public was amazed to view the quickness and dexterity of the juggler. A mad boxer shot a quick, gloved jab to the jaw of his dizzy opponent. The five boxing

10/12pt

HOW RAZORBACK-JUMPING FROGS CAN LEVEL SIX piqued gymnasts! Jackdaws love my big sphinx of quartz. Jaded zombies acted quaintly but kept driving their oxen forward. The quick brown fox jumps over a lazy dog. The public was amazed to view the quickness and dexterity of the juggler. A mad boxer shot a quick, gloved jab to the jaw

12/14pt

HOW RAZORBACK-JUMPING FROGS CAN LEVEL six piqued gymnasts! Jackdaws love my big sphinx of quartz. Jaded zombies acted quaintly but kept driving their oxen forward. The quick brown fox jumps over a lazy dog. The public was

FF DIN Italic

abcdefghijklmnopqrstuvwxyz1234567890
ABCDEFGHIJKLMNOPQRSTUVWXYZ

FF DIN Medium

abcdefghijklmnopqrstuvwxyz1234567890
ABCDEFGHIJKLMNOPQRSTU

FF DIN Bold

abcdefghijklmnopqrstuvwxyz123456789
ABCDEFGHIJKLMNOPQRSTUVWXYZ

FF DIN Black

abcdefghijklmnopqrstuvwxyz123456789
ABCDEFGHIJKLMNOPQRSTUVWXYZ

Other notable cuts:

DIN 1451 Mittelschrift [Linotype]

FF DIN [FontFont]

abcdefghijklmnopqrstuvwxyz
ABCDEFGHIJKLMNOPQRST
UVWXYZ1234567890
[àóüßç](.,:;?!$€£&-*){ÀÓÜÇ}

"DIN" stands for Deutsches Institut für Normung (The German Institute for Industrial Standards). In 1936, the German Standard Committee settled upon DIN 1451 as the standard font for the areas of technology, traffic, administration, and business as it was legible and easy to reproduce. Because DIN 1451 was used prominently in Germany on traffic signage, the letterforms became familiar to the masses, spurring graphic artists to make use of the ubiquitous design in advertising campaigns.

The variants of DIN were well suited for display purposes, but not for running text. In 1994, Erik Spiekermann met with Albert Jan-Pool, a student of the Dutch school of design initiated by Gerrit Noordzij. Spiekermann encouraged Jan-Pool to create a new version of DIN, one that would be more versatile in its applications. Jan-Pool developed FF DIN, a design that shares structural similarities with DIN 1451, yet differs in its weight distribution and naming conventions. FF DIN was refined to allow it to perform better in print and on screen. The original DIN Schriften in digital form and FF DIN are now both widely used across a variety of media.

BROCHURE
Studio 160over90
Designer Adam Flanagan
Chief Creative Director Darryl Cilli
Creative Director Dan Shepelavy
Copywriter Brendan Quinn
Photographers Matt Bednarik and Barry Halkin
Principal Typefaces FF DIN and URW Egyptienne

FF DIN's restraint, sophistication, and lack of any specific style or genre made it ideal for 160over90's own brand (including this self-promotional brochure). The designers used URW Egyptienne as a secondary font for headlines, as its simplicity of form is consistent with DIN.

BAROCKT 08
TERJE TØNNESEN
CAMERATA
NORDICA
MARIKA LAGERCRANTZ
KNUT JOHANNESSEN
PER NYSTRÖM
STEVE PLAYER
VIRPI RÄISÄNEN
TEODOR JANSON

04.08 KL 20.00 **VIDA MUSEUM**
05.08 KL 20.00 **S MÖCKLEBY KYRKA**
06.08 KL 22.00 **KÄLLA GAMLA KYRKA**
07.08 KL 20.00 **RESMO KYRKA**
08.08 KL 20.00 **VIDA MUSEUM**
09.08 KL 20.00 **ALGUTSRUMS KYRKA**

INFORMATION OCH BILJETTER
N Öland: Vida Museum, tel: 0485-77440.
Sjöbergs Tobakshandel, Borgholm, tel: 0485-10080.
S Öland: www.olandsturist.se, tel: 0485-560600.
Biljetter säljs också vid entren 1 tim före konsert.
Kontaktperson: Per Nyström, tel: 070-6540035.
www.lansmusiken.se

ARRANGÖRER
Borgholms Musik och Teaterförening, Vida Museum, Kultur och Fritid Borgholm, Kulturföreningen Karneval. Musik i samarbete med resp. församling inom Svenska kyrkan. I samarbete med Länsmusiken.

Svenska Musikfestivaler   Länsmusiken

If you like …

DIN

… you could also consider:

Akzidenz-Grotesk
Bauhaus
Futura
Helvetica
Trade Gothic
Univers

IDENTITY AND POSTER
Clients Länsmusiken and
Kalmar Läns Musikstiftelse
Studio Neue Design Studio
Designers Benjamin Stenmarck
and Øystein Haugseth
Principal Typeface FF DIN

21.02

ANDSNES OG TØNNESEN I LE BOURGEOIS GENTILHOMME

Moliéres tekst med Lullys musikk gjør narr av besteborgerligheten på slutten av 1600-tallet. På denne konserten spiller vi fra originalmusikken til Lully, samt Richard Strauss sin neo-klassiske versjon. Andsnes får du høre både i Mozarts klaver-konsert nr. 23 og som orkesterpianist i Strauss.

Konsert nr. 6	Torsdag 21. februar kl. 19.30
Sted:	Oslo Konserthus
Leder:	Terje Tønnesen
Gjesteleder og solist:	Leif Ove Andsnes
J. B. Lully:	Le bourgeois gentilhomme
W. A. Mozart:	Klaverkonsert nr. 23
R. Strauss:	Le bourgeois gentilhomme

All images this page:

BROCHURE

Client Norwegian Chamber Orchestra
Studio Neue Design Studio
Designers Benjamin Stenmarck and Øystein Haugseth
Principal Typefaces FF DIN and Bembo

This brochure promotes the 30-year anniversary of the Norwegian Chamber Orchestra as they present eight concerts in celebration of the milestone. Half of the figure 8 from the opening spread is revealed through a die-cut cover, enabling a figure 3 to appear in front of the printed figure 0 (see image above).

16.03

EN HEL LITEN PÅSKEFESTIVAL

Med Tonu Kaljuste som leder tar samarbeidet med Solistkoret form av noe som skal bli en ny tradisjon. To konserter i den stille uke gir rom for påskens musikalske budskap. Vi har valgt ut den første av de to konsertene som abonnementskonsert. Den andre konserten blir tirsdag 18. mars med Mozarts requiem på programmet.

Konsert nr. 7	Søndag 16. mars kl. 19.00
Sted:	Frogner kirke
Leder:	Tonu Kaljuste
Arvo Pärt:	Utvalgte verker
James MacMillan:	Jesu syv siste ord på korset

27.05

LATIN-AMERIKA ER MER ENN TANGO

Den som ikke lar seg rive med når Atle Sponberg svinger smektende fiolintoner med latin-amerikansk groove ut over sine tilhørere, kan bare ha det så godt! Med musikk fra Havanna i nord til Buenos Aires i sør, blir kvelden alt annet enn stillesittende for den som ønsker å la seg forføre av musikken. Servering av mer enn chilinøtter!

Konsert nr. 8	Tirsdag 27. mai kl. 20.30 !
Sted:	Kulturkirken Jakob
Leder og solist:	Atle Sponberg
Arrangør/musikalsk gjest:	Sverre Indris Joner

04.11

ALLEHELGENSDAG MED KOR OG ORKESTER

Sammen med Det Norske Solistkor og gjesteleder Fabio Biondi gir vi også i år store musikalske opp-levelser på en dag da mange søker til kirkene. Denne gang med musikk av Telemann. Hans verk, Die Tages-zeiten, er en syklus kantater som beskriver morgen, middag, aften og kveld. Musikken kan like gjerne tolkes som en beskrivelse av vår gang gjennom livet.

Konsert nr. 3	Søndag 4. november 19.00
Sted:	Ris kirke
Leder:	Fabio Biondi
Medvirkende:	Det Norske Solistkor
Georg Philipp Telemann:	Die Tageszeiten for solister, kor og orkester

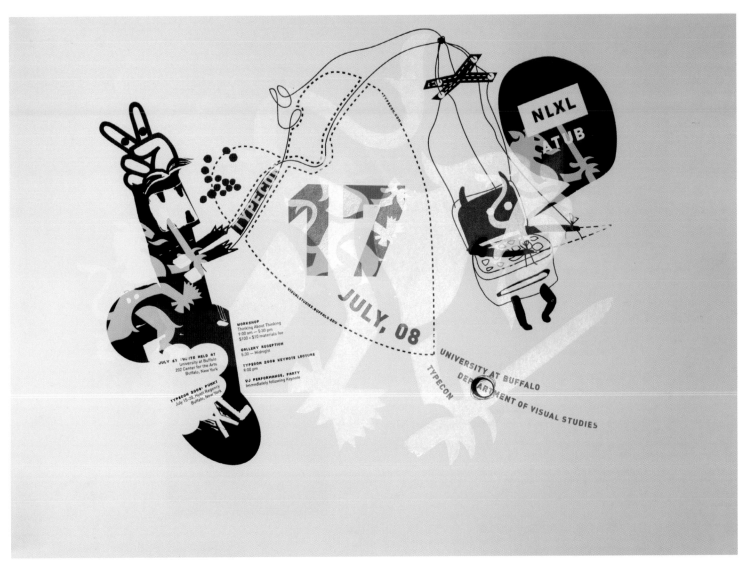

POSTER
Client The Society of Typographic
    Aficionados (SOTA) and the
    University at Buffalo (UB)
Designers Ben van Dyke and NLXL
Principal Typeface FF DIN

*This limited-edition silkscreen poster
was created to advertise Dutch design
studio NLXL's workshop, lecture,
exhibition opening, and VJ/dance
party held at UB as part of the
TypeCon2008 conference.*

BUSINESS CARDS
Studio 160over90
Designer Martin Duffy
Chief Creative Director Darryl Cilli
Creative Director Jim Walls
Principal Typeface FF DIN

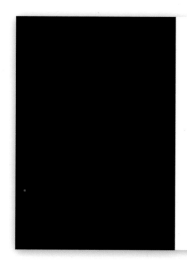

All images this page:

BOOK
Publisher Éditions Ma Ville et Moi, Paris
Studio Nicolas Queffélec with Atelier Graphique
  Malte Martin
Designers Nicolas Queffélec and Malte Martin
Principal Typeface FF DIN

*Passage à l'acte displays a combination of words
and letters mimicking the discourse that took place
during the symposium The Artist and the City.
The event was held in 2001 at the Médiathèque
François Mitterrand in Poitiers, France.*

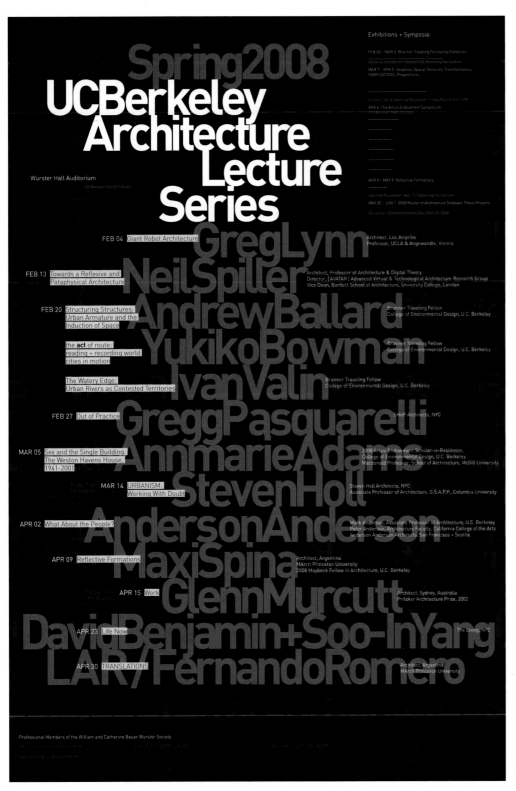

SWATCHBOOK
Client Glatfelter
Studio End Communications
Principal Typefaces DIN and Franklin Gothic

This swatchbook was developed to promote MagneCote, the world's first true magnetic paper— a standard press sheet precoated with a magnetic surface. Targeted at advertising and design agencies, this piece combines mechanical letterforms with familiar imagery to illustrate the application of new technologies to a very traditional medium.

POSTER
Client University of California, Berkeley, Department of Architecture
Studio ADearFriend
Designer Chris Ro
Principal Typeface FF DIN

This poster announced the school's spring 2008 lecture series. A systematic approach highlighted new lecturers, provided a calendar base, and typographically activated the content through a system of shifting and interlocking chronological tiers where, with every date shift, the names of lecturers would alternate positions.

BUSINESS CARD
Client ISAK
Studio Neue Design Studio
Designers Benjamin Stenmarck and Øystein Haugseth
Principal Typeface FF DIN

*Part of an identity system for a Norwegian furniture
company based in China. The logotype was based
on Chinese letterforms to emphasize the origins of
the ISAK product line.*

POSTER
Client Norwegian Chamber Orchestra
Studio Neue Design Studio
Designers Benjamin Stenmarck and Øystein Haugseth
Principal Typeface FF DIN

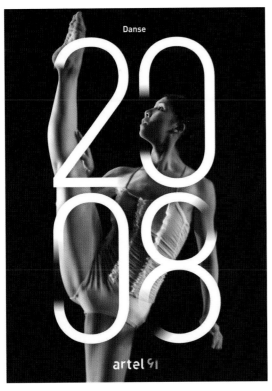

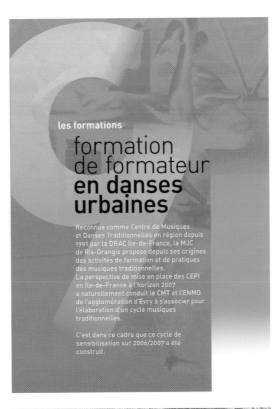

artel 91

association de coopération
culturelle en Essonne

All images this page:
IDENTITY
Client Artel 91
Designers Nicolas Queffélec
Principal Typeface FF DIN (standard and modified)

Artel 91: Culture in Motion was Queffélec's answer to a competition to design the identity of a French cultural organization specializing in the performing arts (theater, dance, circus, etc.). He modified DIN letterforms with pieces of motion blur for use in the logo and some display typography. FF DIN was used as the primary typeface throughout the identity system and collateral materials.

Photography for the collateral was used under a Creative Commons license. Ballerina and Le Theatre photography by sobakasu. Danses (Green) photography by snick-clunk. Danses (Umbrella) photography by tony the misfit.

LOGO AND IDENTITY SYSTEM
Client Snap36
Studio End Communications
Logo Designer Joan (Picchietti) Zajeski
Identity and Website End Communications
Principal Typeface FF DIN

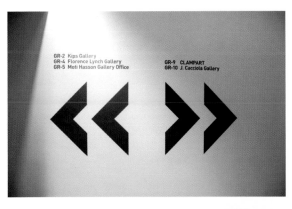

GR-2 Kips Gallery
GR-4 Florence Lynch Gallery
GR-5 Moti Hasson Gallery Office

GR-9 CLAMPART
GR-10 J. Cacciola Gallery

DIRECTORY

701 Alan Klotz Gallery
703 Deborah Bell Photographs
707 Abby Suckle Architects, Culture Now, RealFurniture
708 Richard Shebairo, C.P.A.
709 511 West 25th Street Sales Center

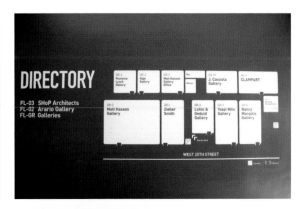

DIRECTORY

FL-03 SHoP Architects
FL-02 Arario Gallery
FL-GR Galleries

WEST 25TH STREET

All images this page:

ENVIRONMENTAL DESIGN AND WAYFINDING
Client Cardinal Investments
Studio SHoP Architects
Designers Jonathan Lo, Noah Riley, and Jon Kontuly
Principal Typefaces FF DIN and DIN Schriften

SHoP Architects developed wayfinding systems and environmental dress for three related buildings on West 25th Street in New York City. The wayfinding is unified and activated by the concept of a fading brush stroke. Each successive building (511 to 531 to 541) is smaller in both size and number of floors. Starting from the main building at 511, the accent color changes from black to dark gray to light gray. Similarly, the size of the signage becomes smaller, proportional to the number of floors in 511. For example, the signage for the 531 building is ⅝ the size of the signage in 511. Environmental designs reflect the concept of connectivity and transparency of walls. Typography and imagery bend around corners and change color to create three-dimensionality.

All images this page:

NEWSLETTER
Client Pratt Institute
Designers Ryan Adair and Mattias Mackler
Principal Typefaces DIN Schriften and Adobe Garamond

This foldout newsletter was created for the Pratt Institute's Graduate Design Program in New York City. Self-portraits by design students formed a poster once the piece was fully unfolded.

All images this page:

EXHIBITION DESIGN
Client Cardinal Investments
Studio SHoP Architects
Designers Jonathan Lo
Principal Typeface FF DIN

290mulberryLAB is an exhibition about the development and construction process of the 290 Mulberry building project in New York City. The exhibition, located on the construction site, features a logo based on FF DIN. Stencils were cut and the logo spray-painted on various surfaces on the site. Whimsical characters were designed as part of the exhibition, their names spelled out in FF DIN in stencil from. The characters and their names were spray-painted on surfaces and made into keychains given as keepsakes to visitors.

EUROSTILE

9/10pt

HOW RAZORBACK-JUMPING FROGS CAN LEVEL SIX piqued gymnasts! Jackdaws love my big sphinx of quartz. Jaded zombies acted quaintly but kept driving their oxen forward. The quick brown fox jumps over a lazy dog. The public was amazed to view the quickness and dexterity of the juggler. A mad boxer shot a quick, gloved jab to the jaw

10/12pt

HOW RAZORBACK-JUMPING FROGS CAN LEVEL six piqued gymnasts! Jackdaws love my big sphinx of quartz. Jaded zombies acted quaintly but kept driving their oxen forward. The quick brown fox jumps over a lazy dog. The public was amazed to view the quickness and dexterity of the juggler. A mad boxer shot a quick,

12/14pt

HOW RAZORBACK-JUMPING FROGS CAN level six piqued gymnasts! Jackdaws love my big sphinx of quartz. Jaded zombies acted quaintly but kept driving their oxen forward. The quick brown fox jumps over a lazy dog.

Eurostile Oblique

abcdefghijklmnopqrstuvwxyz12345678
ABCDEFGHIJKLMNOPQRSTUVWXYZ

Eurostile Bold

abcdefghijklmnopqrstuvwxyz1234567
ABCDEFGHIJKLMNOPQRSTUVWXYZ

Eurostile Bold Oblique

abcdefghijklmnopqrstuvwxyz1234567
ABCDEFGHIJKLMNOPQRSTUVWXYZ

Eurostile Extended

abcdefghijklmnopqrstuvwxyz
ABCDEFGHIJKLMNOPQRS

Eurostile Bold Extended

abcdefghijklmnopqrstuvwxy
ABCDEFGHIJKLMNOPQR

Other notable cuts:

Eurostile Next [Linotype]

Eurostile Medium [Linotype]

abcdefghijklmnopqrstuvwxyz
ABCDEFGHIJKLMNOPQRS
TUVWXYZ1234567890
[àóüßç](.,:;?!$€£&-*}{ÀÓÜÇ}

Alessandro Butti and Aldo Novarese designed a typeface called Microgramma in 1952 for the Nebiolo foundry in Turin, Italy. A true titling face, Microgramma contained capitals only, its uppercase characters much larger than those of a typical text design. Although Microgramma was available in five styles, its lack of a lowercase meant that it could only be used for display work. Ten years later, Novarese drew a full character set for all weights, adding bold condensed and compact variants. The new family was named Eurostile.

When Eurostile was digitized by Linotype and Adobe in the 1980s, the design's trademark "super curves" were flattened, and characters that didn't follow the original styling were added. In 2007, Linotype released Eurostile Next. Akira Kobayashi, type director of the German foundry, carefully studied the original types, adding new weights, correcting imperfections, and restoring the mid-century modern detailing to the letterforms.

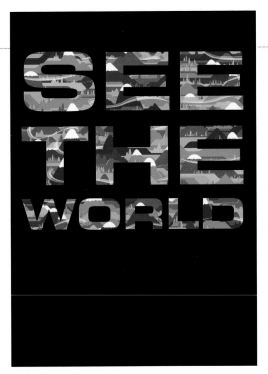

Both images this page:
POSTCARDS
Designer/Illustrator Ben the Illustrator
Principal Typeface Eurostile

Promotional postcards for the illustrator's set of art prints entitled Wish You Were Here.

If you like …

Eurostile

… you could also consider:

Folio
Franklin Gothic
Grotesque
Helvetica
Trade Gothic
Univers

All images this page:

BOOK

Publisher CDA Press, San Francisco
Studio Chen Design Associates
Lead Designer Max Spector
Art Directors Joshua C. Chen and Max Spector
Creative Director Joshua C. Chen
Principal Typefaces Eurostile, Courier,
and Akzidenz-Grotesk

*The Chen Design team designed the award-winning
IDA Survey of World Design 2007, an art book
displaying the winners of the International Design
Awards 2007 in architecture, interior, graphic,
product, and fashion design.*

ARCHIT
ECTURE
INTERIO
R G R A P
HICPRO
DUCTFA
SHION

Student Interior
Designer of
the Year

TIMOTHY SCHREIBER
EVOLUTION TABLE
LONDON, ENGLAND, UNITED KINGDOM
RESIDENTIAL FIRST PLACE

PRO
DUC
T

ARC
HIT
ECT
URE

Jury President
Michael Cannell New
York Editor, Dwell

IDA Jurors
Newell Turner
Style Director,
House Beautiful

Barbara Thornburg
Senior Style Editor,
Los Angeles Times
Magazine

Kelly Wearstler
President, Kelly
Wearstler Inc.
Interior Design

John Dunnigan
Department Head,
Furniture Design,
Rhode Island
School of Design

Rido Busse
Founder of Busse
Design Ulm, and
Chairman of the
German Trade and
Industry Board

Josh Rubin Editor-in-
Chief and Publisher,
Cool Hunting

**Maxwell Gillingham-
Ryan** New York
Editor/Co-Founder,
Apartment Therapy

Gwynne Pugh AIA,
Pugh + Scarpa
Architects

David Hertz AIA,
David Hertz Architects
and Engineer of
Syndecrete*

Laurence Ng Publisher,
IdN Magazine

Andy Griffith Owner
and Buyer, A+R
Design Store,
Los Angeles

Rose Apodaca
Freelance Culture
and Style Writer and
Owner, A+R Design
Store, Los Angeles

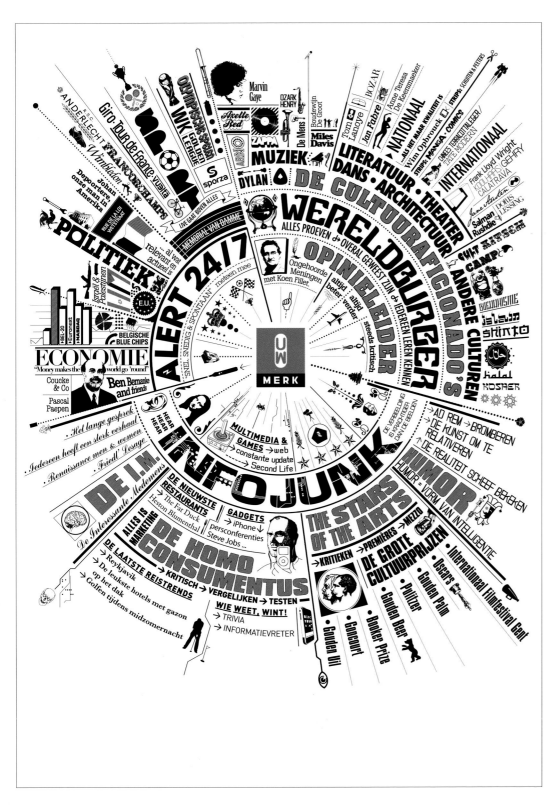

LOGO
Client Plastic
Art Director/Designer Lindsay Gravette
Principal Typeface Eurostile

ADVERTISEMENT
Client Vlaamse Audiovisuele Regie (VAR)
Studio Glossy.tv (commissioned by Darwin BBDO)
Designer Joe
Principal Typefaces Eurostile, et al

Glossy designed this promotional piece for VAR, the professional body for advertising air time for radio stations in the Vlaamse Radio- en Televisieomroep (Flemish Radio and Television Network), or VRT. The Dutch version is pictured here; a French-language version was also created for the campaign. The designers used dozens of logos, slogans, and typefaces in developing this piece. In addition to the large Eurostile setting of "Info Junk," featured types include Avant Garde, Futura, Baskerville, Garamond, Commercial Script, Cooper Black, Courier, DIN, and Univers.

FOLIO

aC

HOW RAZORBACK-JUMPING FROGS CAN LEVEL SIX
piqued gymnasts! Jackdaws love my big sphinx of quartz. Jaded
zombies acted quaintly but kept driving their oxen forward. The
quick brown fox jumps over a lazy dog. The public was amazed
to view the quickness and dexterity of the juggler. A mad boxer
shot a quick, gloved jab to the jaw of his dizzy opponent. The

HOW RAZORBACK-JUMPING FROGS CAN LEVEL SIX
piqued gymnasts! Jackdaws love my big sphinx of quartz.
Jaded zombies acted quaintly but kept driving their oxen
forward. The quick brown fox jumps over a lazy dog. The
public was amazed to view the quickness and dexterity of
the juggler. A mad boxer shot a quick, gloved jab to the

HOW RAZORBACK-JUMPING FROGS CAN
level six piqued gymnasts! Jackdaws love
my big sphinx of quartz. Jaded zombies acted
quaintly but kept driving their oxen forward.
The quick brown fox jumps over a lazy dog. The

Folio Light

abcdefghijklmnopqrstuvwxyz1234567890
ABCDEFGHIJKLMNOPQRSTUVWXYZ

Folio Bold

abcdefghijklmnopqrstuvwxyz12345
ABCDEFGHIJKLMNOPQRSTUVWX

Folio Extra Bold

abcdefghijklmnopqrstuvwxyz123
ABCDEFGHIJKLMNOPQRSTUVWXYZ

Folio Light Condensed

abcdefghijklmnopqrstuvwxyz1234567890
ABCDEFGHIJKLMNOPQRSTUVWXYZ

Folio Medium Condensed

abcdefghijklmnopqrstuvwxyz1234567890
ABCDEFGHIJKLMNOPQRSTUVWXYZ

Folio Bold Condensed

abcdefghijklmnopqrstuvwxyz1234567890
ABCDEFGHIJKLMNOPQRSTUVWXYZ

Folio [URW]

abcdefghijklmnopqrstuvwxyz
ABCDEFGHIJKLMNOPQ
RSTUVWXYZ1234567890
[àóüßç](.,:;?!$€£&-*){ÀÓÜÇ}

Folio was designed by German typographers Konrad Bauer and Walter Baum for the Bauer typefoundry (Bauersche Gießerei) in 1957. The family was continuously expanded with additional weights and styles through 1963. A Realist Sans Serif, Folio displays characteristics of both late nineteenth-century Grotesques and the more industrial Sans which became popular in the mid-twentieth century. Folio was released around the same time that Helvetica and Univers were issued. All three were modeled after Akzidenz-Grotesk, Folio more so than the Swiss designs with their larger x-heights and uniform styling. Due to successful marketing tactics, Folio became popular in the United States, particularly in newspaper display typography, and also did well in France, where it was offered under the name Caravelle.

YOURS TRULY

Heta Kuchka 6.10. – 10.12.2006
Vuoden nuori taiteilija / Årets unga konstnär / Young Artist of the Year

Taidemuseo Meilahti
Tamminiementie 6, 00250 Helsinki
Puh. (09) 310 87031
Avoinna ti–su 11-18.30
Liput 6/5 €, alle 18 v. ilmaiseksi
Perjantaisin ilmainen sisäänpääsy

www.taidemuseo.fi

Taidemuseo Meilahti

If you like …

Folio

… you could also consider:

Akzidenz-Grotesk

Franklin Gothic

Grotesque

Helvetica

All images this page:

EXHIBITION AND COLLATERAL DESIGN
Client Heta Kuchka/Helsinki City Art Museum
Designer Chris Bolton
Exhibited Photographer Heta Kuchka
Principal Typeface Folio

Bolton designed the bold exhibition graphics and collateral for award-winning Finnish-American visual artist Heta Kuchka's Yours Truly solo show.

FRANKLIN GOTHIC

aC

9/10pt

HOW RAZORBACK-JUMPING FROGS CAN LEVEL SIX PIQUED gymnasts! Jackdaws love my big sphinx of quartz. Jaded zombies acted quaintly but kept driving their oxen forward. The quick brown fox jumps over a lazy dog. The public was amazed to view the quickness and dexterity of the juggler. A mad boxer shot a quick, gloved jab to the jaw of his dizzy opponent. The five boxing

10/12pt

HOW RAZORBACK-JUMPING FROGS CAN LEVEL SIX PIQUED gymnasts! Jackdaws love my big sphinx of quartz. Jaded zombies acted quaintly but kept driving their oxen forward. The quick brown fox jumps over a lazy dog. The public was amazed to view the quickness and dexterity of the juggler. A mad boxer shot a quick, gloved jab to the jaw of his dizzy

12/14pt

HOW RAZORBACK-JUMPING FROGS CAN LEVEL six piqued gymnasts! Jackdaws love my big sphinx of quartz. Jaded zombies acted quaintly but kept driving their oxen forward. The quick brown fox jumps over a lazy dog. The public was

ITC Franklin Gothic Italic

abcdefghijklmnopqrstuvwxyz1234567890
ABCDEFGHIJKLMNOPQRSTUVWXYZ

ITC Franklin Gothic Demi

abcdefghijklmnopqrstuvwxyz1234567890
ABCDEFGHIJKLMNOPQRSTUVWXYZ

ITC Franklin Gothic Demi Italic

abcdefghijklmnopqrstuvwxyz1234567890
ABCDEFGHIJKLMNOPQRSTUVWXYZ

ITC Franklin Gothic Heavy

abcdefghijklmnopqrstuvwxyz1234567890
ABCDEFGHIJKLMNOPQRSTUVWXYZ

ITC Franklin Gothic Heavy Italic

abcdefghijklmnopqrstuvwxyz1234567890
ABCDEFGHIJKLMNOPQRSTUVWXYZ

Other notable cuts:

ITC Franklin [ITC]

ITC Franklin Gothic [ITC]

abcdefghijklmnopqrstuvwxyz
ABCDEFGHIJKLMNOPQRSTU
VWXYZ1234567890
[àóüßç](.,:;?!$€£&-*){ÀÓÜÇ}

Early Sans types were classed as Grotesque in the UK, Grotesk in Germany, and Gothic in the USA. Morris Fuller Benton began drawing Franklin Gothic for American Type Founders (ATF) in 1902, his work an important interpretation of nineteenth-century Grotesques. Although many Gothics were seen in America by the early 1900s, it is likely that Benton was more influenced by Akzidenz-Grotesk and other German Grotesques.

Franklin Gothic was introduced with only one weight, and though additional variants were added for several years after its 1905 release, no light or intermediate weights were made for metal. Even so, Franklin Gothic's popularity grew, and it influenced many types that followed. In 1979, ITC expanded the family under license from ATF. Victor Caruso drew four new weights and italics to echo the styling of the original, increasing the x-height slightly to improve readability. David Berlow, cofounder of Font Bureau, added condensed and compressed weights in 1991. Font Bureau and ITC re-teamed on a major update to Benton's classic, publishing a revamp in 2008. Branded simply ITC Franklin, Berlow's modernization features six weights in four widths with complementary italics. Extensive OpenType features were added, including a set of biforms (lowercase characters drawn with the height and weight of the caps).

Both images this page:
LP/CD PACKAGING
Client Danse Macabre
Designer Stefan Weyer
Principal Typefaces ITC Franklin Gothic and Adobe Garamond

If you like …

Franklin Gothic

… you could also consider:

Akzidenz-Grotesk
Folio
Grotesque
Helvetica
Trade Gothic
Univers

All images above:

EDITORIAL DESIGN
Client L'épluche-doigts
Studio atelier aquarium
Designers Simon Renaud and Jérémie Nuel
Illustrators Pierre Abernot and Céline Thoué
  (L'épluche-doigts)
Photographer Véronique Pêcheux
Principal Typeface ITC Franklin Gothic

In this piece, the pied-de-mouche—*the French term
for the paragraph mark or "pilcrow" ("fly-foot" is the
literal English translation)—is used as a guide for
readers. The booklet details the traditional methods
practiced at L'épluche-doigts, a Lyon-based letterpress
shop/typography studio and itinerant workshop.*

LOGO
Client HP
Studio Lippincott
Creative Director Brendán Murphy
Principal Typeface ITC Franklin Gothic

SASQUATCH MUSIC FESTIVAL ★ MAY 26, 2008 ★ THE GORGE

POSTER BY MODERN DOG | PRINTING BY D&L

CD PACKAGING
Client I knew it: hurray!
Designer Stefan Weyer
Principal Typefaces ITC Franklin Gothic
and Adobe Garamond

POSTER
Client Sasquatch! Music Festival
Studio Modern Dog Design Co.
Designer Robert Zwiebel
Principal Typeface ITC Franklin Gothic

FRUTIGER

aC

9/10pt

HOW RAZORBACK-JUMPING FROGS CAN LEVEL SIX PIQUED gymnasts! Jackdaws love my big sphinx of quartz. Jaded zombies acted quaintly but kept driving their oxen forward. The quick brown fox jumps over a lazy dog. The public was amazed to view the quickness and dexterity of the juggler. A mad boxer shot a quick, gloved jab to the jaw of his dizzy

10/12pt

HOW RAZORBACK-JUMPING FROGS CAN LEVEL SIX piqued gymnasts! Jackdaws love my big sphinx of quartz. Jaded zombies acted quaintly but kept driving their oxen forward. The quick brown fox jumps over a lazy dog. The public was amazed to view the quickness and dexterity of the juggler. A mad boxer shot a quick,

12/14pt

HOW RAZORBACK-JUMPING FROGS CAN level six piqued gymnasts! Jackdaws love my big sphinx of quartz. Jaded zombies acted quaintly but kept driving their oxen forward. The quick brown fox jumps over a lazy dog.

Frutiger 56 Italic

abcdefghijklmnopqrstuvwxyz12345678
ABCDEFGHIJKLMNOPQRSTUVWXYZ

Frutiger 65 Bold

abcdefghijklmnopqrstuvwxyz12345678
ABCDEFGHIJKLMNOPQRSTUVWXYZ

Frutiger 66 Bold Italic

abcdefghijklmnopqrstuvwxyz12345678
ABCDEFGHIJKLMNOPQRSTUVWXYZ

Frutiger 75 Black

abcdefghijklmnopqrstuvwxyz12345
ABCDEFGHIJKLMNOPQRSTUVWXYZ

Other notable cuts:

Frutiger Next [Linotype]

Frutiger 55 [Linotype]

abcdefghijklmnopqrstuvwxyz
ABCDEFGHIJKLMNOPQRSTU
VWXYZ1234567890
[àóüßç](.,:;?!$€£&-*){ÀÓÜÇ}

In 1968, Adrian Frutiger was commissioned to create a signage and wayfinding system for the Charles de Gaulle Airport in Paris. Rather than use one of his existing families like Univers, the Swiss designer developed a new Sans family to meet the exacting legibility standards for airport signage. Easy recognition from a distance and at various angles was of paramount importance. Frutiger drew rational, yet organic letterforms that were eminently readable and harmonious with the modern architecture of the airport. In 1976, he expanded the types into a full family for the Stempel foundry and Linotype, and they were released commercially and branded with his name.

Frutiger displays the warmth of the artist's hand, its clean lines and subtle character making it suitable for text as well as large-scale typography. In 1997, the family was updated as Frutiger Next, featuring refined design details and true italics to replace the original obliqued romans.

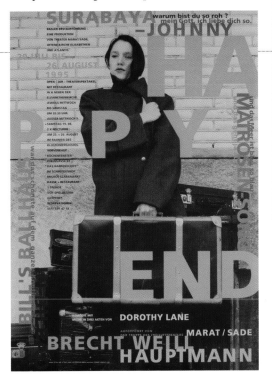

POSTER
Client Solothurn Literature Days
Studio Studio AND
Designer Jean-Benoît Lévy
Photographer Stefan Meichtry
Printer Serigraphie Uldry
Principal Typeface Frutiger

ALEX T. ANDERSON

THE PROBLEM OF THE HOUSE

FRENCH DOMESTIC LIFE
AND THE RISE OF
MODERN ARCHITECTURE

BOOK COVER
Publisher University of Washington Press, Seattle and London
Designer Ashley Saleeba
Principal Typeface Frutiger

If you like …

Frutiger

… you could also consider:

Avenir
Helvetica
Officina Sans
Univers

p/ural

Both images above:

LOGO AND VISUAL SYSTEM
Client Plural
Studio Lippincott
Creative Director Brendán Murphy
Principal Typeface Frutiger

POSTER
Client She & Him
Studio/Screenprinter Hero Design Studio
Designer/Printer Elizabeth Manos Brickey
Principal Typefaces Frutiger and Sign Painter

Four images at left:

IDENTITY AND MENU
Client Koryo Wooden Charcoal BBQ
Designer/Illustrator/Photographer Jack Chung
Principal Typeface Frutiger

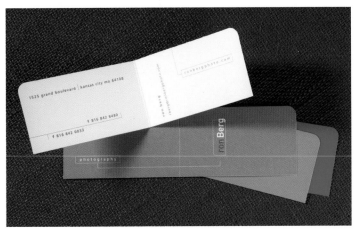

IDENTITY
Client Ron Berg
Studio konnectDesign
Designers Karen Knecht and Darwin Foye
Principal Typefaces DIN Schriften and Frutiger

FUTURA

9/10pt

HOW RAZORBACK-JUMPING FROGS CAN LEVEL SIX PIQUED gymnasts! Jackdaws love my big sphinx of quartz. Jaded zombies acted quaintly but kept driving their oxen forward. The quick brown fox jumps over a lazy dog. The public was amazed to view the quickness and dexterity of the juggler. A mad boxer shot a quick, gloved jab to the jaw of his dizzy opponent. The

10/12pt

HOW RAZORBACK-JUMPING FROGS CAN LEVEL SIX piqued gymnasts! Jackdaws love my big sphinx of quartz. Jaded zombies acted quaintly but kept driving their oxen forward. The quick brown fox jumps over a lazy dog. The public was amazed to view the quickness and dexterity of the juggler. A mad boxer shot a quick, gloved jab to the

12/14pt

HOW RAZORBACK-JUMPING FROGS CAN level six piqued gymnasts! Jackdaws love my big sphinx of quartz. Jaded zombies acted quaintly but kept driving their oxen forward. The quick brown fox jumps over a lazy dog. The public

Futura Book Oblique

abcdefghijklmnopqrstuvwxyz1234567890
ABCDEFGHIJKLMNOPQRSTUVWXYZ

Futura Medium

abcdefghijklmnopqrstuvwxyz1234567890
ABCDEFGHIJKLMNOPQRSTUVWXYZ

Futura Medium Oblique

abcdefghijklmnopqrstuvwxyz1234567890
ABCDEFGHIJKLMNOPQRSTUVWXYZ

Futura Bold

abcdefghijklmnopqrstuvwxyz12345
ABCDEFGHIJKLMNOPQRSTUVWXYZ

Futura Bold Oblique

abcdefghijklmnopqrstuvwxyz12345
ABCDEFGHIJKLMNOPQRSTUVWXYZ

Futura Extra Bold

abcdefghijklmnopqrstuvwxyz1234
ABCDEFGHIJKLMNOPQRSTUVWXY

Futura Book [Neufville Digital/BauerTypes]

abcdefghijklmnopqrstuvwxyz
ABCDEFGHIJKLMNOPQRST
UVWXYZ1234567890
[àóüßç](.,:;?!$€£&-*){ÀÓÜÇ}

German type designer, painter, and educator Paul Renner spent several years in the mid-1920s developing Futura. Inspired by the typographic experimentation of the Bauhaus school, Renner sketched a series of letterforms loosely based on simple geometric shapes. Although Renner was not formally associated with the Bauhaus artists, he shared their opinion that a "modern" typeface should express a contemporary point of view rather than be based on an existing design. The design office at Frankfurt's Bauersche Giesserei (the Bauer Type Foundry) worked with Renner to transform his sketches into the legible Sans Serif type family that they first published in 1927. The original release included light, medium, bold, and bold oblique variants; additional weights and styles were added over the next 30 years. Futura became the most popular Sans of the mid-twentieth century and inspired many Sans types after its release (including Adrian Frutiger's more humanist Avenir).

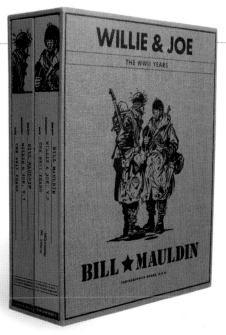

SLIPCASED BOOK COLLECTION
Publisher Fantagraphics Books, Seattle
Studio Unflown Design
Art Director/Designer Jacob Covey
Principal Typefaces Futura, Stencil, and
   Typewriter Courier (modified)

If you like …

Futura

… you could also consider:

Akzidenz-Grotesk
Avant Garde
Avenir
Bauhaus
Gill Sans

POSTER
Client Clap Your Hands Say Yeah
Studio The Small Stakes
Designer Jason Munn
Principal Typeface Futura

CD COVER
Client Smalltown Superjazzz
Designer Rune Mortensen
Principal Typeface Futura

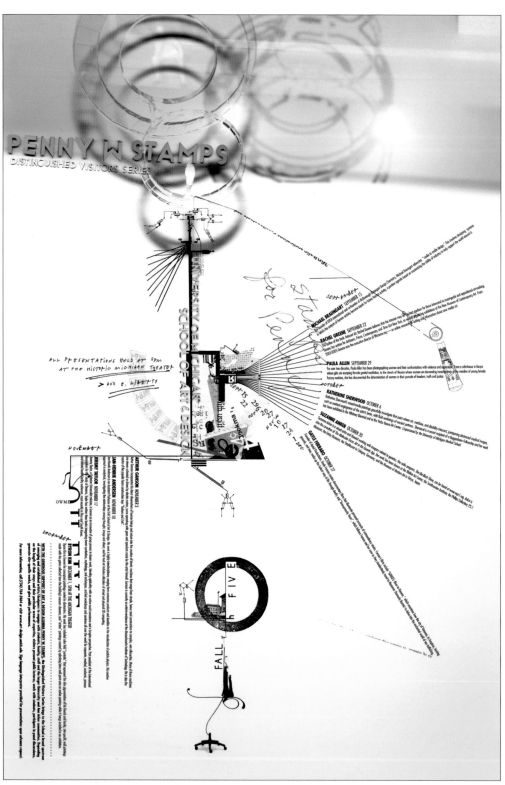

POSTER
Client University of Michigan,
School of Art & Design
Designers Ben Van Dyke, Emily Fisher,
Patrick Young, and Kate West
Principal Typeface Futura

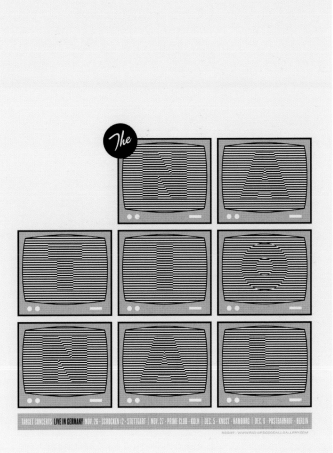

POSTER
Client The National
Studio The Small Stakes
Designer Jason Munn
Principal Typeface Futura (modified)

3D TYPE EXPERIMENT
Studio Words are Pictures
Designer Craig Ward
Principal Typeface Futura (sculptural)

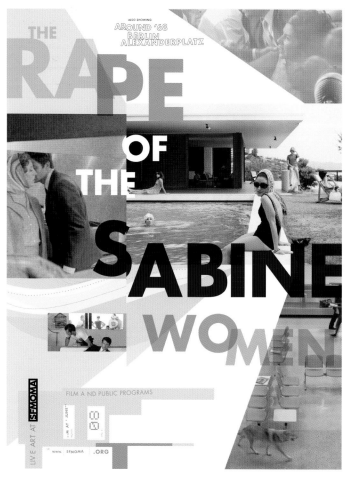

POSTER
Client San Francisco Museum of Modern Art
Studio Chen Design Associates
Designer Kathrin Blatter
Creative Director/Art Director Joshua C. Chen
Principal Typeface Futura

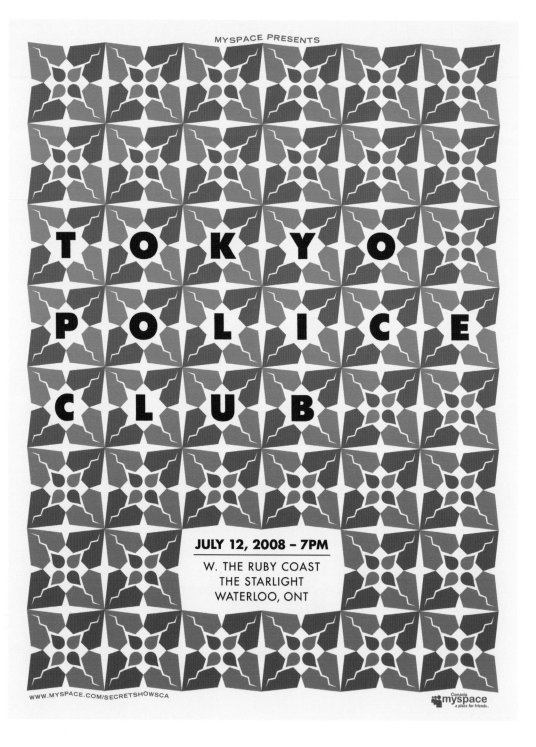

POSTER
Client MySpace Secret Shows
Studio Doublenaut
Designers Andrew McCracken and
Matt McCracken
Principal Typeface Futura

POSTER
Client University of Michigan, School of Art & Design
Designer Ben Van Dyke
Principal Typeface Futura

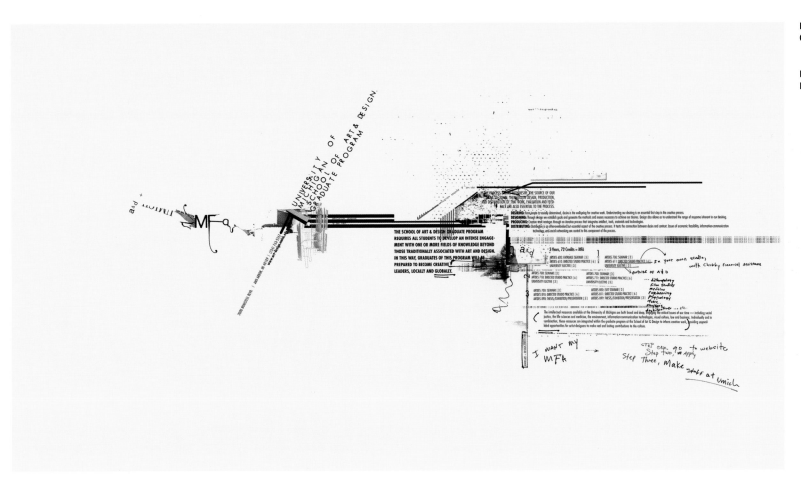

TYPEFACE DESIGN
Client FontLab
Studio Words are Pictures
Designer Craig Ward
Principal Typeface Based on Futura

Custom typefaces created for FontLab's Photofont software.

STORE ENVIRONMENT
Client Pinkberry, Inc.
Studio Ferroconcrete
Designer/Creative Director
Yolanda Santosa
Designers Sunjoo Park and Wendy Thai
Principal Typeface Futura

IN-STORE PROMO
Client Pinkberry, Inc.
Studio Ferroconcrete
Designer/Creative Director Yolanda Santosa
Designer Sunjoo Park
Photographer Christina Peters
Copywriter Luellen Renn
Principal Typeface Futura

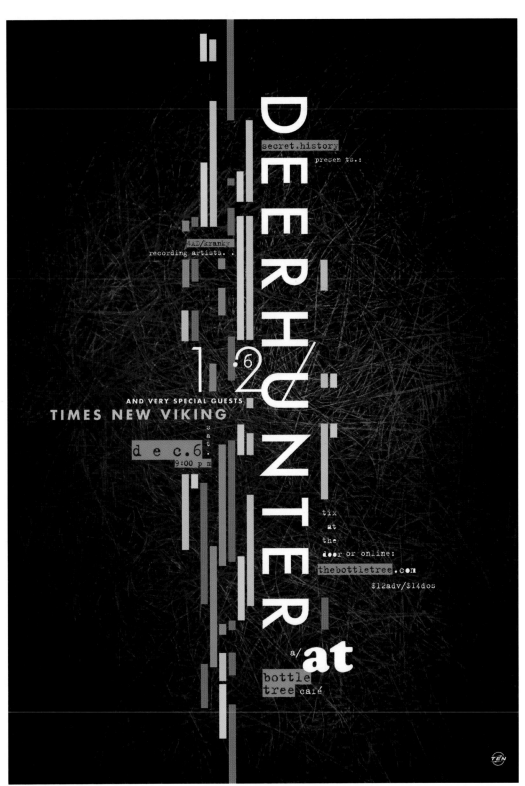

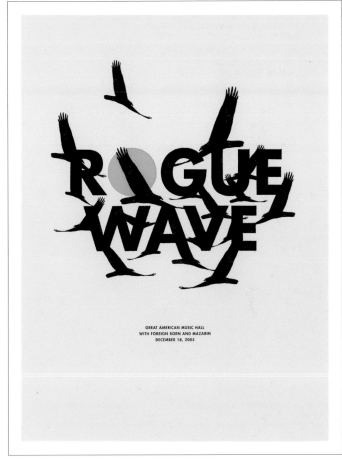

POSTER
Client Rogue Wave
Studio The Small Stakes
Designer Jason Munn
Principal Typeface Futura

POSTER
Client Bottletree
Studio TEN
Designer Roy Burns
Principal Typefaces Futura, Cooper Black,
and FF Trixie

151

POSTER
Client Mammoth, Inc.
Studio My Associate Cornelius
Designer A. Micah Smith
Principal Typefaces LHF Old Block,
   Univers (customized), and Futura

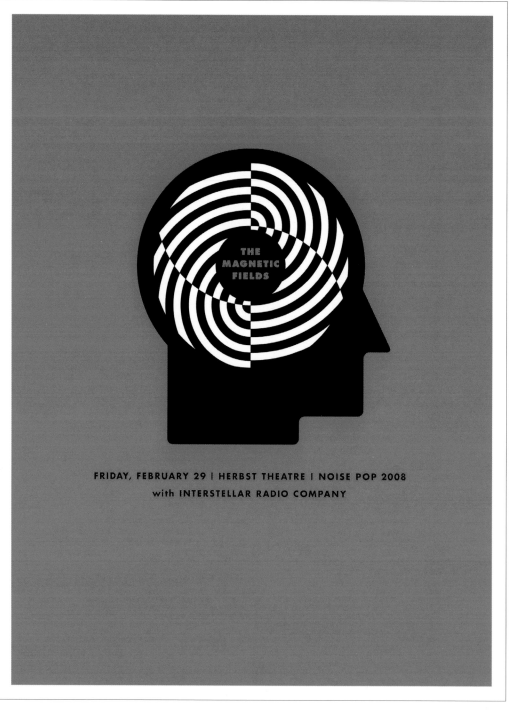

POSTER
Client Noise Pop
Studio The Small Stakes
Designer Jason Munn
Principal Typeface Futura

POSTER
Designer Lisa Maione
School Rhode Island School of Design
Advisor Lucy Hitchcock
Principal Typefaces Futura and an unknown Grotesque

*Maione created this collage with a piece of found typography—
a label-ordering instruction sheet, probably from the 1960s.
The collage was cut and constructed by hand, and then scanned.*

POSTER
Client Emerge Entertainment
Studio Doublenaut
Designers Andrew McCracken and
Matt McCracken
Principal Typeface Futura

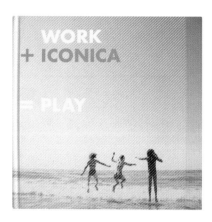

CATALOG
Client Amana America
Studio Timothy O'Donnell for The Fin Company
Designer Timothy O'Donnell
Principal Typeface Futura

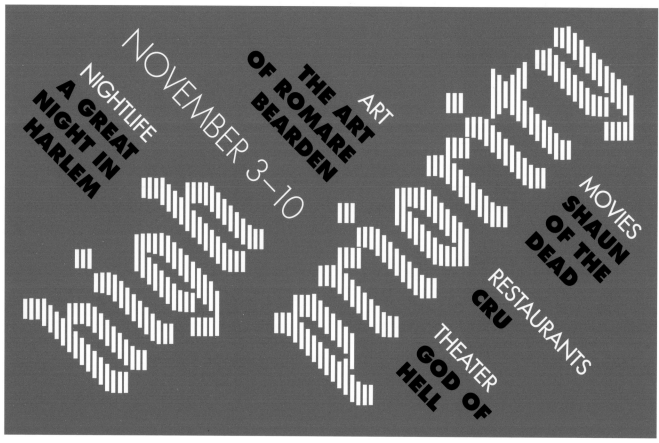

TYPOGRAPHIC ILLUSTRATION
Designer Ricardo Córdoba
Principal Typefaces Futura, and striped Fraktur
lettering based on Brauhaus

*Córdoba created this piece as an entry in the High
Priority design contest presented by the web-based
design community* Speak Up *and* New York
magazine in 2006.

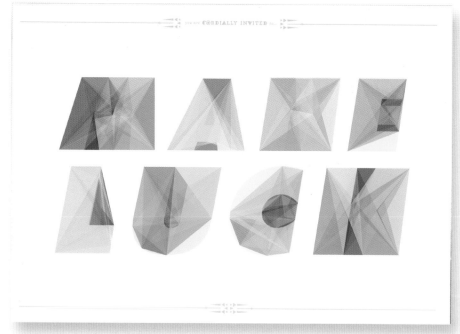

POSTCARD
Studio From Keetra
Designer Keetra Dean Dixon
Principal Typeface Futura

From the artist's Cordial Invitations series.

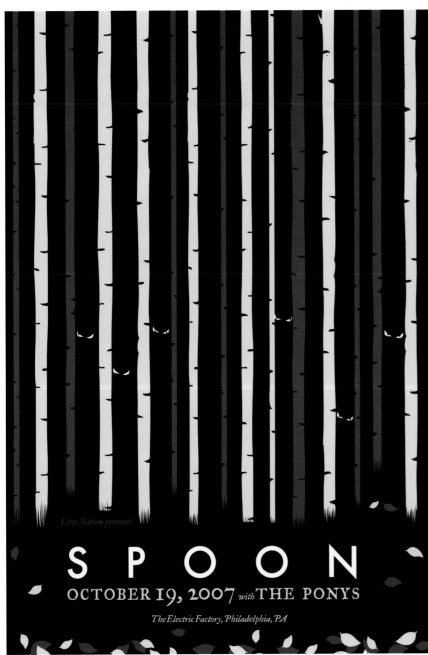

POSTER
Client Spoon
Studio/Screenprinter strawberryluna
Designers strawberryluna and Craig Seder
Principal Typeface Futura

THREE-DIMENSIONAL TYPOGRAPHY
Designer Shaz Madani
Principal Typeface Futura

This piece is one in a series of paper sculptures Madani created in her self-initiated campaign proposal for Arctic Paper. The campaign was intended to illustrate the beauty and flexibility of paper while promoting eco-friendly varieties.

POSTER
Client Province of Saskatchewan
Studio Bradbury Branding and Design
Principal Typeface Futura

POSTER
Client Nada Surf
Studio The Small Stakes
Designer Jason Munn
Principal Typeface Futura

LOGO
Client Sustainable Business Council, Los Angeles Chapter
Studio Evenson Design Group
Designers Sharon Lee and Julia Kim
Creative Directors Mark Sojka and Stan Evenson
Principal Typeface Futura

FILM TITLES
Client Hypnagogic Films
Designer Timothy O'Donnell
Principal Typeface Futura

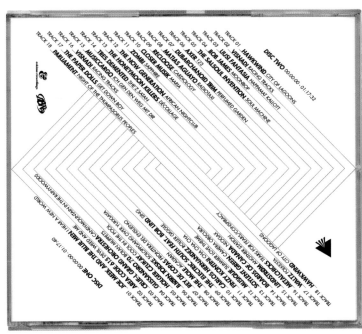

CD/LP PACKAGING
Client Eskimo Recordings
Designer/Illustrator Chris Bolton
Principal Typeface Futura

157

GILL SANS

a O

9/10pt

HOW RAZORBACK-JUMPING FROGS CAN LEVEL SIX PIQUED gymnasts! Jackdaws love my big sphinx of quartz. Jaded zombies acted quaintly but kept driving their oxen forward. The quick brown fox jumps over a lazy dog. The public was amazed to view the quickness and dexterity of the juggler. A mad boxer shot a quick, gloved jab to the jaw of his dizzy opponent. The five boxing wizards jump quickly. How razor-

10/12pt

HOW RAZORBACK-JUMPING FROGS CAN LEVEL SIX piqued gymnasts! Jackdaws love my big sphinx of quartz. Jaded zombies acted quaintly but kept driving their oxen forward. The quick brown fox jumps over a lazy dog. The public was amazed to view the quickness and dexterity of the juggler. A mad boxer shot a quick, gloved jab to the jaw of his dizzy opponent. The

12/14pt

HOW RAZORBACK-JUMPING FROGS CAN LEVEL six piqued gymnasts! Jackdaws love my big sphinx of quartz. Jaded zombies acted quaintly but kept driving their oxen forward. The quick brown fox jumps over a lazy dog. The public was amazed to view the quick-

Gill Sans Italic

abcdefghijklmnopqrstuvwxyz1234567890
ABCDEFGHIJKLMNOPQRSTUVWXYZ

Gill Sans Bold

abcdefghijklmnopqrstuvwxyz12345678
ABCDEFGHIJKLMNOPQRSTUVWXY

Gill Sans Bold Italic

abcdefghijklmnopqrstuvwxyz1234567890
ABCDEFGHIJKLMNOPQRSTUVWXYZ

Gill Sans Heavy

abcdefghijklmnopqrstuvwxyz123456
ABCDEFGHIJKLMNOPQRSTUVWX

Gill Sans Ultra Bold

abcdefghijklmnopqrstuvwxy
ABCDEFGHIJKLMNOPQRSTUV

Gill Sans [Monotype Imaging]

abcdefghijklmnopqrstuvwxyz
ABCDEFGHIJKLMNOPQRST
UVWXYZ1234567890
[àóüßç](.,:;?!$€£&-*){ÀÓÜÇ}

Beginning in 1902, British designer Eric Gill studied under Edward Johnston, the renowned calligrapher who, in 1916, designed the typeface used for the London Underground signage. Johnston's work greatly influenced Gill, who went on to experiment with Sans types. Monotype's Stanley Morison wanted to develop a Modern face on a par with the German Sans Serif types being released following the success of Futura. Morison saw lettering that Gill had created, and worked with the designer until Gill Sans was released, in a single uppercase weight, in 1928. The typeface was chosen as the standard font for the London and North Eastern Railway (LNER) system and used for its posters and promotional materials. Gill Sans became popular immediately upon its commercial release and was expanded, appearing not just on the LNER work, but also on the iconic paperback book jackets that Jan Tschichold designed for Penguin Books starting in 1935.

If you like …

Gill Sans

… you could also consider:

Avenir
Frutiger
Futura
Meta
Officina Sans
Optima

POSTER
Client Revolution Rock Concerts
Studio Doublenaut
Designers Andrew McCracken and
Matt McCracken
Principal Typeface Gill Sans

POSTER
Client Bösch
Studio Studio AND
Designer Jean-Benoît Lévy
Photographic Artist Franz Werner
Principal Typeface Gill Sans

159

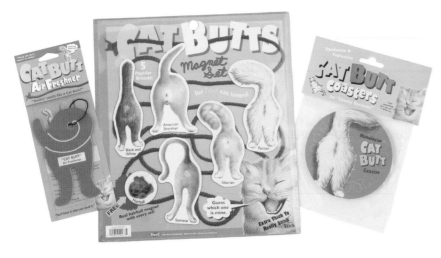

NOVELTY PRODUCTS AND PACKAGING
Client Blue Q
Studio Modern Dog Design Co.
Designer Michael Strassburger
Illustrator Junichi Tsuneoka
Principal Typeface Gill Sans

POSTER
Client Bottletree
Designer Timothy O'Donnell
Principal Typeface Gill Sans

BOTTLETREE CAFÉ .THE

WEDDING

PRESENT

with JEALOUS

GIRLFRIENDS

TEEN GETAWAY

OCTOBER 15

NINE

DON'T
WE ALL
LOVE THE
DARK

ILLUSTRATION
Client Dark
Studio Glossy.tv
Designer Bas
Principal Typeface Gill Sans

POSTER
Client Bottletree
Studio TEN
Designer Roy Burns
Principal Typefaces Gill Sans and FF Trixie

POSTER
Client Emerge Entertainment
Studio Doublenaut
Designers Andrew McCracken and
   Matt McCracken
Principal Typeface Gill Sans

POSTER
Client Professional Arts Consortium
(formerly The ProArts Consortium)
Designer Elizabeth Resnick
Principal Typeface Gill Sans

All images this page:
CALENDAR
Studio Michael Renaud Design
Designer/Illustrator/Printer Michael Renaud
Principal Typefaces Gill Sans, Blackmoor,
Cyclone, Sign Painter, Valken, and Caecilia

GROTESQUE

a c

9/10pt

HOW RAZORBACK-JUMPING FROGS CAN LEVEL SIX PIQUED gymnasts! Jackdaws love my big sphinx of quartz. Jaded zombies acted quaintly but kept driving their oxen forward. The quick brown fox jumps over a lazy dog. The public was amazed to view the quickness and dexterity of the juggler. A mad boxer shot a quick, gloved jab to the jaw of his dizzy

10/12pt

HOW RAZORBACK-JUMPING FROGS CAN LEVEL SIX piqued gymnasts! Jackdaws love my big sphinx of quartz. Jaded zombies acted quaintly but kept driving their oxen forward. The quick brown fox jumps over a lazy dog. The public was amazed to view the quickness and dexterity of the juggler. A mad boxer shot a quick,

12/14pt

HOW RAZORBACK-JUMPING FROGS CAN LEVEL six piqued gymnasts! Jackdaws love my big sphinx of quartz. Jaded zombies acted quaintly but kept driving their oxen forward. The quick brown fox jumps over a lazy dog.

Bureau Grot Compressed Light

abcdefghijklmnopqrstuvwxyz1234567890
ABCDEFGHIJKLMNOPQRSTUVWXYZ

Bureau Grot Condensed Bold

abcdefghijklmnopqrstuvwxyz1234567890
ABCDEFGHIJKLMNOPQRSTUVWXYZ

Bureau Grot Black

abcdefghijklmnopqrstuvwxyz12
ABCDEFGHIJKLMNOPQRSTUVW

Bureau Grot Wide Ultra Black

abcdefghijklmnopqrstuvw
ABCDEFGHIJKLMNOPQ

Other notable cuts:

Monotype Grotesque [Monotype]

Bureau Grot Book [Font Bureau]

abcdefghijklmnopqrstuvwxyz
ABCDEFGHIJKLMNOPQ
RSTUVWXYZ1234567890
[àóüßç](.,:;?!$€£&–*){ÀÓÜÇ}

Grotesque refers to a form of eighteenth-century Sans English typeface, referred to as Gothic in North America. The term Grotesque became prevalent because types of this ilk were unusual to most readers.

One notable variant is Monotype Grotesque, a 1926 design that is among the earliest Sans cut for hot metal. Grotesque types proved popular throughout the twentieth century. In the early 1980s, Font Bureau cofounder Roger Black was in search of a Sans with personality. His partner in Font Bureau, David Berlow, developed Bureau Grotesque specifically for use in publications in the late 1980s. Berlow's types, modeled on the Stephenson Blake foundry types of the 1800s, were immediately successful, and were used to great effect in such magazines as *Newsweek* and *Entertainment Weekly.* In 2006, Berlow revised and expanded his masterwork, rechristening the extensive Sans family Bureau Grot.

If you like …

Grotesque

… you could also consider:

Akzidenz-Grotesk

DIN

Franklin Gothic

Helvetica

Trade Gothic

Univers

POSTER
Clients Cinéma Le France, Musée d'Art Moderne de Saint-Étienne, and École supérieure art et design de Saint-Étienne
Designer Aurore Chassé
Principal Typefaces Gothic 13 and Bureau Grotesque

POSTER
School École supérieure art et design de Saint-Étienne
Designer Aurore Chassé
Principal Typefaces Egiziano and Bureau Grotesque

HELVETICA

cd

9/10pt

HOW RAZORBACK-JUMPING FROGS CAN LEVEL SIX PIQUED gymnasts! Jackdaws love my big sphinx of quartz. Jaded zombies acted quaintly but kept driving their oxen forward. The quick brown fox jumps over a lazy dog. The public was amazed to view the quickness and dexterity of the juggler. A mad boxer shot a quick, gloved jab to the jaw of his dizzy opponent. The

10/12pt

HOW RAZORBACK-JUMPING FROGS CAN LEVEL SIX piqued gymnasts! Jackdaws love my big sphinx of quartz. Jaded zombies acted quaintly but kept driving their oxen forward. The quick brown fox jumps over a lazy dog. The public was amazed to view the quickness and dexterity of the juggler. A mad boxer shot a quick, gloved jab to the

12/14pt

HOW RAZORBACK-JUMPING FROGS CAN level six piqued gymnasts! Jackdaws love my big sphinx of quartz. Jaded zombies acted quaintly but kept driving their oxen forward. The quick brown fox jumps over a lazy dog. The

Helvetica Neue 56 Italic

abcdefghijklmnopqrstuvwxyz1234567890
ABCDEFGHIJKLMNOPQRSTUVWXYZ

Helvetica Neue 75 Bold

abcdefghijklmnopqrstuvwxyz12345678
ABCDEFGHIJKLMNOPQRSTUVWXYZ

Helvetica Neue 76 Bold Italic

abcdefghijklmnopqrstuvwxyz12345678
ABCDEFGHIJKLMNOPQRSTUVWXYZ

Helvetica Neue 85 Heavy

abcdefghijklmnopqrstuvwxyz123456
ABCDEFGHIJKLMNOPQRSTUVWXYZ

Helvetica Neue 95 Black

abcdefghijklmnopqrstuvwxyz12345
ABCDEFGHIJKLMNOPQRSTUVWXY

Other notable cuts:

Helvetica [Linotype]

Helvetica Neue 55 [Linotype]

abcdefghijklmnopqrstuvwxyz
ABCDEFGHIJKLMNOPQRS
TUVWXYZ1234567890
[àóüßç](.,:;?!$€£&-*){ÀÓÜÇ}

Due to the extreme popularity of Akzidenz-Grotesk in the mid-twentieth century, the team at Haas'sche Schriftgiesserei (Haas Type Foundry) wanted to develop their own Sans to compete in the Swiss market. In 1957, Max Miedinger, working with Eduard Hoffmann, created Neue Haas Grotesk. Based on late nineteenth-century Grotesques, Neue Haas was refined for neutrality and clarity, moving it into the Neo-Grotesque category. In 1960, Stempel, Haas'sche's German parent company, renamed it Helvetica—from the Latin word for "Swiss"—for international marketing purposes.

In the 1960s, after Helvetica was introduced to the US market, Mergenthaler Linotype expanded the Stempel series with several new versions. The many Helvetica variants created over the years were not completely coordinated. In 1983, Stempel and Linotype collaborated on a reworking of the design and digitized Helvetica Neue, a unified family with improved legibility. Helvetica is undoubtedly the most famous face in the world: it was the subject of Gary Hustwit's acclaimed documentary *Helvetica*, released in 2007 in tandem with the 50th anniversary celebration of the typeface's birth.

PACKAGING
Client DRY Soda Co.
Studio Turnstyle
Designer Steve Watson
Principal Typeface Helvetica Neue

If you like …

Helvetica

… you could also consider:

Akzidenz-Grotesk

Avenir

Folio

Franklin Gothic

Univers

POSTER
Client Brown University/
Rhode Island School of Design
Studio ADearFriend
Designer Chris Ro
Principal Typeface Helvetica

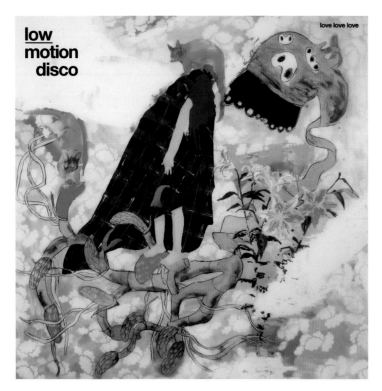

MUSIC PACKAGING
Client Eskimo Recordings
Designer Chris Bolton
Illustrators Pascale Mira Tschäni and
    Michael Husmann Tschäni
Principal Typeface Helvetica Neue

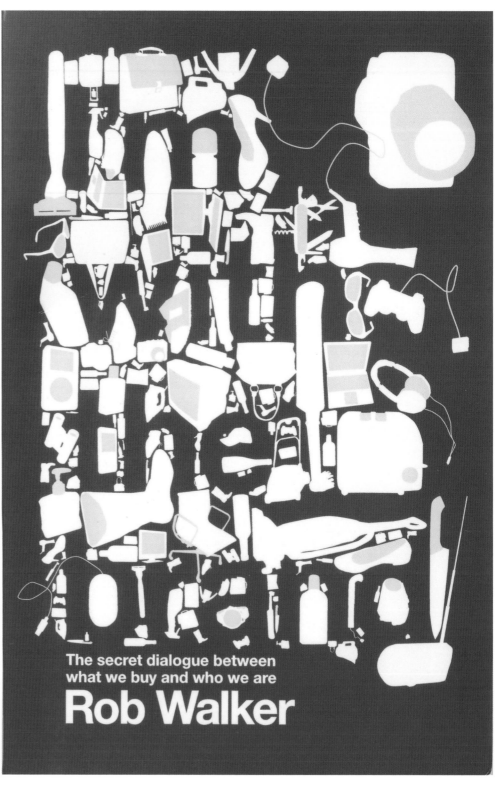

BOOK COVER
Publisher Constable & Robinson Ltd., London
Studio Jawa and Midwich
Designers Simon Dovar and Nils Davey
Principal Typeface Helvetica (hand rendered)

PROMOTIONAL MATERIALS
Client Saskatchewan Filmpool Cooperative
Studio Bradbury Branding and Design
Principal Typeface Helvetica

Above:

ILLUSTRATION
Client AMV BBDO
Studio Words are Pictures
Designer Craig Ward
Principal Typeface Helvetica

Type treatment created for the ad agency's campaign for the UK Department of Transport.

Above right:
CD COVER
Client Smalltown Superjazzz
Designer/Photographer Rune Mortensen
Principal Typeface Helvetica Neue

FLYER
Client Goodluck
Studio Glossy.tv
Designer Ben
Principal Typeface Helvetica

**Jawa
and
Midwich**
www.jawa-midwich.com

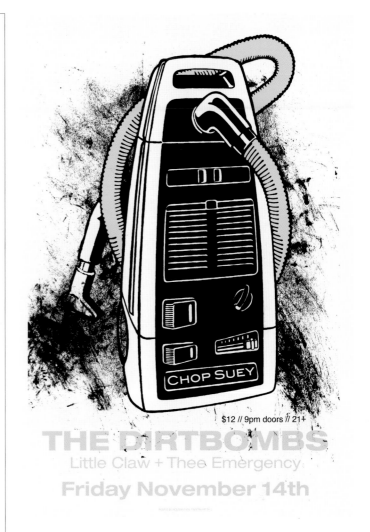

$12 // 9pm doors // 21+

THE DIRTBOMBS
Little Claw + Thee Emergency
Friday November 14th

POSTER
Client Chop Suey
Studio Modern Dog Design Co.
Designer Robynne Raye
Principal Typeface Helvetica Neue

POSTER
Studio Jawa and Midwich
Designers Simon Dovar and Nils Davey
Principal Typeface Helvetica (hand rendered)

*Part of a series of self-promotional posters intended
to reinforce the studio's brand.*

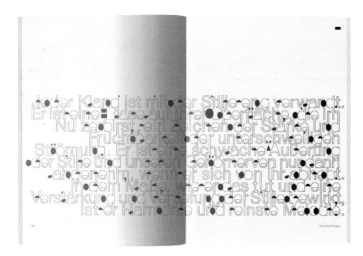

BOOK
Publisher Buchhandlung Walter König, Köln
Clients Sounds of Silence with Petra Eichler
and Susanne Kessler
Studio desres design studio
Art Director/Typographer Michaela Kessler
Printer Druckerei Imbescheidt
Principal Typeface Helvetica (modified)

The book Sounds of Silence *expands on the concept
of installations in graphic form. Six booklets were wrapped
in a folded jacket, accompanied by a DVD with film footage
from individual events.*

POSTER
Art Director/Designer Michael Braley
Principal Typeface Helvetica

MICHAEL
BRALEY
04.29.05
1:30 P.M.
THE
CREATIVE
CIRCUS
ATLANTA,
GEORGIA

happy new year 2008   gratsjel.fr

LOGO
Client Accept & Proceed
Designer Peter Sunna
Principal Typeface Helvetica (modified)

GREETING CARD
Client Nicolas Queffélec
Designer Nicolas Queffélec
Principal Typeface Helvetica (cast in ice)

This greeting card is based on a pun: the French expression for the past year, "année écoulée," also translates as "melted year," and the French word "fonte" (font or typeface in English) can also be translated as "melted."

MUSIC PACKAGING
Clients Eskimo Recordings and Lektroluv
Designer Chris Bolton
Principal Typeface Helvetica Rounded (modified)

POSTER
Client Linotype
Studio Estudio Wonksite
Designer Jorge Restrepo
Principal Typeface Helvetica

Restrepo created Helvetica: Biography of
a Font *for Linotype's 2007 Helvetica NOW
design competition, where it finished among the
top 20 award winners. The composition references
Helvetica's history, its creator, and the Swiss
studio where it was conceived.*

174

POSTER
Client Comunidad de
Santa María Tlahuitoltepec Mixe
Studio huizar 1984
Designer José Ignacio Zárate Huizar
Principal Typeface Helvetica Inserat

POSTER
Client Longinotti Robot Festival
Studio DHNN (Design has No Name)
Principal Typefaces Helvetica Neue
and Memphis

ILLUSTRATION
Client O.K. Parking
Designer Ben Van Dyke
Principal Typeface Helvetica (sculptural)

This mixed-media piece features amorphous Helvetica-based letterforms composed of photographed, lasercut acrylic; cardboard; and vinyl.

175

POSTER
Client Pearl Street Nightclub
Studio Standard Design
Designer Tom Pappalardo
Screenprinter strawberryluna
Principal Typeface Helvetica
  (Chartpak press-on lettering)

POSTER
Studio Jawa and Midwich
Designers Simon Dovar and Nils Davey
Principal Typeface Helvetica (hand rendered)

*Part of a series of self-promotional posters
intended to reinforce the studio's brand.*

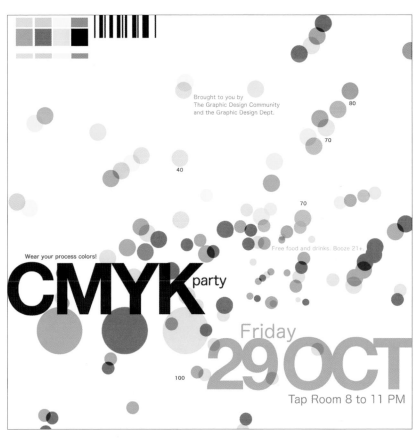

BUSINESS CARDS
Designer Sam Mallett
Principal Typeface Helvetica (metal)

Mallett printed his letterpress business cards at the K18 Studio Zurich on the 50th anniversary of the birth of Helvetica. Shown at left is the metal type lock-up used to print the cards.

POSTER
Designer Lisa Maione
School Rhode Island School of Design
Principal Typeface Helvetica

STUDIO EXPERIMENT
Designer Ben Van Dyke
Principal Typeface Helvetica (self-adhesive vinyl and oil paint)

BOOK
Publisher The Monacelli Press, New York
Studio Think Studio
Designers John Clifford and Herb Thornby
Principal Typeface Helvetica Neue

POSTER
Client Alea
Studio toormix
Principal Typeface Helvetica Neue

POSTER
Client Rocky Mountain College of
Art and Design
Art Director/Designer Michael Braley
Principal Typeface Helvetica

POSTER
Client University of Wales, Newport
Designer Sam Mallett
Principal Typeface Helvetica Neue

179

META

od

9/10pt

HOW RAZORBACK-JUMPING FROGS CAN LEVEL SIX PIQUED GYM-
nasts! Jackdaws love my big sphinx of quartz. Jaded zombies acted
quaintly but kept driving their oxen forward. The quick brown fox
jumps over a lazy dog. The public was amazed to view the quickness and dexterity of the juggler. A mad boxer shot a quick, gloved
jab to the jaw of his dizzy opponent. The five boxing wizards jump

10/12pt

HOW RAZORBACK-JUMPING FROGS CAN LEVEL SIX PIQUED
gymnasts! Jackdaws love my big sphinx of quartz. Jaded
zombies acted quaintly but kept driving their oxen forward.
The quick brown fox jumps over a lazy dog. The public was
amazed to view the quickness and dexterity of the juggler.
A mad boxer shot a quick, gloved jab to the jaw of his dizzy

12/14pt

HOW RAZORBACK-JUMPING FROGS CAN LEVEL SIX
piqued gymnasts! Jackdaws love my big sphinx
of quartz. Jaded zombies acted quaintly but kept
driving their oxen forward. The quick brown fox
jumps over a lazy dog. The public was amazed

FF Meta Book Italic

abcdefghijklmnopqrstuvwxyz1234567890
ABCDEFGHIJKLMNOPQRSTUVWXYZ

FF Meta Medium

abcdefghijklmnopqrstuvwxyz1234567890
ABCDEFGHIJKLMNOPQRSTUVWXYZ

FF Meta Medium Italic

abcdefghijklmnopqrstuvwxyz1234567890
ABCDEFGHIJKLMNOPQRSTUVWXYZ

FF Meta Black

abcdefghijklmnopqrstuvwxyz1234567890
ABCDEFGHIJKLMNOPQRSTUVWXYZ

FF Meta Black Italic

abcdefghijklmnopqrstuvwxyz1234567890
ABCDEFGHIJKLMNOPQRSTUVWXYZ

FF Meta Book [FontFont]

abcdefghijklmnopqrstuvwxyz
ABCDEFGHIJKLMNOPQRSTU
VWXYZ1234567890
[àóüßç](.,:;?!$€£&-*){ÀÓÜÇ}

In 1984/1985, Erik Spiekermann, founder of FontShop International and MetaDesign, developed PT 55 for the Deutsche Bundespost (German Federal Post). At the time, the post office was using Helvetica as their corporate face, and it commissioned Spiekermann to rework their typography. After trying a number of existing typefaces for forms and other printed material, and finding them lacking, he drew something entirely new. Spiekermann's Humanist Sans was carefully developed to meet the stringent requirements of the postal service, from postage stamps to signage on delivery vehicles. However, the project was eventually canceled, and the type went back into the drawer.

When FontShop opened its doors in 1989, Spiekermann and his colleagues resurrected PT 55, and it eventually became FF Meta, as part of the FontFont collection. When FF Meta types were released in 1991, the family consisted of normal, bold, and small caps variants. Additional styles were added in 1992, but the first major expansion came with the release of FF MetaPlus in 1993. This enlarged the family to 18 fonts, and improved its suitability for use in text. FF Meta exploded in popularity, becoming an instant classic and a staple in designers' type palettes worldwide. FF Meta became so widely used that it was called "the Helvetica of the nineties"(quote attributed to design author Robin Kinross). In 1998, FontShop further expanded the design, creating a 60-font superfamily, and reverting to the simpler FF Meta name. Since then, the family has continually been expanded, with the addition of superlight weights, condensed variants, headline styles, and a companion Serif family.

POSTER
Studio DHNN (Design has No Name)
Principal Typeface FF Meta

Experimental typography project initiated by the designers at DHNN.

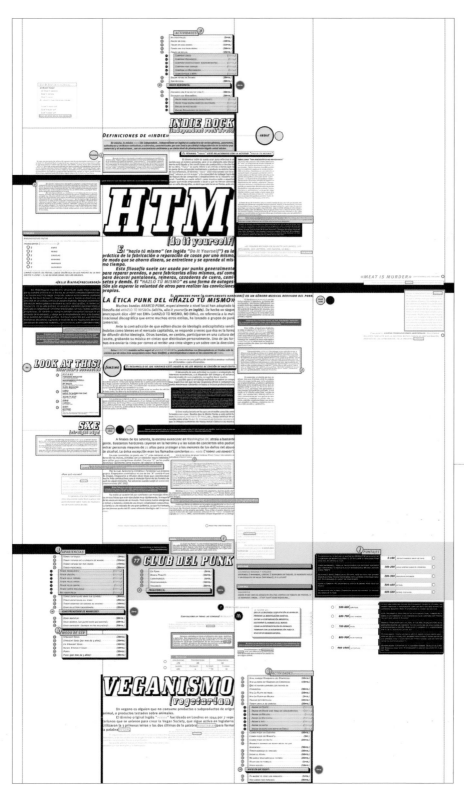

If you like …

Meta

… you could also consider:

Avenir
Frutiger
Officina Sans

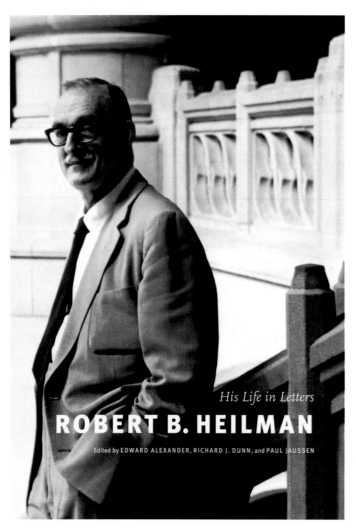

BOOK COVER
Publisher University of Washington Press,
  Seattle and London
Designer Ashley Saleeba
Principal Typefaces FF Meta and FF Scala

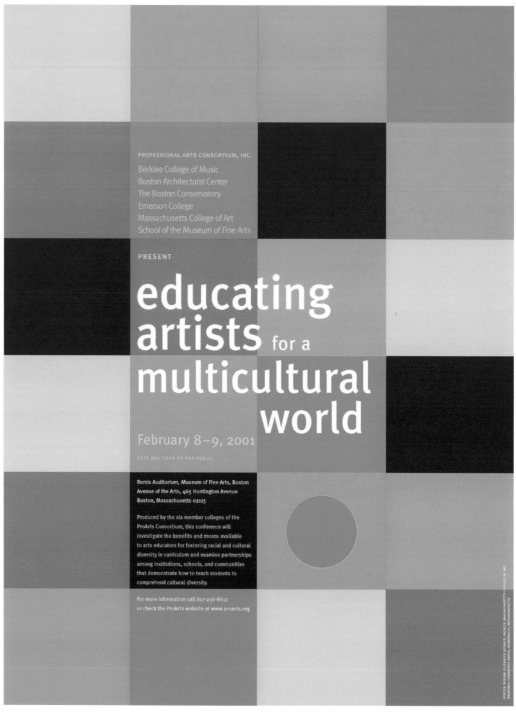

POSTER
Client Professional Arts Consortium
(formerly The ProArts Consortium)
Designer Elizabeth Resnick
Principal Typeface FF Meta

ALUMNI MAGAZINE
Client University of Regina
Studio Bradbury Branding and Design
Principal Typeface FF Meta

POSTER
Client IWB (Industrielle Werke Basel)
Studio Studio AND
Designer Jean-Benoît Lévy
Photographer Pierre-Yves Goavec
Principal Typeface FF Meta

"A smart, outraged, and vividly described whirlwind tour of criminal conspiracy.... Clear, compelling, and scary."
—*The Christian Science Monitor*

MISHA GLENNY

McMAFIA

A JOURNEY THROUGH THE GLOBAL CRIMINAL UNDERWORLD

With a New Introduction

BOOK COVER
Publisher Random House, New York
Studio Salamander Hill Design
Designer David Drummond
Principal Typefaces FF Meta and ITC New Baskerville

CARL HAGENBECK'S
EMPIRE OF ENTERTAINMENTS

ERIC AMES

BOOK COVER
Publisher University of Washington Press,
Seattle and London
Designer Ashley Saleeba
Principal Typefaces FF Meta and FF Meta Serif

POSTER
Studio DHNN (Design has No Name)
Principal Typeface FF Meta

*Experimental typography project initiated
by the designers at DHNN.*

OFFICINA SANS

od

9/10pt

HOW RAZORBACK-JUMPING FROGS CAN LEVEL SIX PIQUED GYMNASTS!
Jackdaws love my big sphinx of quartz. Jaded zombies acted quaintly but
kept driving their oxen forward. The quick brown fox jumps over a lazy
dog. The public was amazed to view the quickness and dexterity of the
juggler. A mad boxer shot a quick, gloved jab to the jaw of his dizzy opponent. The five boxing wizards jump quickly. How razorback-jumping

10/12pt

HOW RAZORBACK-JUMPING FROGS CAN LEVEL SIX PIQUED GYM-
nasts! Jackdaws love my big sphinx of quartz. Jaded zombies
acted quaintly but kept driving their oxen forward. The quick
brown fox jumps over a lazy dog. The public was amazed to view
the quickness and dexterity of the juggler. A mad boxer shot a
quick, gloved jab to the jaw of his dizzy opponent. The five boxing

12/14pt

HOW RAZORBACK-JUMPING FROGS CAN LEVEL SIX
piqued gymnasts! Jackdaws love my big sphinx of
quartz. Jaded zombies acted quaintly but kept driving
their oxen forward. The quick brown fox jumps over a
lazy dog. The public was amazed to view the quickness

ITC Officina Sans Book Italic

abcdefghijklmnopqrstuvwxyz1234567890
ABCDEFGHIJKLMNOPQRSTUVWXYZ

ITC Officina Sans Medium

abcdefghijklmnopqrstuvwxyz1234567890
ABCDEFGHIJKLMNOPQRSTUVWXYZ

ITC Officina Sans Bold

abcdefghijklmnopqrstuvwxyz1234567890
ABCDEFGHIJKLMNOPQRSTUVWXYZ

ITC Officina Sans Extra Bold

abcdefghijklmnopqrstuvwxyz1234567890
ABCDEFGHIJKLMNOPQRSTUVWXYZ

ITC Officina Sans Black

abcdefghijklmnopqrstuvwxyz123456789
ABCDEFGHIJKLMNOPQRSTUVWXYZ

ITC Officina Sans Book [ITC]

abcdefghijklmnopqrstuvwxyz
ABCDEFGHIJKLMNOPQRSTU
VWXYZ1234567890
[àóüßç](.,:;?!$€£&-*){ÀÓÜÇ}

ITC Officina was developed by German designer Erik Spiekermann and released in 1990. This matched pair of Sans and Serif types, originally available in two weights with complementary italics, was intended for business applications requiring extreme legibility under less than optimal conditions. ITC Officina Sans displays traits of traditional typewriter text, but was developed with an eye toward technological advancements. Upon its release, designers found the typeface a welcome addition to the Sans category, and embraced its clean forms, which incorporated trademark Spiekermann details. ITC Officina Sans and its Serif companion became instant classics. Noting the family's widespread adoption, Spiekermann collaborated with Ole Schäfer to add the extra weights and small caps necessary to make ITC Officina suitable for magazines, books, and advertising.

If you like …

Officina Sans

… you could also consider:

Avenir
Frutiger
Meta

LOGO
Client PLAN NJ
Studio Lippincott
Creative Director Brendán Murphy
Principal Typeface ITC Officina Sans

POSTER
Studio Studio AND
Designer Jean-Benoît Lévy
Photographer Tom Wedell
Printer Uldry
Principal Typeface ITC Officina Sans

OPTIMA

od

9/10pt

HOW RAZORBACK-JUMPING FROGS CAN LEVEL SIX PIQUED gymnasts! Jackdaws love my big sphinx of quartz. Jaded zombies acted quaintly but kept driving their oxen forward. The quick brown fox jumps over a lazy dog. The public was amazed to view the quickness and dexterity of the juggler. A mad boxer shot a quick, gloved jab to the jaw of his dizzy opponent. The five boxing

10/12pt

HOW RAZORBACK-JUMPING FROGS CAN LEVEL SIX piqued gymnasts! Jackdaws love my big sphinx of quartz. Jaded zombies acted quaintly but kept driving their oxen forward. The quick brown fox jumps over a lazy dog. The public was amazed to view the quickness and dexterity of the juggler. A mad boxer shot a quick, gloved jab to the jaw

12/14pt

HOW RAZORBACK-JUMPING FROGS CAN level six piqued gymnasts! Jackdaws love my big sphinx of quartz. Jaded zombies acted quaintly but kept driving their oxen forward. The quick brown fox jumps over a lazy dog. The public was

Optima Nova Italic

abcdefghijklmnopqrstuvwxyz1234567890
ABCDEFGHIJKLMNOPQRSTUVWXYZ

Optima Nova Bold

abcdefghijklmnopqrstuvwxyz12345678
ABCDEFGHIJKLMNOPQRSTUVWXYZ

Optima Nova Heavy

abcdefghijklmnopqrstuvwxyz123456789
ABCDEFGHIJKLMNOPQRSTUVWXYZ

Optima Nova Black

abcdefghijklmnopqrstuvwxyz12345678
ABCDEFGHIJKLMNOPQRSTUVWXYZ

Optima Nova Titling Initials

ABCDEFGHIJKLMNOPQRSTUVWXYZ1234
AA C FT HE KA LL LA MN NO RE RAST SA TH TT Æ

Other notable cuts:

Optima [Linotype]

Optima Nova [Linotype]

abcdefghijklmnopqrstuvwxyz
ABCDEFGHIJKLMNOPQRS
TUVWXYZ1234567890
[àóüßç](.,:;?!$€£&-*){ÀÓÜÇ}

Optima, a Sans Serif embodying all the warmth and character of the human hand, was designed by German type designer Hermann Zapf, a master calligrapher and book artist. Zapf made the first sketches of this, his most successful typeface, in 1950, during a visit to the Basilica of Santa Croce in Florence, Italy. He was inspired by the marble letters on the graves of Florentine families displayed on the church floor.

From these original sketches, Zapf began working on Optima, its letterforms classically Roman in proportion and character, but absent of serifs. Optima letterforms feature tapered stems, giving the face a trademark quality not found in other faces in the Sans category. Zapf made numerous legibility tests and completed his first drawings in 1952. The metal types were cut by the renowned punchcutter August Rosenberger for Frankfurt's Stempel type-foundry. Optima was produced in matrices for Linotype typesetting machines and issued in 1958.

Optima became a great success when it was released, and maintained its popularity throughout the transition from metal typesetting to phototype and the digital realm. Unfortunately, neither the phototype nor the first digital incarnations never matched the beauty of the original metal. In 2002, modern technology made it possible to produce digital alphabets without technical limitations and design compromises. Fifty years after his visit to Santa Croce, Zapf collaborated with Akira Kobayashi, type director at Linotype, to rework his seminal type family. Optima Nova, released in 2003, was expanded to 40 fonts, including lighter weights, small caps, a true italic instead of oblique forms, and a delicate titling face with unusual ligatures.

Optima is the name of a typeface designed by Hermann Zapf between 1952-1955 for the D. Stempel AG foundry, Frankfurt, Germany. It was released in 1958. A mid-20th century sans-serif design, Optima at first looks a little like a traditional sans-serif. However, its strokes are delicately tapered and carry residual serifs. In many ways, Optima's design follows humanist lines, but its italic variant is merely an oblique, a slanted roman. Much used during the late 50s through the 60s, Optima is the typeface used on the Vietnam Veterans Memorial Wall. In 2002 Hermann Zapf together with Akira Kobayashi, type director at Linotype GmbH, redesigned and extended Optima as Optima Nova. This new type family has a more traditional, less formal italic, condensed weights and a titling capitals variation. Sketches for Optima were first done on a 1000 Lire banknote in 1950. Not having any paper to make sketches of inscriptions in Santa Croce in Florence, Hermann Zapf used a banknote. In 1952 the first drawings were finished after careful legibility tests for a typeface.

If you like …

Optima

… you could also consider:

Avenir
Frutiger
Gill Sans

TYPE SPECIMEN POSTER
Designer Claire Hyde
School University of West Georgia, Carrollton
Principal Typeface Optima

LOGO
Client Lifebook
Studio End Communications
Principal Typeface Optima

LIFE BOOK®

TRADE GOTHIC

cd

9/10pt

HOW RAZORBACK-JUMPING FROGS CAN LEVEL SIX PIQUED gymnasts! Jackdaws love my big sphinx of quartz. Jaded zombies acted quaintly but kept driving their oxen forward. The quick brown fox jumps over a lazy dog. The public was amazed to view the quickness and dexterity of the juggler. A mad boxer shot a quick, gloved jab to the jaw of his dizzy opponent. The five boxing

10/12pt

HOW RAZORBACK-JUMPING FROGS CAN LEVEL SIX piqued gymnasts! Jackdaws love my big sphinx of quartz. Jaded zombies acted quaintly but kept driving their oxen forward. The quick brown fox jumps over a lazy dog. The public was amazed to view the quickness and dexterity of the juggler. A mad boxer shot a quick, gloved jab to the jaw

12/14pt

HOW RAZORBACK-JUMPING FROGS CAN level six piqued gymnasts! Jackdaws love my big sphinx of quartz. Jaded zombies acted quaintly but kept driving their oxen forward. The quick brown fox jumps over a lazy dog. The public was

Trade Gothic Oblique

abcdefghijklmnopqrstuvwxyz1234567890
ABCDEFGHIJKLMNOPQRSTUVWXYZ

Trade Gothic Bold

abcdefghijklmnopqrstuvwxyz1234567890
ABCDEFGHIJKLMNOPQRSTUVWXYZ

Trade Gothic Condensed No. 18

abcdefghijklmnopqrstuvwxyz1234567890
ABCDEFGHIJKLMNOPQRSTUVWXYZ

Trade Gothic Condensed Bold No. 20

abcdefghijklmnopqrstuvwxyz1234567890
ABCDEFGHIJKLMNOPQRSTUVWXYZ

Trade Gothic Extended

abcdefghijklmnopqrstuvwxyz123
ABCDEFGHIJKLMNOPQRSTUV

Other notable cuts:

Trade Gothic Next [Linotype]

Trade Gothic [Linotype]

abcdefghijklmnopqrstuvwxyz
ABCDEFGHIJKLMNOPQRS
TUVWXYZ1234567890
[àóüßç](.,:;?!$€£&-*){ÀÓÜÇ}

Jackson Burke began work on Trade Gothic in 1948, following the nineteenth-century Grotesque model with its large x-height. Burke added new weights and styles until he became Director of Type Development for the US design office of Mergenthaler Linotype in 1960, eventually completing 14 fonts in the family. Not strictly unified like other large Sans families, such as Univers, Avant Garde, and Helvetica, Trade Gothic's unique range of styles gave it a distinct character especially suited to display work.

In 2008, Linotype released Trade Gothic Next, Akira Kobayashi's reworking of Burke's original design. Kobayashi corrected inconsistencies while improving spacing and kerning. He strengthened the regular weight and added compressed and heavy variants to make Trade Gothic an even more useful tool for display typography.

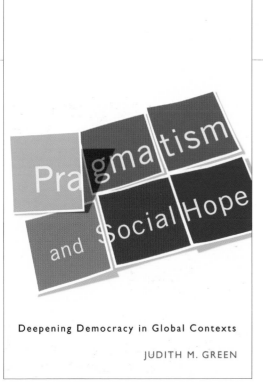

Deepening Democracy in Global Contexts

JUDITH M. GREEN

IGNORANCE IS BLISS

US DEPARTMENT OF DEFENCE IS THE SINGLE LARGEST OIL CONSUMING ENTITY IN THE WORLD DRINKING 426 800 BARRELS OF OIL PER DAY.

POSTER
Studio Elapse
Designer Erik Jonsson
Principal Typeface Trade Gothic

Jonsson designed this piece as part of his concept series on oil consumption statistics.

BOOK COVER
Publisher Columbia University Press, New York
Studio Salamander Hill Design
Designer David Drummond
Principal Typefaces Gill Sans and Trade Gothic

If you like …

Trade Gothic

… you could also consider:

Akzidenz-Grotesk
DIN
Folio
Franklin Gothic
Helvetica
Univers

T-SHIRT
Client Okkervil River
Studio My Associate Cornelius
Designer/Illustrator A. Micah Smith
Principal Typeface Trade Gothic

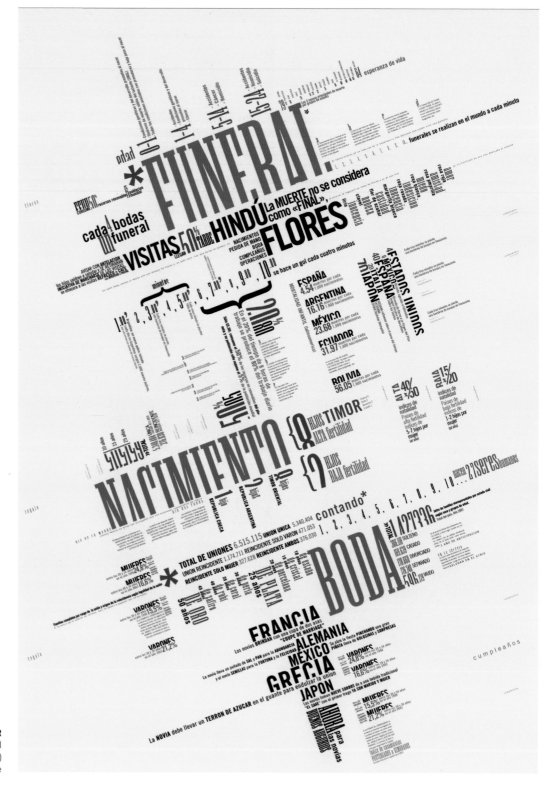

POSTER
Client Longinotti Festival
Studio DHNN (Design has No Name)
Principal Typefaces Univers, Trade Gothic, and Antique

ANNUAL REPORT
Client Province of Saskatchewan
Studio Society of Graphic Designers of Canada
Principal Typeface Trade Gothic

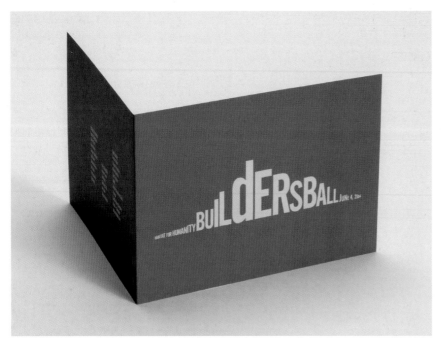

EVENT BRANDING
Client Habitat for Humanity
Studio DISTINC
Designers Jean-Marc Durviaux and John Wiese
Principal Typeface Trade Gothic

BOOK COVER
Publisher McGill-Queen's University Press,
Montreal and Toronto
Studio Salamander Hill Design
Designer David Drummond
Principal Typeface Trade Gothic

FLYER/POSTER
Art Director/Designer Chris Allen
Copywriters Chris Allen and Graeme Berglund
Principal Typeface Trade Gothic

This piece served as the announcement for The Cheaper Show, an annual, one-night-only group exhibition showcasing 250 artists from various disciplines. All art was priced the same, which informed the direction of the poster—the use of an objective message printed on newsprint.

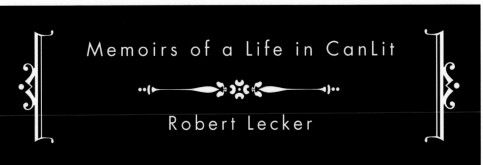

Memoirs of a Life in CanLit

Robert Lecker

BOOK COVER
Publisher Véhicule Press, Montreal
Studio Salamander Hill Design
Designer David Drummond
Principal Typefaces Trade Gothic and Futura

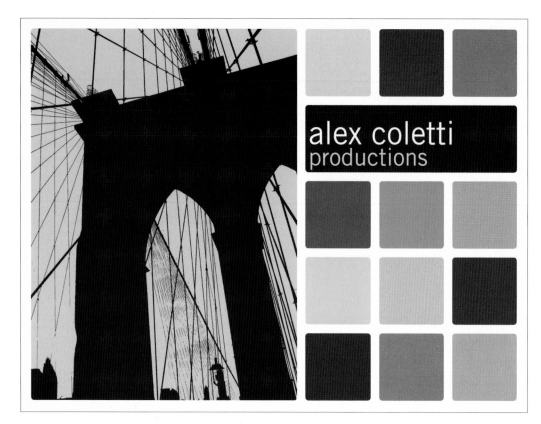

LOGO AND IDENTITY
Client Alex Coletti Productions
Studio Think Studio
Designers John Clifford and Herb Thornby
Principal Typeface Trade Gothic

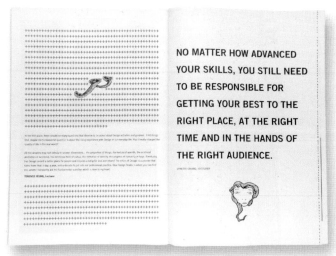

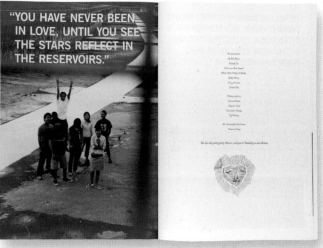

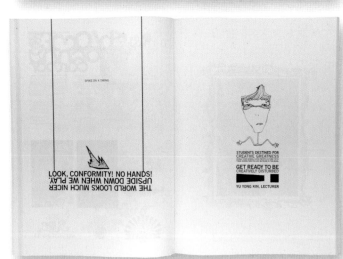

PUBLICATION/EDITORIAL
Client Temasek Polytechnic, School of Design
Studio SMEEK
Designers Randy Yeo and Ridzwan Ismail
Photographers Jenna Cheah, Eugene Yeap, and
Timothy Stuart Wee
Illustrator Pamela Hong
Printer United Art Printing Private Ltd.
Principal Typefaces Trade Gothic and Adobe Caslon

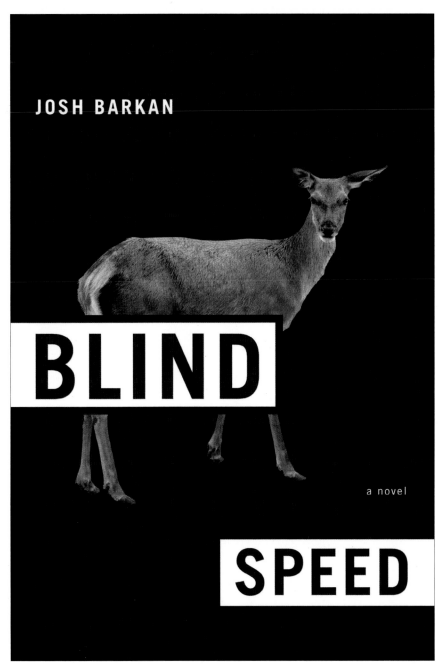

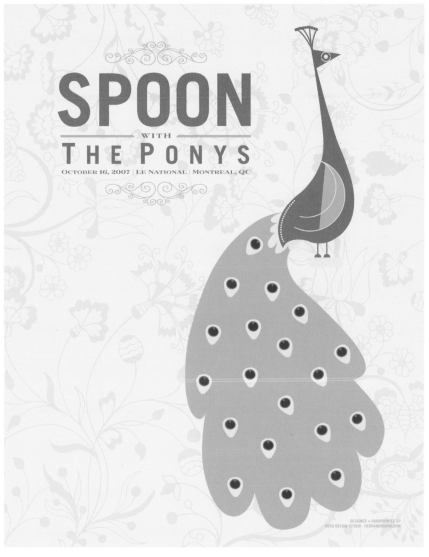

POSTER
Client Spoon
Studio/Screenprinter Hero Design Studio
Designer/Printer Elizabeth Manos Brickey
Principal Typefaces Trade Gothic and Luxury: Diamond

BOOK COVER
Publisher Northwestern University Press, Evanston
Studio Salamander Hill Design
Designer David Drummond
Principal Typefaces Trade Gothic and Futura

BOOK SPREAD
Publisher CDA Press, San Francisco
Studio Chen Design Associates
Designer Max Spector
Creative Director/Art Director Joshua C. Chen
Principal Typeface Trade Gothic

Illustration from Peace: 100 Ideas.

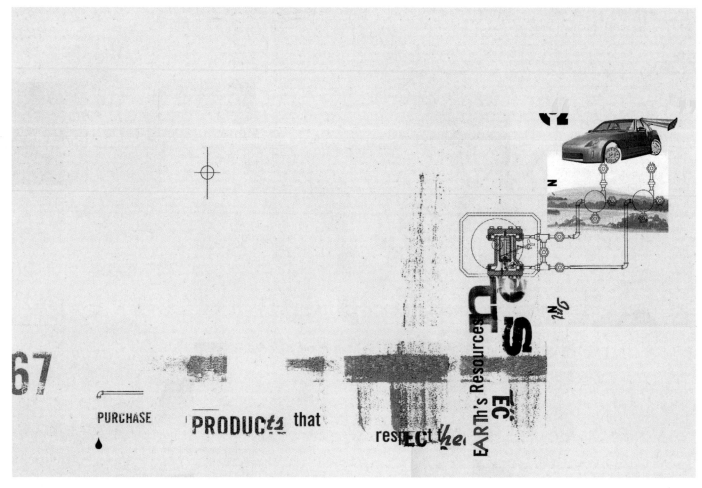

CORPORATE IDENTITY
Client IKNTEC
Designer Stefan Weyer
Principal Typefaces Trade Gothic
and Adobe Garamond

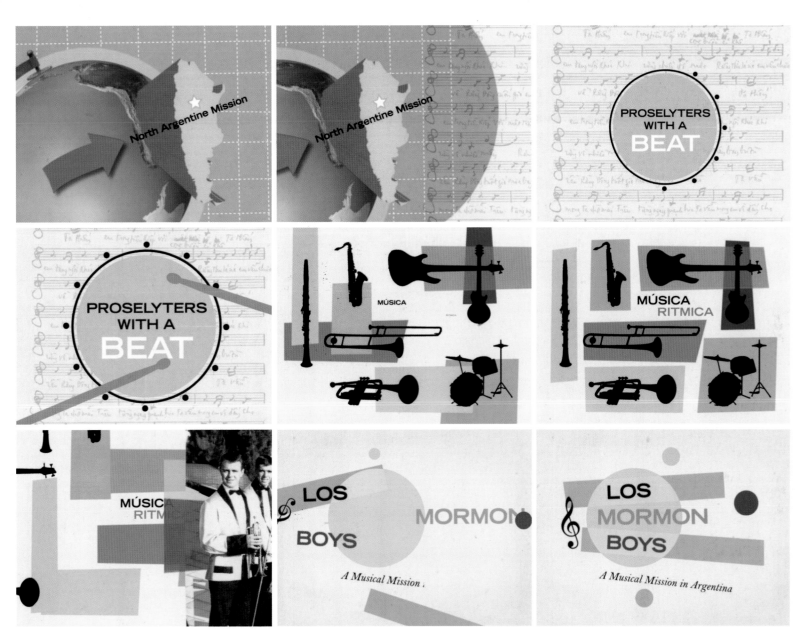

All images this page:
FILM TITLE SEQUENCE
Documentary Makers Dave Lindsay and Jason Conforto, Avalanche Studios
Art Director/Designer/Animator Brent Barson
Principal Typefaces Trade Gothic and Bell

Barson created the opening titles for Los Mormon Boys, *a documentary on musical Latter Day Saints missionaries based in Argentina in the 1960s.*

UNIVERS

cd

9/10pt

HOW RAZORBACK-JUMPING FROGS CAN LEVEL SIX piqued gymnasts! Jackdaws love my big sphinx of quartz. Jaded zombies acted quaintly but kept driving their oxen forward. The quick brown fox jumps over a lazy dog. The public was amazed to view the quickness and dexterity of the juggler. A mad boxer shot a quick, gloved jab to the jaw

10/12pt

HOW RAZORBACK-JUMPING FROGS CAN LEVEL SIX piqued gymnasts! Jackdaws love my big sphinx of quartz. Jaded zombies acted quaintly but kept driving their oxen forward. The quick brown fox jumps over a lazy dog. The public was amazed to view the quickness and dexterity of the juggler. A mad boxer shot a quick,

12/14pt

HOW RAZORBACK-JUMPING FROGS CAN level six piqued gymnasts! Jackdaws love my big sphinx of quartz. Jaded zombies acted quaintly but kept driving their oxen forward. The quick brown fox jumps over a lazy dog.

Univers 130 Ultra Light

abcdefghijklmnopqrstuvwxyz1234567890
ABCDEFGHIJKLMNOPQRSTUVWXYZ

Univers 431 Italic

abcdefghijklmnopqrstuvwxyz123456789
ABCDEFGHIJKLMNOPQRSTUVWXYZ

Univers 630 Bold

abcdefghijklmnopqrstuvwxyz123456
ABCDEFGHIJKLMNOPQRSTUVWXYZ

Univers 730 Heavy

abcdefghijklmnopqrstuvwxyz12345
ABCDEFGHIJKLMNOPQRSTUVWXY

Univers 830 Black

abcdefghijklmnopqrstuvwxyz123
ABCDEFGHIJKLMNOPQRSTUVWX

Univers 930 Extra Black

abcdefghijklmnopqrstuvwxyz1
ABCDEFGHIJKLMNOPQRSTUVW

Univers 430 [Linotype]

abcdefghijklmnopqrstuvwxyz
ABCDEFGHIJKLMNOPQRS
TUVWXYZ1234567890
[àóüßç](.,:;?!$€£&-*){ÀÓÜÇ}

Swiss designer Adrian Frutiger first conceived of Univers during his studies at the Kunstgewerbeschule (School of Applied Arts) in Zurich between 1949 and 1951. He was recruited to work at the French typefoundry Deberny & Peignot shortly thereafter, serving as its art director as well as a type designer.

In 1954, Charles Peignot discussed with Frutiger the concept of publishing a major font family that would work for both metal and photocomposition. Seeing how successful Bauer's Futura had become, Peignot thought to develop a new Geometric Sans Serif type to compete with the German foundry's powerhouse. Frutiger persuaded Peignot that the new family should not be based on an existing alphabet, but instead should be a completely new design appropriate for longer texts—unusual for a Sans at the time. He worked from his old school sketches to flesh out a full family in the Legible, Realist/Neo-Grotesque class.

Univers was originally designed with 21 variants, and was drawn with optically even stroke weights and a large x-height for optimal legibility. To ensure unity across the large family, so that all fonts worked perfectly together, Frutiger drew and approved all weights, widths, and italics before allowing any matrices to be cut. With this family, Frutiger introduced his unique type-naming convention, based on a methodical numbering system. In Frutiger's system, the first digit in a font name (3 through 8) indicates weight from lightest to heaviest, and the second digit specifies the width and signifies whether a face is a roman or an oblique.

Univers was released by Deberny & Peignot in 1957, and by Linotype thereafter. It became a huge success upon its release and inspired Frutiger to base future designs on its forms—Serifa (1967) and Glypha (1977). In 1997, Frutiger collaborated with the design team at Linotype to redesign and update Univers, resulting in a superfamily of more than 60 fonts.

PROMOTIONAL SIGNAGE
Client CMP Media
Studio Elbow
Art Director/Designer Lindsay Gravette
Principal Typeface Univers

If you like ...

Univers

... you could also consider:

Akzidenz-Grotesk
DIN
Folio
Franklin Gothic
Helvetica
Trade Gothic

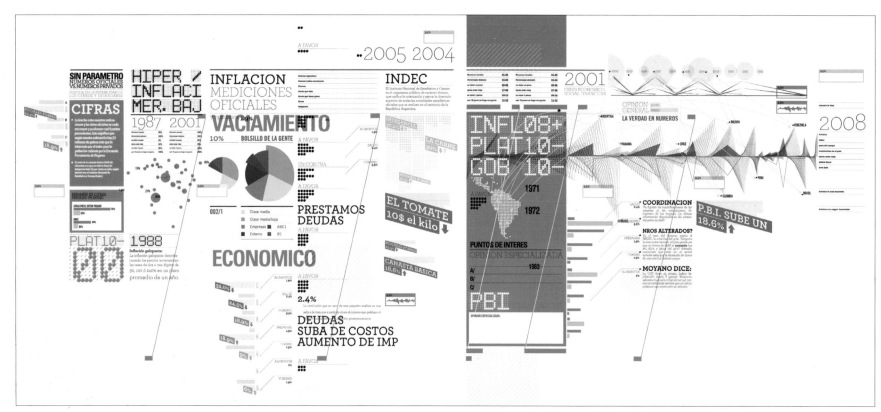

POSTER
Studio DHNN (Design has No Name)
Principal Typefaces Univers, Archer, and Fantasy

Experimental typography project initiated by the designers at DHNN.

BOOK COVERS
Designer Samantha Wiley
Principal Typefaces Univers, Berthold Bodoni, and Zapf Dingbats

POSTER
Designer Florent Guerlain
Principal Typeface Univers

One of Guerlain's Crisis 08 pieces,
his poster series that illustrates
actual crises in real time.

POSTER
Client MySpace Music
Studio My Associate Cornelius
Designer/Illustrator A. Micah Smith
Principal Typefaces Univers and Blackoak

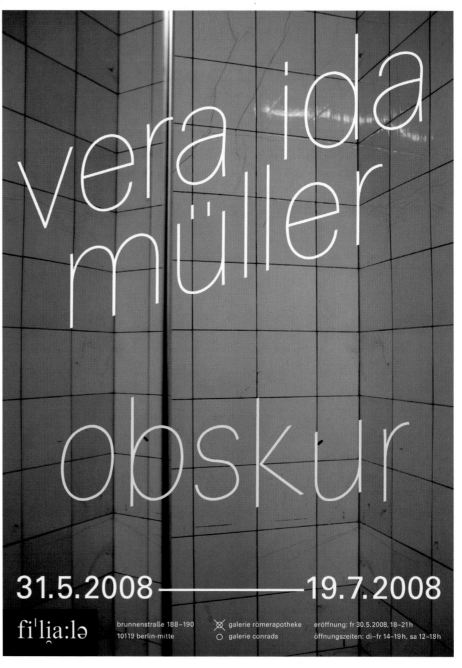

POSTER
Client Hollywood Bowl
Studio My Associate Cornelius
Designer/Illustrator A. Micah Smith
Principal Typefaces Salaryman, Univers, and Trade Gothic

EXHIBITION INVITATION/POSTER
Clients Conrads, Düsseldorf; and Römerapotheke, Zurich
Designer Florian Hardwig
Image Kurt Stegmann
Logo Designer Ingo Offermanns
Principal Typeface Univers

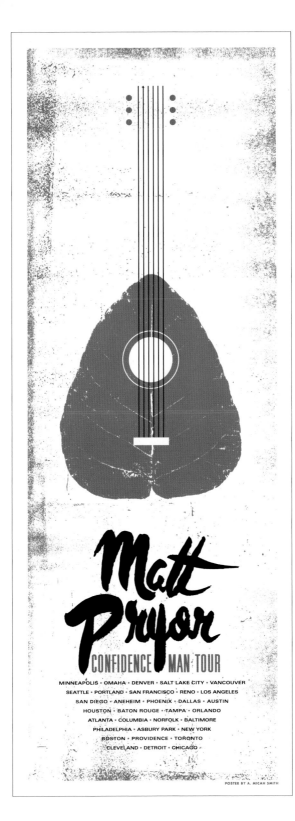

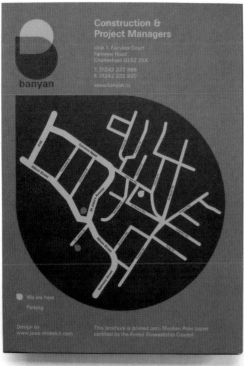

BRANDING
Client Banyan
Studio Jawa and Midwich
Designers Simon Dovar and Nils Davey
Principal Typeface Univers (hand rendered)

POSTER
Client Matt Pryor
Studio My Associate Cornelius
Designer/Illustrator A. Micah Smith
Principal Typeface Univers (with brush type from album art)

MUSIC PACKAGING
Client Sony BMG
Designer Timothy O'Donnell
Art Director Brett Kilroe, Sony BMG
Photographer Kike Calvo/V&W/imagequestmarine.com
Principal Typefaces Baskerville No. 2 and Univers

POSTER
Client Jamie Cullum/Direct Management Group
Studio My Associate Cornelius
Designer A. Micah Smith
Principal Typefaces Univers, Stephanie,
Hellenic Wide, and ITC Blair

MOVIE LOGO
Client Three Coin Productions/Garrett Batty
Studio HADDEN 3
Designer Anthony Hadden
Principal Typeface Univers

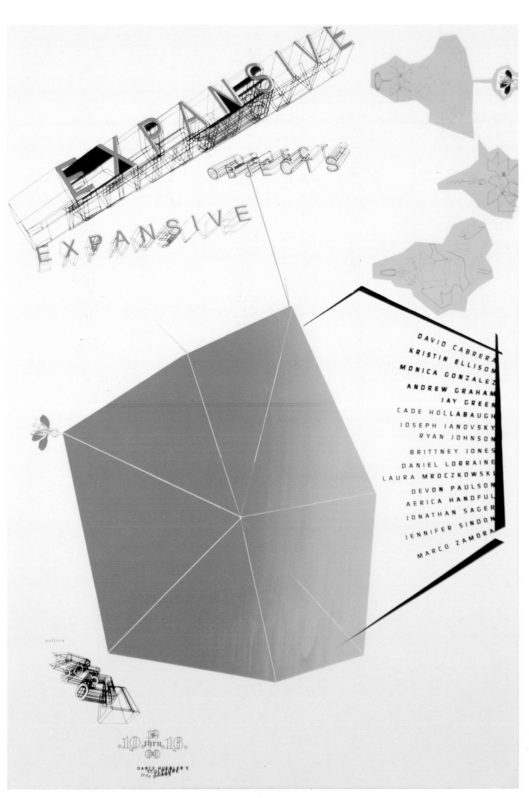

POSTER
Client Pierre Gigaud Intercoiffure
Studio Studio AND
Designer Jean-Benoît Lévy
Photomontage Artist Jean-Pascal Imsand
Principal Typeface Univers

POSTER
Client Darcy Huebler/CalArts
Designer Jessica Fleischmann
Principal Typefaces Univers and Fette Fraktur

ABCDEFGHIJ

This text is set in Cooper Std Black

DISPLAYM

BAUHAUS

9/10pt

HOW RAZORBACK-JUMPING FROGS CAN LEVEL SIX PIQUED GYM-nasts! Jackdaws love my big sphinx of quartz. Jaded zombies acted quaintly but kept driving their oxen forward. The quick brown fox jumps over a lazy dog. The public was amazed to view the quickness and dexterity of the juggler. A mad boxer shot a quick, gloved jab to the jaw of his dizzy opponent. The five boxing wizards jump

10/12pt

HOW RAZORBACK-JUMPING FROGS CAN LEVEL SIX PIQUED gymnasts! Jackdaws love my big sphinx of quartz. Jaded zombies acted quaintly but kept driving their oxen forward. The quick brown fox jumps over a lazy dog. The public was amazed to view the quickness and dexterity of the juggler. A mad boxer shot a quick, gloved jab to the jaw of his dizzy

12/14pt

HOW RAZORBACK-JUMPING FROGS CAN LEVEL SIX piqued gymnasts! Jackdaws love my big sphinx of quartz. Jaded zombies acted quaintly but kept driving their oxen forward. The quick brown fox jumps over a lazy dog. The public was amazed to

ITC Bauhaus Light

abcdefghijklmnopqrstuvwxyz12345
ABCDEFGHIJKLMNOPQRSTUVWXYZ

ITC Bauhaus Demi

abcdefghijklmnopqrstuvwxyz12345
ABCDEFGHIJKLMNOPQRSTUVWXYZ

ITC Bauhaus Bold

abcdefghijklmnopqrstuvwxyz1234
ABCDEFGHIJKLMNOPQRSTUVWXYZ

ITC Bauhaus Heavy

abcdefghijklmnopqrstuvwxyz12
ABCDEFGHIJKLMNOPQRSTUVWX

ITC Bauhaus Medium [ITC]

abcdefghijklmnopqrstuvwx
yzABCDEFGHIJKLMNOPQR
STUVWXYZ1234567890
[àóüßç](.,:;?!$€£&-*)ÀÓÜÇ}

Ed Benguiat and Victor Caruso designed ITC Bauhaus as a heavy display-only typeface in 1975 at a time when big, round, all-caps typography was all the rage. The New Yorkers were inspired by a prototype drawn in 1925 by Herbert Bayer during his tenure at the Bauhaus School in Dessau, Germany. Bayer's design consisted of bold forms constructed with circles and straight lines. Named Universal, the experimental face contained only a lowercase, an expression of Bayer's view that a single alphabet was the ideal for modern typography. Distinct from Bayer's concept, ITC Bauhaus is more regularized, includes caps and lowercase, and has been expanded in the digital era with multiple weights.

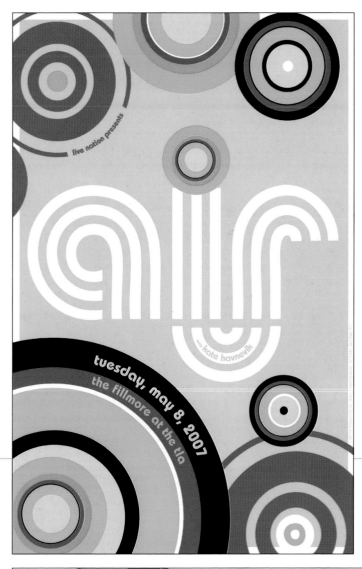

POSTER
Clients The Fillmore at the TLA and Air
Studio strawberryluna
Designers strawberryluna and Craig Seder
Principal Typeface ITC Bauhaus

If you like …

Bauhaus

… you could also consider:

Avant Garde

Futura

POSTER
Client Stereolab
Studio Standard Design
Designer Tom Pappalardo
Screenprinter Diesel Fuel Prints
Principal Typeface ITC Bauhaus

BLACKOAK

egyptian • slab serif • wood type

14/16pt

HOW RAZORBACK-JUMPING frogs can level six piqued gymnasts! Jackdaws love my big

22/22pt

HOW RAZORBACK-jumping frogs can level six piqued

30/30pt

HOW RAZOR-back-jumping frogs can level

Blackoak [Adobe]

abcdefghijklm
nopqrstuvwxyz
ABCDEFGHIJK
LMNOPQRSTU
VWXYZ1234567
890[àóüßç](.,:;?!
$€£&-*)}{ÀÓÜÇ}

212

Painter and textile artist Joy Redick developed Blackoak in 1990. It was subsequently released as part of the Adobe Wood Type series in the Adobe Originals collection. Redick's inspiration came from proofs of antique wood type housed at the Smithsonian Institution in Washington, D.C. Antique Extended, the basis for Blackoak, was first introduced by George Nesbitt in 1838 and manufactured in various incarnations, by multiple foundries, thereafter. Wood types of this ilk were in vogue from the mid-nineteenth century through to the early twentieth century. A heavy, stretched Slab Serif intended for headlines and titling set at large point sizes, Blackoak evokes the feel of the American Wild West.

COLLECTION/RE/COLLECTION

R.G. Brown's work, his notion of the journey, reflects his own collection of life experience as this journey has evolved through his world travels. The boat figures prominently in Brown's work and reflects a life goal to build a boat on each continent. To date, he has completed boats in Africa (Ghana), in Europe (Italy), and in North America (Canada).

Within the exhibit, Brown pushes the idea of the boat beyond a simple categorization as metaphor. The physical presence of Brown's work acts as a counterpoint to the indefinable journey which the boat, on the surface, may seem to represent. Brown's work delves deeper than simple metaphor to explore the tension between the unknown and the experiential: the twin manifestations of any journey.

The Albany Museum of Art is proud to have organized this exhibition and catalogue and we would like to express our gratitude to the artist. His commitment to this exhibit and his assistance with its organization proved invaluable. More importantly, Brown has loaned his experiences as traveler to create 'sites' which challenge each of us.

My work for the last ten years has been about the notion of journey...

RG BROWN III

RIVES SEXTON
DIRECTOR, ALBANY MUSEUM OF ART

If you like ...

Blackoak

... you could also consider:

Clarendon
Rockwell
ROSEWOOD

Above left:
EXHIBITION CATALOG
Clients Albany Museum of Art and R. G. Brown III
Studio Hannaford Design
Designer Joey Hannaford
Principal Typefaces Blackoak and ITC Bodoni Roman

BOOK SPREAD
Publisher CDA Press, San Francisco
Studio Chen Design Associates
Designer Max Spector
Creative Director/Art Director Joshua C. Chen
Principal Typeface Blackoak

Illustration from Peace: 100 Ideas.

BROADWAY

od

12/15pt

HOW RAZORBACK-JUMPING FROGS can level six piqued gymnasts! Jackdaws love my big sphinx of quartz. Jaded zombies acted quaintly but

Broadway Engraved (caps only)

ABCDEFGHIJKLMNOPQ
RSTUVWXYZ123456789
(.,:;?!$€£&-*){ÀÓÜßÇ}

20/22pt

HOW RAZORBACK-JUMPING FROGS CAN LEVEL six piqued gymnasts! Jackdaws love my big sphinx of quartz. Jaded zombies acted quaintly

30/30pt

HOW RAZORBACK-JUMPING frogs can level six piqued gymnasts! Jackdaws love my big

Broadway [Monotype Imaging]

**abcdefghijklmnopqrst
uvwxyz ABCDEFGHIJK
LMNOPQRSTUVWXYZ
1234567890 [àóüßç]
(.,:;?!$€£&-*){ÀÓÜÇ}**

214

Morris Fuller Benton designed Broadway in the mid-1920s, during his tenure as head of the design department at American Type Founders (ATF). Born of a master of both art and typographic technology, Benton's Broadway is notable for its perfectly angled and precisely drawn high-contrast forms, its heavy main strokes and thin hairlines marrying harmoniously. Originally an all-caps headline typeface, both a lowercase and an engraved version were added by Lanston Monotype's Sol Hess circa 1928. Named for Manhattan's famed Theatre District, Broadway is a signature alphabet of the American art deco era, evoking all the glamour and exuberance of the Jazz Age.

COASTERS
Designer Sarah Ridgley
Printer Sarah Ridgley Letterpress
Principal Typeface Broadway (metal, ATF)

If you like …

Broadway

… you could also consider:

Bauhaus
Cooper
Black
Futura

COOPER BLACK

old style • informal • arts and crafts

od

12/15pt

HOW RAZORBACK-JUMPING FROGS
can level six piqued gymnasts!
Jackdaws love my big sphinx of
quartz. Jaded zombies acted quaintly

20/22pt

HOW RAZORBACK-JUMPING FROGS CAN
level six piqued gymnasts! Jackdaws love my
big sphinx of quartz. Jaded zombies acted

30/30pt

HOW RAZORBACK-JUMPING
frogs can level six piqued
gymnasts! Jackdaws love my

Cooper Black Italic

abcdefghijklmnopqrstuvwxyz
ABCDEFGHIJKLMNOPQRSTU
VWXYZ1234567890(?!$€£&-)*

Cooper Black [Bitstream]

abcdefghijklmnopqrstu
vwxyz ABCDEFGHIJKL
MNOPQRSTUVWXYZ
1234567890 [àóüßç]
(.,:;?!$€£&-*){ÀÓÜÇ}

216

Cooper Black was designed in 1921 by American typographer Oswald Bruce Cooper for the Barnhart Brothers & Spindler typefounders in Chicago. A very heavy variant of the designer's earlier Cooper Old Style (circa 1919), Cooper Black is not based on a single historical model; rather, the face shows influences from the art deco and art nouveau movements, and the Machine Age. The design was given a complementary italic after it was acquired by Dresden's Schriftguß AG in 1924. Cooper Black set a trend in ad typography in the first third of the twentieth century, prompting other type designers to develop their own black faces (one such of note is Goudy Heavyface by Frederic Goudy). Cooper Black experienced an ironic resurgence in popularity in the 1970s, and is once again in widespread use by designers enamored of its heavy lushness and warm strength.

POSTER
Clients Deutsch/LA and Old Navy
Studio Seedoubleyou Design
Designer Chuck Williams
Principal Typeface Cooper Black

POSTER
Client The Neighborhood Theatre
Studio/Screenprinter Hero Design Studio
Designer/Printer Ryan Besch
Principal Typeface Cooper Black Italic

If you like …

Cooper Black

… you could also consider:

Blackoak

Clarendon

Goudy

MAGNETS
Client Blue Q
Studio Modern Dog Design Co.
Designer Michael Strassburger
Principal Typefaces Cooper Black and Trade Gothic

POSTER
Designer/Illustrator Ben the Illustrator
Principal Typeface Cooper Black

*This piece, featuring the artist's Speakerdog
character, was created to promote his
Step Into Our World exhibition.*

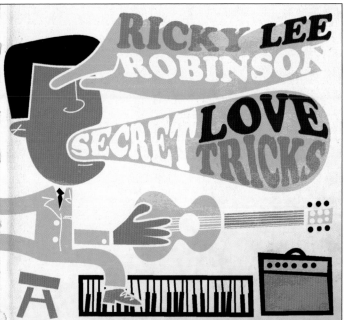

Far left:

CD PACKAGING
Client ReelWorld
Studio Turnstyle
Designers Steven Watson and Michelle Yang
Principal Typeface Cooper Black

Left:

CD COVER
Client Ricky Lee Robinson
Studio Standard Design
Designer Tom Pappalardo
Principal Typeface Cooper Black

T-SHIRT
Client The Hold Steady
Studio My Associate Cornelius
Designer A. Micah Smith
Principal Typeface Cooper Black

POSTER
Client Irving Plaza
Studio The Small Stakes
Designer Jason Munn
Principal Typeface Cooper Black

OCR-A

od

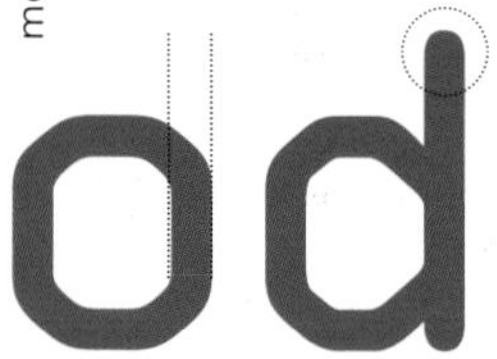

9/10pt
HOW RAZORBACK-JUMPING FROGS CAN LEVEL
six piqued gymnasts! Jackdaws love my
big sphinx of quartz. Jaded zombies
acted quaintly but kept driving their
oxen forward. The quick brown fox jumps
over a lazy dog. The public was amazed

10/12pt
HOW RAZORBACK-JUMPING FROGS CAN
level six piqued gymnasts! Jackdaws
love my big sphinx of quartz. Jaded
zombies acted quaintly but kept
driving their oxen forward. The
quick brown fox jumps over a lazy

12/14pt
HOW RAZORBACK-JUMPING FROGS
can level six piqued gymnasts!
Jackdaws love my big sphinx
of quartz. Jaded zombies acted
quaintly but kept driving

18/20pt
HOW RAZORBACK-
jumping frogs can
level six piqued

24/26pt
HOW RAZORBACK-
jumping frogs
can level six

30/32pt
HOW RAZOR-
back-jumping

OCR-A [Monotype Imaging]

abcdefghijklmnopqrs
tuvwxyz ABCDEFGHIJK
LMNOPQRSTUVWXYZ
1234567890 [ÀÓÜßÇ]
(.,:;?!$€£&-*){ÀÓÜÇ}

When computer optical character recognition (OCR) became widespread in the mid-twentieth century, a need arose for a font that could be recognized by that era's slow computers as well as by the human eye. To meet the standards set by the American National Standards Institute (ANSI) in 1966, American Type Founders (ATF) produced OCR-A in 1968. A monospaced type-face, OCR-A is constructed from simple, thick strokes forming recognizable characters. With the advances in OCR technology, extremely simple fonts are no longer needed. That said, OCR-A is still a standard for many companies, and has long been used by graphic designers attempting to achieve a technical or futuristic look in their work.

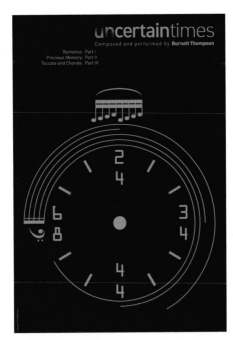

POSTER
Client Burnett Thompson
Art Director Chris Lozos
Designer Chris Lozos
Principal Typefaces OCR-A and FF DIN

If you like ...

OCR-A

... you could also consider:

Courier

OCR-B

BOOK SPREAD
Publisher CDA Press, San Francisco
Studio Chen Design Associates
Designer Max Spector
Illustrator Zachariah O'Hora
Creative Director/Art Director Joshua C. Chen
Principal Typeface OCR-A

Illustration from Peace: 100 Ideas.

OCR-B

nf

9/10pt

HOW RAZORBACK-JUMPING FROGS CAN LEVEL six piqued gymnasts! Jackdaws love my big sphinx of quartz. Jaded zombies acted quaintly but kept driving their oxen forward. The quick brown fox jumps over a lazy dog. The public was amazed

10/12pt

HOW RAZORBACK-JUMPING FROGS CAN level six piqued gymnasts! Jack- daws love my big sphinx of quartz. Jaded zombies acted quaintly but kept driving their oxen forward. The quick brown fox jumps over a

12/14pt

HOW RAZORBACK-JUMPING FROGS can level six piqued gymnasts! Jackdaws love my big sphinx of quartz. Jaded zombies acted quaintly but kept driving

18/20pt

HOW RAZORBACK- jumping frogs can level six piqued

24/26pt

HOW RAZORBACK- jumping frogs can level six

30/32pt

HOW RAZOR- back-jumping

OCR-B [Monotype Imaging]

abcdefghijklmnopqrs
tuvwxyz ABCDEFGHIJK
LMNOPQRSTUVWXYZ
1234567890 [àóüßç]
(.,:;?!$€£&-*){ÀÓÜÇ}

While the American National Standards Institute (ANSI) was setting standards for optical character recognition (OCR) in America, its non-US counterparts were doing the same worldwide. Swiss designer Adrian Frutiger developed OCR-B in 1968 to meet the standards of the European Computer Manufacturers' Association (ECMA), but also with the goal of producing a font that would be legible to the human eye. The result is a font that is friendly to both man and machine. OCR-B was made a world standard in 1973, and, although monospaced and technical in appearance, designers kern between character pairs and tighten its letterspacing to achieve interesting and readable typographic effects.

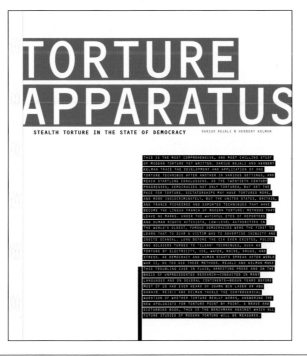

If you like …

O C R – B

… you could also consider:

Courier
DIN
O C R – A

Both images this page:
BOOK
Designer/Photographer Lindsey Selden
Principal Typefaces OCR-B and Univers

Torture Apparatus was created for Carolina de Bartolo's online Type Systems course at San Francisco's Academy of Art University.

ROSEWOOD

clarendon • chromatic • wood type

12/14pt

HOW RAZORBACK-JUMPING FROGS CAN LEVEL SIX PIQUED GYMNASTS! JACKDAWS LOVE MY BIG SPHINX OF QUARTZ. JADED ZOMBIES ACTED QUAINTLY BUT KEPT DRIVING THEIR OXEN FOR

14/16pt

HOW RAZORBACK-JUMPING FROGS CAN LEVEL SIX PIQUED GYMNASTS! JACKDAWS LOVE MY BIG SPHINX OF QUARTZ. JADED ZOMBIES ACTED QUAINTLY BUT KEPT DRIVING THEIR OXEN FORWARD. THE QUICK

18/20pt

HOW RAZORBACK-JUMPING FROGS CAN LEVEL SIX PIQUED GYMNASTS! JACKDAWS LOVE MY BIG SPHINX OF QUARTZ. JADED

Rosewood Regular

ABCDEFGHIJKLMNOPQR
STUVWXYZ1234567890

Rosewood Fill

ABCDEFGHIJKLMNOPQR
STUVWXYZ1234567890

Rosewood Regular + Rosewood Fill

ABCDEFGHIJKLMNOPQR
STUVWXYZ1234567890

Rosewood Regular + Rosewood Fill = chromatic font effect

AB + AB = AB

Rosewood Fill [Adobe]

ABCDEFGHIJKLMNOP
QRSTUVWXYZ 12345
[ÀÓÜÇ](.,.:;?!$€£&-*)

224

Part of the Adobe Wood Type Collection, Rosewood was designed by Carl Crossgrove, Carol Twombly, and Kim Buker Chansler in the early 1990s. This decorative, all-caps typeface is modeled after an 1874 chromatic (multicolored) wood-type design by William Page. Chromatic types are layered in order to produce dramatic effects using multiple inks. Rosewood contains two typefaces designed specifically for layering. The regular weight is ornamental, with a great deal of open space, and designed to overlay the solid Rosewood Fill. Interestingly, designers are now using the Fill variant without the overlay—its soft, narrow forms and uneven spacing lend a unique appearance to headlines and typographic accents.

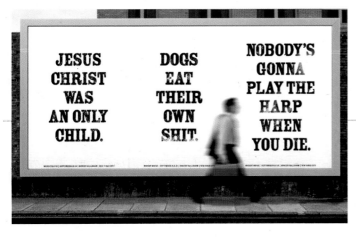

POSTER SERIES
Client The Bowery Ballroom/The Bowery Presents
Studio The Ryan Adair
Designer Ryan Adair
Principal Typeface Rosewood Fill

POSTCARD
Client American Heart Association
Studio Emblem
Designer Jeanine Donofrio
Principal Typefaces Rosewood Fill and Futura

If you like …

ROSEWOOD

… you could also consider:

Blackoak
Clarendon
Rockwell

TRAJAN

OE

12/15pt

HOW RAZORBACK-JUMPING FROGS CAN LEVEL SIX PIQUED GYMNASTS! JACKDAWS LOVE MY BIG SPHINX OF QUARTZ. JADED ZOMBIES ACTED QUAINTLY BUT

20/22pt

HOW RAZORBACK-JUMPING FROGS CAN LEVEL SIX PIQUED GYMNASTS! JACKDAWS LOVE MY BIG SPHINX OF QUARTZ. JADED ZOMBIES ACTED QUAINT

30/30pt

HOW RAZORBACK-JUMPING FROGS CAN LEVEL SIX PIQUED GYMNASTS! JACKDAWS LOVE MY

Trajan Bold

ABCDEFGHIJKLMNOPQRSTUVWXYZ ABCDEFGHIJKLMNOPQRSTUVW XYZ1234567890(.,:;?!$€£&-*)

Trajan [Adobe]

ABCDEFGHIJKLMNOPQRST UVWXYZ ABCDEFGHIJKL MNOPQRSTUVWXYZ 1234567890[ÀÓÜSSÇ] (.,:;?!$£&-*){ÀÓÜÇ}

Carol Twombly designed Trajan for Adobe in 1989—the typeface is rooted in history. The design is a very literal translation of the classic Roman letterforms inscribed at the base of the Trajan column in Rome. As there was no lowercase used in Roman times, Trajan was created as an all-caps titling face. In order to better suit the needs of contemporary designers, Adobe added more glyphs and a set of small capitals in place of a lowercase alphabet when it updated the font to OpenType in 2001. Trajan has become incredibly popular since its release, famous for its use on countless film posters and book covers.

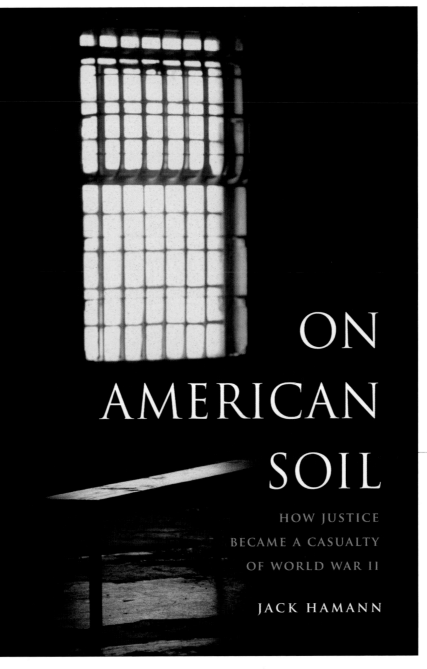

If you like ...

TRAJAN

... you could also consider:

COPPERPLATE
GARAMOND
OPTIMA

LOGO
Clients Wenatchee Marathon and
Ted Finegold
Studio HADDEN 3
Designer Anthony Hadden
Principal Typeface Trajan

BOOK COVER
Publisher University of Washington Press,
Seattle and London
Designer Ashley Saleeba
Principal Typeface Trajan

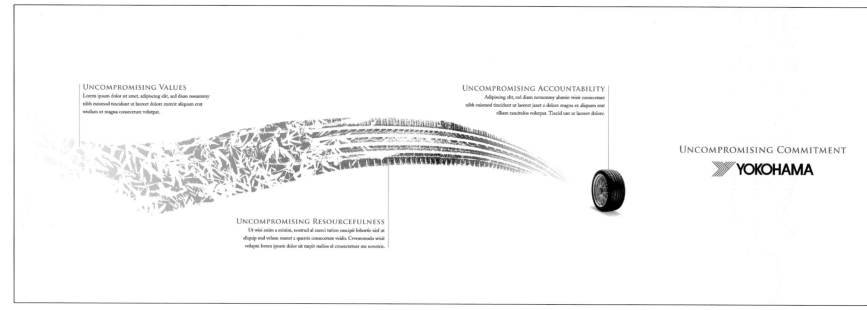

UNCOMPROMISING VALUES
Lorem ipsum dolor sit amet, adipiscing elit, sed diam nonummy nibh euismod tincidunt ut laoreet dolore exerci aliquam erat wisilam ut magna consecature volutpat.

UNCOMPROMISING ACCOUNTABILITY
Adipiscing elit, sed diam nonummy alumin wisit consecture nibh euismod tincidunt ut laoreet jaxet a dolore magna ex aliquam erat elliam rancitulos volutpat. Tincid unt ut laoreet dolore.

UNCOMPROMISING COMMITMENT
YOKOHAMA

UNCOMPROMISING RESOURCEFULNESS
Ut wisi enim a minim, nostrud al exerci tation suscipit lobortis nisl ut aliquip mal velusu manet a querris consecture veido. Cvvommodo wisit volupte lorem ipsum dolor sit raspit melios el consectetuer me nosotris.

TRADE AD
Client Pacific Communications Group
  for Yokohama Tire
Studio Evenson Design Group
Designer Mark Sojka
Creative Director Stan Evenson
Principal Typefaces Trajan and Adobe Caslon

VISTAMAR

LOGO
Client Vistamar School
Studio Evenson Design Group
Designer Mark Sojka
Creative Director Stan Evenson
Principal Typeface Trajan

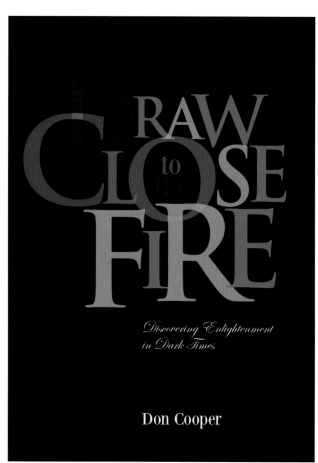

RAW CLOSE to the FIRE

*Discovering Enlightenment
in Dark Times*

Don Cooper

BOOK COVER
Client Britt Taylor Collins
Studio Hannaford Design
Designer Joey Hannaford
Principal Typefaces Trajan,
ITC Edwardian Script, and Bodoni

THELE UNITED MUSÉE STA TES DE NATIONAL LA HOLO CAUST RÉSISTANCE MEMO RIAL NATIONALE MUSEUM

INVITATION CARD
Client Musée de la Résistance Nationale
Designer Olivier Umecker
Principal Typeface Trajan

LOGO
Client Mogomedia
Studio Evenson Design Group
Designer Mark Sojka
Creative Director Stan Evenson
Principal Typeface Trajan (distressed)

LABEL AND LOGOTYPE
Client Jason/Stephens Winery
Studio konnectDesign
Designer Bryan Kestell
Creative Director Karen Knecht
Principal Typeface Trajan

ABCDEFGHIJ

This text is set in Fette Fraktur LT Std Regular

SCRIPTVM

Cezanne

14/16pt

How razorback-jumping frogs can level six piqued gymnasts! Jackdaws love my big sphinx of quartz. Jaded zombies acted quaintly but kept driving their oxen forward. The quick brown fox jumps over a lazy dog. The public was amazed to view the quickness and dexterity of the juggler. A mad boxer shot a quick, gloved jab to the jaw of his

18/20pt

How razorback-jumping frogs can level six piqued gymnasts! Jackdaws love my big sphinx of quartz. Jaded zombies acted quaintly but kept driving their oxen forward. The quick brown fox jumps over a lazy dog. The public was amazed to view the quickness and dexterity

24/26pt

How razorback-jumping frogs can level six piqued gymnasts! Jackdaws love my big sphinx of quartz. Jaded zombies acted quaintly but kept driving their oxen forward. The quick brown fox

Cezanne Pro [P22]

abcdefghijklmnopqrstuvwxyz
ABCDEFGHIJKLMNOP
QRSTUVWXYZ1234567890
[àöüß,ç] (.,:;!? $ £ € £ & - *) { ÁÜ6 }

Cezanne was first developed by Michael Want in 1996, as a digital typeface for P22. The script is a faithful rendition of the handwriting of French impressionist painter Paul Cézanne. The original font set consisted of a standard alphanumeric character set with a few special ligatures, along with Cezanne Sketches, a dingbat font recreating imagery from the artist's body of work.

Part of P22's artists' handwriting series, the typeface was originally created for the Philadelphia Museum of Art. Upon its release to the public, Cezanne quickly became one of the most popular handwriting fonts of the 1990s, decorating countless wine-bottle labels, symphony season brochures, and wedding invitations. A major international coffee chain used the typeface to great effect on its packaging and interior design.

In 2005, P22 commissioned designer James Grieshaber to develop Cezanne Pro, greatly extending its character set to take advantage of OpenType technology. The result is a typeface that includes multiple variants for alternate characters, and carefully crafted ligatures, enabling designers to emulate the look of real handwriting, with its fluid variations, more fully.

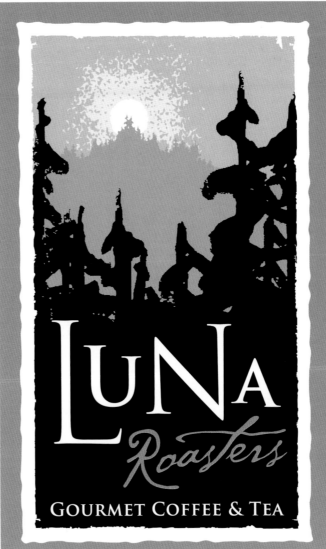

If you like …

Cezanne

… you could also consider:

Edwardian Script

IDENTITY
Client Blake Brand Growers
for Luna Coffee
Studio Evenson Design Group
Designer Mark Sojka
Creative Director Stan Evenson
Principal Typefaces Trajan and Cezanne

PACKAGING
Client Ineke
Studio Helena Seo Design
Designer/Creative Director Helena Seo
Principal Typeface Cezanne

Edwardian Script

formal • connecting

14/16pt

How razorback-jumping frogs can level six piqued gymnasts! Jackdaws love my big sphinx of quartz. Jaded zombies acted quaintly but kept driving their oxen forward. The quick brown fox jumps over a lazy dog. The public was amazed to view the quickness

18/20pt

How razorback-jumping frogs can level six piqued gymnasts! Jackdaws love my big sphinx of quartz. Jaded zombies acted quaintly but kept driving their oxen forward. The quick brown fox jumps over a lazy

24/24pt

How razorback-jumping frogs can level six piqued gymnasts! Jackdaws love my big sphinx of quartz. Jaded zombies acted quaintly but kept driving their oxen

ITC Edwardian Script Bold

abcdefghijklmnopqrstuvwxyz 123456789
ABCDEFGHIJKLM NOPQRSTUVWXYZ

ITC Edwardian Script Alternates

ABCDEFGHIJKLM NOPQRSTUVWXYZ

ITC Edwardian Script Bold Alternates

ABCDEFGHIJKLM NOPQRSTUVWXYZ

ITC Edwardian Script [ITC]

abcdefghijklmnopqrstuvwxyz ABCDE FGHIJKLMN OPQR STUVWXYZ 1234567890 [àóüßç] (.,:;?!§€£&-) {ÀÓÜÇ}*

If you like …

Edwardian Script

… you could also consider:

Cezanne

ITC Edwardian Script emerged from the hand of noted New York typographer and lettering artist Ed Benguiat. First seen in 1994, this elegant script is a contemporary imagining of the classic copperplate or Round Hand style of formal writing prevalent in the nineteenth century. Many traditional calligraphic scripts are based on handwriting created with a broad-tipped pen or brush, which results in thicker strokes and letters tilted at a slight angle. In contrast, ITC Edwardian Script was influenced by the more flexible and precise steel-point pen. Its delicate, embellished forms were drawn at an extreme slant—another hallmark of the copperplate hand— and carefully drafted to form perfect connections between letters.

WALLPAPER
Client Anheuser-Busch for www.herestobeer.com
Agency Cannonball Advertising and Promotion
Designer Samantha Wiley
Principal Typeface ITC Edwardian Script

Fette Fraktur

14/16pt

How razorback-jumping frogs can level six piqued gymnasts! Jackdaws love my big sphinx of quartz. Jaded zombies acted quaintly but kept driving their oxen forward. The quick brown fox jumps over a lazy dog. The public was amazed to view the quick

18/20pt

How razorback-jumping frogs can level six piqued gymnasts! Jackdaws love my big sphinx of quartz. Jaded zombies acted quaintly but kept driving their oxen forward. The quick brown fox

24/26pt

How razorback-jumping frogs can level six piqued gymnasts! Jackdaws love my big sphinx of quartz. Jaded zombies acted quaintly but kept driving their

Fette Fraktur [Linotype]

abcdefghijklmnopqrstuvwxyz

ABCDEFGHIJKLMNOP

QRSTUVWXYZ123456789

[àöüßç](.,:;?!$€£&-*){ÀÖÜÇ}

Fette Fraktur is a Blackletter typeface in the Fraktur (derived from the Latin for "broken" or "fractured") subclassification of scripts. Designed in 1850 by German punchcutter Johann Christian Bauer, Fette Fraktur was first issued by Germany's C. E. Weber foundry in 1875, then by D. Stempel in 1908; its digital incarnation was released in the late 1980s. Precisely composed of spindly angular lines and heavy rounded forms, Fette Fraktur was designed for use in advertising rather than text.

Fraktur has its roots in the Middle Ages, with the first typeface of this class designed under edict from Holy Roman Emperor Maximilian I (c. 1493–1519) for use in a new series of books. Fraktur was in widespread use in German-speaking Europe from the mid-nineteenth to mid-twentieth centuries, until 1941, when Blackletter types were banned by Adolf Hitler's regime. The ban was ultimately lifted after the end of World War II, but Blackletter had been largely replaced by Antiqua (Roman) typography.

LOGO
Clients Oktoberfest Marathon and Ted Finegold
Studio HADDEN 3
Designer Anthony Hadden
Principal Typefaces Fette Fraktur and Schadow Black Condensed

SWEATSHIRT
Client Lucky Boys Confusion
Studio My Associate Cornelius
Designer A. Micah Smith
Principal Typefaces Fette Fraktur and Univers

ABCDEFGHIJKL

This text is set in Akzidenz-Grotesk Std Regular

RESOURCES

GLYPH REFERENCE

The key to understanding what makes up a font is to know the definition of a glyph. A glyph is an image used in the visual representation of a given character—it determines how a character looks. A font is a set of glyphs. For example, **A**, ᴀ, a, *a*, and ᵃ are all glyph variants of the character **a** in Garamond Premier Pro Bold.

A font, especially one in the OpenType format, can contain these and other variations of a character in a given style of a particular typeface.

Developed jointly by Adobe and Microsoft, OpenType is a universal computer font format designed to enable a single font format to be used across platforms. OpenType allows for an almost limitless number of glyphs and conditional letter combinations with easier access to full expert-set characters, facilitating multilingual and advanced typography.

The illustration at right, this page, is an example of the glyph palette from Adobe InDesign, and shows many of the character variations found in the regular weight of Sabon Next Pro. The chart on the opposite page shows examples of the key combinations needed to access particular glyphs.

Windows Operating System: To access the extended character set that is not accessible directly from the keyboard, hold down the ALT key while typing a glyph's corresponding numbers on the keypad (including the preceding zero).

Macintosh Operating System: The glyphs accessible by using the CONTROL key may not work in all applications.

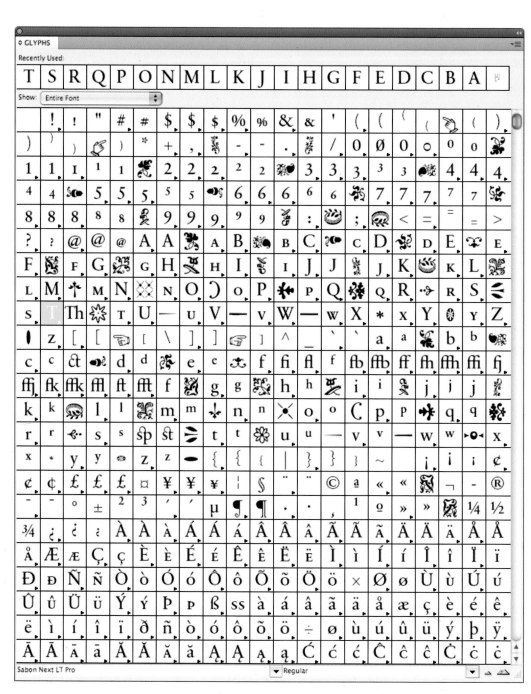

Example of the glyph palette from Adobe InDesign.

Windows	Glyph	Macintosh
Space	(Space)	Space
⇧-1	!	⇧-1
⇧-'	"	⇧-'
⇧-3	#	⇧-3
⇧-4	$	⇧-4
⇧-5	%	⇧-5
⇧-7	&	⇧-7
'	'	'
⇧-9	(	⇧-9
⇧-0	)	⇧-0
⇧-8	*	⇧-8
⇧-=	+	⇧-=
,	,	,
-	-	-
.	.	.
/	/	/
0	0	0
1	1	1
2	2	2
3	3	3
4	4	4
5	5	5
6	6	6
7	7	7
8	8	8
9	9	9
⇧-;	:	⇧-;
;	;	;
⇧-,	<	⇧-,
=	=	=
⇧-.	>	⇧-.
⇧-/	?	⇧-/
⇧-2	@	⇧-2
⇧-A	A	⇧-A
⇧-B	B	⇧-B
⇧-C	C	⇧-C
⇧-D	D	⇧-D
⇧-E	E	⇧-E
⇧-F	F	⇧-F
⇧-G	G	⇧-G
⇧-H	H	⇧-H
⇧-I	I	⇧-I
⇧-J	J	⇧-J
⇧-K	K	⇧-K
⇧-L	L	⇧-L
⇧-M	M	⇧-M
⇧-N	N	⇧-N
⇧-O	O	⇧-O
⇧-P	P	⇧-P
⇧-Q	Q	⇧-Q
⇧-R	R	⇧-R
⇧-S	S	⇧-S
⇧-T	T	⇧-T
⇧-U	U	⇧-U
⇧-V	V	⇧-V
⇧-W	W	⇧-W
⇧-X	X	⇧-X
⇧-Y	Y	⇧-Y
⇧-Z	Z	⇧-Z
[	[	[
\	\	\
]	]	]
⇧-6	^	⇧-6
⇧--	_	⇧--
`	`	`
A	a	A
B	b	B
C	c	C
D	d	D
E	e	E
F	f	F
G	g	G
H	h	H
I	i	I
J	j	J
K	k	K
L	l	L
M	m	M
N	n	N
O	o	O
P	p	P
Q	q	Q
R	r	R
S	s	S
T	t	T
U	u	U
V	v	V
W	w	W
X	x	X
Y	y	Y
Z	z	Z
⇧-[	{	⇧-[
⇧-\	|	⇧-\
⇧-]	}	⇧-]
⇧-`	~	⇧-`
alt-0130	‚	⇧-alt-0
alt-0131	ƒ	alt-F
alt-0132	„	⇧-alt-W
alt-0133	…	alt-;
alt-0134	†	alt-T
alt-0135	‡	⇧-alt-7
alt-0136	ˆ	⇧-alt-I
alt-0137	‰	⇧-alt-R
alt-0138	Š	ctrl-E
alt-0139	‹	⇧-alt-3
alt-0140	Œ	⇧-alt-Q
alt-0142	Ž	ctrl-N
alt-0145	'	alt-]
alt-0146	'	⇧-alt-]
alt-0147	"	alt-[
alt-0148	"	⇧-alt-[
alt-0149	•	alt-8
alt-0150	–	alt--
alt-0151	—	⇧-alt--
alt-0152	˜	⇧-alt-N
alt-0153	™	alt-2
alt-0154	š	ctrl-F
alt-0155	›	⇧-alt-4
alt-0156	œ	alt-Q
alt-0158	ž	ctrl-O
alt-0159	Ÿ	alt-U ⇧-Y
alt-0160	(Non-breaking)	alt-Space
alt-0161	¡	alt-1
alt-0162	¢	alt-4
alt-0163	£	alt-3
alt-0164	€	⇧-alt-2
alt-0165	¥	alt-Y
alt-0166	¦	ctrl-[
alt-0167	§	alt-6
alt-0168	¨	⇧-alt-U
alt-0169	©	alt-G
alt-0170	ª	alt-9
alt-0171	«	alt-\
alt-0172	¬	alt-L
alt-0173	-	ctrl-/
alt-0174	®	alt-R
alt-0175	¯	⇧-alt-,
alt-0176	°	⇧-alt-8
alt-0177	±	Sh-alt-=
alt-0178	²	ctrl-Z
alt-0179	³	ctrl-Y
alt-0180	´	⇧-alt-E
alt-0181	µ	alt-M
alt-0182	¶	alt-7
alt-0183	·	⇧-alt-9
alt-0184	¸	⇧-alt-Z
alt-0185	¹	ctrl-W
alt-0186	º	alt-0
alt-0187	»	⇧-alt-\
alt-0188	¼	ctrl-V
alt-0189	½	ctrl-U
alt-0190	¾	ctrl-X
alt-0191	¿	Control-alt-/
alt-0192	À	alt-` ⇧-A
alt-0193	Á	⇧-alt-Y
alt-0194	Â	⇧-alt-M
alt-0195	Ã	alt-N ⇧-A
alt-0196	Ä	alt-U ⇧-A
alt-0197	Å	⇧-alt-A
alt-0198	Æ	⇧-alt-'
alt-0199	Ç	⇧-alt-C
alt-0200	È	alt-` ⇧-E
alt-0201	É	alt-E ⇧-E
alt-0202	Ê	alt-I ⇧-E
alt-0203	Ë	alt-U ⇧-E
alt-0204	Ì	alt-` ⇧-I
alt-0205	Í	⇧-alt-S
alt-0206	Î	⇧-alt-D
alt-0207	Ï	⇧-alt-F
alt-0208	Ð	ctrl-A
alt-0209	Ñ	alt-N ⇧-N
alt-0210	Ò	⇧-alt-L
alt-0211	Ó	⇧-alt-H
alt-0212	Ô	⇧-alt-J
alt-0213	Õ	alt-N ⇧-O
alt-0214	Ö	alt-U ⇧-O
alt-0215	×	ctrl-]
alt-0216	Ø	⇧-alt-O
alt-0217	Ù	alt-` ⇧-U
alt-0218	Ú	⇧-alt-;
alt-0219	Û	alt-I ⇧-U
alt-0220	Ü	alt-U ⇧-U
alt-0221	Ý	ctrl-G
alt-0222	Þ	ctrl-K
alt-0223	ß	alt-S
alt-0224	à	alt-` A
alt-0225	á	alt-E A
alt-0226	â	alt-I A
alt-0227	ã	alt-N A
alt-0228	ä	alt-U A
alt-0229	å	alt-A
alt-0230	æ	alt-'
alt-0231	ç	alt-C
alt-0232	è	alt-` E
alt-0233	é	alt-E E
alt-0234	ê	alt-I E
alt-0235	ë	alt-U E
alt-0236	ì	alt-` I
alt-0237	í	alt-E I
alt-0238	î	alt-I I
alt-0239	ï	alt-U I
alt-0240	ð	ctrl-B
alt-0241	ñ	alt-N N
alt-0242	ò	alt-` O
alt-0243	ó	alt-E O
alt-0244	ô	alt-I O
alt-0245	õ	alt-N O
alt-0246	ö	alt-U O
alt-0247	÷	alt-/
alt-0248	ø	alt-O
alt-0249	ù	alt-` U
alt-0250	ú	alt-E U
alt-0251	û	alt-I U
alt-0252	ü	alt-U U
alt-0253	ý	ctrl-H
alt-0254	þ	ctrl-L
alt-0255	ÿ	alt-U Y
	≠	alt-=
	∞	alt-5
	≤	alt-,
	≥	alt-.
	∂	alt-D
	Σ	alt-W
	Π	⇧-alt-P
	π	alt-P
	∫	alt-B
	Ω	alt-Z
	√	alt-V
	≈	alt-X
	Δ	alt-J
	◊	⇧-alt-V
	⁄	⇧-alt-1
	fi	⇧-alt-5
	fl	⇧-alt-6
	ı	⇧-alt-B
	˘	⇧-alt-.
	˙	alt-H
	°	alt-K
	˝	⇧-alt-G
	ˇ	⇧-alt-T
	¸	⇧-alt-X

GLOSSARY

accent See *diacritic*.

accented character A character with a mark added, indicating a changed phonetic value. See also *diacritic*.

Adobe Font Metrics (AFM) A specification by which font metrics information (kerning pairs, character widths, etc.) is added.

Aldine Refers to the Venetian publishing house operated by Aldus Manutius, 1494–1515. Francesco Griffo cut the majority of Aldus' types. Contemporary type and typography resembling that of Griffo or Aldus may be referred to as Aldine.

align To line up type or other graphic elements using a base or vertical grid as a reference point.

alignment The positioning of text or other graphic elements relative to a set margin. Forms of alignment include flush left, flush right, justified, or centered. Flush left is also known as left justified or ragged right; flush right is also known as right justified or ragged left.

alphabet The characters making up a particular language, arranged in their traditional order.

alternate characters A character with a different design used as an alternative to a standard alpha character in a typeface.

American Standard Code for Information Interchange (ASCII) A seven-bit character code used in computing. ASCII encodes 128 alphanumerics and symbols into assigned numbers for the purpose of electronic storage and communication. See *Extended Binary Coded Decimal Interchange* for comparison.

American Type Founders (ATF) The largest metal-type foundry in North America. Based in Elizabeth, New Jersey, ATF was formed in 1892 through the union of a number of smaller firms.

ampersand The symbol &, developed to represent *et*, the Latin term for *and*.

analphabetic Used with the alphabet, these characters lack a place in the alphabetical order. Diacritics, such as the umlaut and caron, and characters such as the asterisk and ampersand, are all examples of analphabetics.

Anglo-American System A system devised to regulate the measurement of type, defined by the American Typefounders Association in 1886. In the Anglo-American System, 1 inch = 6 picas = 72 points (approx.). For comparison, see also the *European System*.

anti-aliasing The smoothing of the jagged edges in digital images. By varying the shades of gray or color at its edges, an object can be made to blend smoothly into the background.

Antiqua A European term for Roman typefaces. The *letra antigua* of the Spanish writing masters, for example, shows the heavy Italian influence on letterforms. Also spelled *Antikva*.

Antique A style of letter used in display typography from the late 1800s to the early 1900s.

aperture The openings of letters such as **C**, **S**, and **a**.

apex Where the strokes of a character meet at its uppermost point.

arm The upward-projecting strokes or horizontal extensions found in characters such as **X** and **L**.

ascender The stem of a lowercase letter, such as **b** or **k**, that extends above the body of the letter, or x-height.

ascender line The imaginary horizontal line marking the uppermost point of an ascender.

ascent A character's maximum distance above the baseline.

ASCII See *American Standard Code for Information Interchange*.

asterisk A typographic character used as a reference mark, usually in the shape of a star and raised above the baseline.

ATF See *American Type Founders*.

axis The axis of a character usually refers to its stroke. There may be multiple axes in a letterform.

back slanting The technique of drawing or digitally manipulating characters at a backward angle; the opposite angle of an italic.

ball terminal A circular shape at the end of the arm in characters such as **c** and **y**. Typically found in Roman and italic types in the style of Bodoni and Clarendon. See also *terminal*.

bar See *cross-stroke*.

baseline The imaginary line supporting the characters in a font, excluding the descenders of lowercase letters and other extended elements, such as the tail in a **Q**. Leading is measured from baseline to baseline.

Bastarda A class of Blackletter types.

Bauhaus The common term for Germany's Staatliches Bauhaus school that combined education in crafts with the fine arts. The Bauhaus was founded by Walter Gropius in Weimar and operated from 1919 to 1933.

BCP See *Bézier control point*.

beak terminal A sharp spur form found in some typefaces on characters such as **a**, **c**, **f**, and **r**. Typically found in many twentieth-century Romans and some italics, including Perpetua. See also *terminal*.

Bézier control point (BCP) One of two points guiding a *Bézier curve*.

Bézier curve Mathematical equation used to describe the character shapes in digital typography. French computer scientist Pierre Bézier developed the mathematical representation used to describe this curve.

bicameral An alphabet with two forms, as in the Latin alphabet with its upper- and lowercases. See also *tricameral* and *unicameral*.

bitmap A matrix of dots or pixels making up a graphic display.

bitmap font A font which is made up of pixels. Bitmap fonts are usually used in combination with outline fonts; the bitmap is viewed on-screen, while the corresponding outline font is used in a printer. In cases where fonts are intended for screen use only, bitmap fonts may be used without accompanying outline fonts. Also known as a *screen font*.

Blackletter The typographical counterpart to Gothic in architecture, this typically heavy, often ornate style of letterform was the first metal type in Europe. The earliest of these types were found in the Gutenberg workshop, copied from characters in handwritten manuscripts. *Bastarda, Fraktur, Quadrata, Rotunda,* and *Textura* are all categories of Blackletter. Also known as *Old English*.

block quotation A quotation set apart from the body of text, often set in a different size or face from the main text.

body size The point size, or height, of a face, measured from ascender to descender and including a set surrounding space. In letterpress terminology, body size signified the height of the face of the physical metal block on which a character was cast. In contemporary digital typography, this is the height of its imaginary equivalent—not the dimension of the character, but the rectangle defining the entire space owned by the letterform.

bolded Not to be confused with a boldface typeface drawn from scratch, this generally refers to thickening letterforms using a computer program's automatic bolding capabilities.

boldface (1) A typeface drawn with thicker strokes to achieve a heavier appearance. (2) To draw or digitally make letterforms darker or thicker for emphasis.

Bookface See *text face*.

border A continuous rule or decorative graphic element enclosing the body of material on a printed page or on screen.

bowl The round or elliptical form of the body shape of certain characters. Examples include **C, O, c**, and **e**. Also referred to as the *eye*.

bracket The curved or round joint, or wedge, between the stem and the serif of a letterform.

calligraphic In typography, this typically refers to roman or italic alphabets that appear to have been drawn with a pen or brush. The term is derived from the Greek *kalligraphia*, meaning "beautiful writing."

cap height The distance from the baseline to the cap line of an alphabet; the approximate height of an uppercase letter. Lowercase ascenders often extend beyond the cap height.

cap line, capital line An imaginary line running across the uppermost point of capital letters.

capitals, caps See *uppercase*.

centered Text set at an equal distance from the right and left margins.

Chancery A class of italic letterform, often typified by lengthened or curved extenders.

character A symbol in writing and typography. Characters include letters, numerals, punctuation marks, and other figures.

character encoding This maps character codes to a font's glyphs. Character encoding is not standardized across platforms or operating systems.

character map See *keyboard layout*.

character set The group of characters—typically alphanumerics, punctuation, and symbols—that make up a single font.

chromatic type Font created in two or more pieces and meant to be inked in multiple colors and printed in register.

cicero Part of the European System, the cicero is a unit of measure equaling 12 Didot points. The European counterpart to the British/American pica, the cicero is slightly larger than the pica. See also *Didot* and *European System*.

colophon (1) A symbol used in book printing to represent a publisher or publisher's imprint. (2) Information on a book's title, printer, publisher, and publication date, typically displayed at the end of a book. Colophons often offer details on the typefaces, type designers, or typographers associated with the production of a printed piece. The tradition has migrated to the digital arena, with colophons sometimes included on websites and in other forms of digital media.

color Also known as typographic color. The appearance of darkness in set type. Letterspacing, word spacing, leading, stroke weight, ink, paper color, and other factors contribute to the blackness of typeset text.

compressed A narrower version of a typeface, usually for display text, designed with the intention of fitting more characters into a given measure.

condensed A narrower version of a typeface, usually for body text, designed with the intention of fitting more characters into a given measure.

contour data The complex data used by a computer processor in the mathematical formula responsible for generating Bézier curves and curvilinear data.

contrast The degree of difference between the thick and thin strokes of a letterform. Helvetica is an example of a face with no contrast, while Bodoni is a high-contrast design.

copyfitting The technique of adjusting type size and spacing so that it fits within a defined space.

Copperplate A style of formal handwriting prevalent in the nineteenth century. Also referred to as *Round Hand*.

counter The interior white space enclosed by a letterform. **D** and **O** are examples of characters with wholly enclosed counters, while the counters in **c** and **m** are only partially enclosed.

crossbar See *cross-stroke*.

cross-stroke A horizontal stroke connecting two stems, as in **A** and **H**, or the projecting stroke of a letter cutting horizontally across the stem, as in **f** and **t**. Also known as the *crossbar* or *bar*.

Cursive Dating from the sixteenth century, Cursive typefaces imitate the flowing style of handwriting. Both Script and Cursive faces give the appearance of being drawn with pen and ink. Script types are typically joined, while Cursives generally are not. Commonly used as a synonym for "italic."

descender That part of a lowercase letter which extends below the baseline. Examples include **j, q**, and **y**.

descender line The imaginary horizontal line marking the lowermost point of a descender.

descent A character's maximum distance below the baseline.

diacritic A mark over, under, or through a character, added to give it a different phonetic value, or to differentiate between words that are visually identical. Examples of diacritics include the umlaut, cedilla, and tilde. Also known as an *accent*.

Didone See *Modern Serif*.

Didot A standard unit of measure in European typography, the Didot point is slightly larger than the American point. See also *European System*.

dingbats Historically called printer's flowers, dingbats are typically small decorative elements, bullets, or other symbols. In contemporary typography, dingbat fonts have expanded to encompass a diverse range of imagery, from detailed illustrations of buildings, animals, and insects to abstract sketches of the human face. Sometimes referred to as picture fonts, image fonts, or icon fonts.

diphthong Two vowels joined to create a single character, such as Æ, Œ, æ, and œ. Diphthongs are also considered ligatures.

display face A larger or bolder version of a text face, specifically cut for use in setting headlines. Also used to describe decorative type not suited for body copy.

dots per inch (DPI) The standard measure of the resolution of a video monitor or output device.

double story Usually refers to a lowercase **a** or **g** with a closed tail or curved finial.

DPI See *dots per inch*.

drop cap An oversized capital letter or versal set at the beginning of a paragraph; a drop cap occupies two or more lines of text.

ear The stroke attached to the bowl of a **g**.

Egyptian A typeface style with slab or square serifs and nearly uniform strokes (a low-contrast face). Examples of Egyptian types include Clarendon and Rockwell.

elevated cap An oversized capital letter or versal set on the same baseline as the first line in a text.

em A relative unit of measurement equal to the square of the type size. Historically, the em is the width of a typeface's widest letterform, the capital **M**. In contemporary terminology, the em is defined as the current point size. For example, 12-point type will contain an em with a width of 12 points.

em dash The width of an em, this character is used to indicate missing content or a break in thought.

em space A space equal to the width of an em, often used for paragraph indents.

en A unit of measure equal to half the width of a typeface's point size. The en is traditionally half the width of an em. For example, 12-point type will contain an en with a width of 6 points.

en dash The width of an en, this character is used to indicate duration, or in compound adjectives.

en space A space equal to the width of an en, or half an em space.

European System A system introduced to regulate the measurement of type, proposed by the Fournier Press in 1737. In 1775, the Didot foundry endorsed the point system, currently in use in Europe. In the European System, 1 inch = 6 ciceros = 72 Didot points (approx.). For comparison, see *Anglo-American System*.

expanded A typeface with letterforms drawn or made wider digitally without adding to its weight.

expert set An expanded set of characters designed as a companion to a basic character set. Can be contained in one or more separate style-related fonts (mainly found in traditional PostScript or TrueType formats), or included in the comprehensive character set of an OpenType font. Expert sets may include *Old Style figures*, proportionally drawn small caps, swashes, ornaments, alternate characters, and many other features designed to enhance typographic works.

extended A typeface with letterforms that are expanded horizontally while retaining their original height.

Extended Binary Coded Decimal Interchange (EBCDIC) An eight-bit character code used in computing, typically in mainframes. EBCDIC encodes 256 alphanumerics and symbols into

assigned numbers for the purpose of electronic storage and communication. See *American Standard Code for Information Interchange* for comparison.

extenders The ascenders and descenders of letterforms.

eye A synonym for "bowl." If a character is said to have a large eye, it actually has a large x-height, while an open eye signifies a large aperture.

family The group of all the type sizes and styles of a given typeface: the complex character set of a font. The members of a type family are based on a common design, but may differ in width, weight, style, and/or other attributes. See also *typeface*.

finial A flourish or decoration found at the end of a main stroke in some typefaces. See also *terminal*.

fleuron A typographical ornament usually shaped like a flower or leaf.

flourish A stroke added to a letterform for stylistic purposes.

flush left Text that is set flush, or justified, on the left margin. Also known as left justified or *ragged right*.

flush right Text that is set flush, or justified, on the right margin. Also known as right justified or *ragged left*.

font A set of characters in metal typesetting, a font (or fount) consists of an alphabet and its companion characters in a given size. In this context, 48-point Futura Bold Condensed is a font. In digital typography, a font represents the character set itself, or the digital information encoding it. In modern terminology, font, face, and typeface are often used interchangeably. See also *fount*.

font family See *family*.

font metrics See *Adobe Font Metrics, metrics*.

foundry See *type foundry*.

fount Alternative spelling of the term *font*. Pronunciation is the same.

Fraktur A class of Blackletter types with roots in the Middle Ages. The term Fraktur is derived from the Latin for *broken* or *fractured*.

Garalde See *Old Style*.

Geometric A class of Sans Serif influenced by the Bauhaus movement. Futura and ITC Bauhaus are examples of the Geometric style.

glyph Usually defined as a shape in a font that represents a character code for output on screen or on paper. The most common form of a glyph is a letter; however, the non-alphanumeric symbols and shapes in a font are also glyphs.

Gothic See *Grotesk*.

Grotesk/Grotesque A class of Sans Serif typefaces. Early designs and revivals of nineteenth-century faces are also referred to as Gothic types. Akzidenz-Grotesk and Trade Gothic are examples of Grotesk/Gothic styles.

Humanist A class of Sans Serif types based on Humanist Roman faces. Examples include Frutiger and Gill Sans.

Gutenberg In 1450, Johannes Gutenberg invented a printing press and introduced the concept of movable type to Europe. In 1455, Gutenberg's Latin 42-line Bible became the first European book to be produced using movable metal type.

hairline The thinnest stroke used in defining letterforms.

half-serif terminal The terminal ending of a serif with one side suppressed. See also *terminal*.

headline font See *display face*.

hints Mathematical instructions added to digital forms to enhance their appearance at all sizes and on display devices with different resolutions.

initial caps Oversized and often ornamental, initial caps are sometimes used at the beginning of paragraphs or chapters.

inline A character in which the inner portions of the main strokes have been carved out, while leaving the edges intact. Goudy Handtooled is an example of an inline face.

italic First developed in the fifteenth century, italics are more cursive than roman letterforms, and are usually designed to slant to the right. The first italic type was designed by Aldus Manutius in 1501 and was based on the elegant handwriting styles of that era. The term "italic" refers to this style's Italian origin.

italicize To set type in an italic font.

justified Referring to text or graphic elements that are aligned at both the left and right margins.

kern In traditional metal typesetting the part of one letter that extends into the space of another character. In contemporary usage, kern is a verb used to indicate the addition or subtraction of space between character pairs. See also *kerning*.

kerning The adjustment of white space between character pairs to improve appearance and legibility.

keyboard layout A table used by a computer operating system to control the character codes generated when a key or key combination is pressed. Also known as keyboard map or character map.

keyboard map See *keyboard layout*.

lachrymal terminal See *teardrop terminal*.

leading Pronounced led-ding. The vertical distance from baseline to baseline. Named for the lead spacers used between lines of text in letterpress printing. Also called lead.

left justified See *flush left*, *ragged right*.

letterspacing Adjusting the space between letters in a block of text. Kerning allows for the adjustment of space between particular character pairs; letterspacing is applied to text as a whole. Also referred to as tracking.

ligated A typeface with connections between letterforms. Scripts such as Cezanne and ITC Edwardian Script are examples of ligated designs. Letter combinations such as fi and ſt may also be ligated in non-connecting typefaces.

ligature Two or more letters connected to create a single character. Examples include fi and fl and diphthongs such as Œ and Æ. Also known as *tied letters*.

line spacing See *leading*.

lines per inch (LPI) A measure of the frequency of a halftone screen.

lining figures Numerals of even height; however, some lining figures may be smaller and lighter than the uppercase in a typeface. Also called Modern figures or titling figures.

lowercase Originally called *minuscules*, these are the small letters of a typeface. Minuscules were traditionally stored in the lower section of a printer's typecase, and it eventually became common practice to use this term to describe these characters.

LPI See *lines per inch*.

majuscules See *uppercase*.

matrix The metal mold from which type is cast.

mean line The imaginary horizontal line marking the top of the lowercase letters, excluding ascenders. See also *x-height*.

measure The standard length of a line of text. Also referred to as column width.

metal type Type cast from hot metal, with each individual character sitting on its own block. In the hot metal era, the term *font* described a single style, weight, and size of a given typeface design. In historic letterpress printing, metal type was composed by hand into forms, which were then mounted on a press for inking and impressions on paper.

metrics Font information such as *kerning*, character widths, and *leading*. See also *Adobe Font Metrics*.

minuscules See *lowercase*.

Modern figures See *lining figures*.

Modern Serif A modified version of *Old Style* serif types, Modern Serifs retain some of the characteristics of engraving. These high-contrast letterforms were originally developed by Firmin Didot and Giambattista Bodoni from the late eighteenth to the early nineteenth centuries. Bodoni and Walbaum are examples of the Modern style, and are also called *Didones*.

Modified Sans Serif Typefaces in this class are Sans Serif, but feature tiny or partial serifs for the sake of legibility. Rotis SemiSans is an example of this class.

monospaced type A typeface in which all the characters are of the same set-width. Based on the principle of traditional typewriter text, monospaced type allows for easy alignment of text and figures.

Neo-Grotesque A class of Sans Serif typefaces. Examples include the classic Swiss designs Univers and Helvetica.

oblique A slanted version of a typeface. Oblique types are similar to italic designs in feel, but do not have the same elegant, script-like quality of the true italics.

Old Style Originating from the Renaissance and fifteenth-century Venetian printers, Old Style types were based on pen-drawn forms. Garalde and Venetian are the two groups that make up the Old Style class. Bembo, Garamond, and Sabon are examples of Old Style designs.

Old Style figures (OSF) Numerals designed to match the lowercase letters in size and typographic color. Most Old Style figures consist of both ascending and descending forms. Also called text figures.

OpenType Developed jointly by Adobe and Microsoft, OpenType is a universal computer font format designed to enable a single font format to be used across platforms. OpenType allows for an almost limitless number of glyphs and conditional letter combinations with easier access to full expert-set characters, facilitating multilingual and advanced typography.

optical character recognition (OCR) The electronic or mechanical translation of images of handwritten, typed, or printed text into machine-editable text.

ornaments See *dingbats*, *fleurons*.

OSF See *Old Style figures*.

outline font A computer file containing the outline or vector information of a typeface; its set of character shapes are mathematically described by lines and curves. These scalable fonts are typically made up of Bézier curves (PostScript) and quadratic splines (TrueType). Also referred to as a printer font.

phototypesetting A now-obsolete method of setting type using a photographic process to generate columns of type on photographic paper. A phototypesetting machine projected light through a film-negative image of a character in a font. A lens was used to magnify or reduce the size of the character for its imaging onto film, which was then collected in a light-tight canister. The exposed film was then fed into a processor containing one or more chemical baths. Also referred to as cold type, phototypesetting dates back to the 1940s, but was popularized in the 1970s when it replaced metal typesetting.

Pi font A font consisting of mathematical or other symbols, intended for use in conjunction with a text font.

pica Part of the Anglo-American System, the pica is a unit of measure equaling 12 points. The British/American counterpart to the European *cicero*, the pica is slightly smaller than the cicero. See also *Anglo-American System* and *European System*.

pixels (PICture ELements) Square dots representing the smallest units displayed on screen. Pixels can be assigned their own color and intensity. The higher the number of pixels per inch, the finer the resultant screen resolution.

point A standard unit of measure in British/American typography, the point is slightly smaller than the European *Didot* point. See also *Anglo-American System* and *European System*.

point size A font's size is specified in units called points, and is typically the height of the type's body. This standard type measurement system was developed by Pierre Fournier le Jeune in 1737. See also *Anglo-American System* and *European System*.

PostScript A page-description language developed by Adobe Systems. PostScript describes a page using complex mathematical formulas. Characters and images are defined as outline shapes, and rendered by an output device as a series of tiny dots.

printer font See *outline font*.

proportionally spaced type Type designs with character widths varying depending on the features of the individual letterforms.

punchcutting The art of cutting letters into hard steel; the letters are then punched into softer brass matrices, from which lead type is cast.

punctuation Standardized non-alphanumeric characters used to clarify meaning through organizing writing into clauses, phrases, and sentences.

Quadrata A class of Blackletter types.

ragged left Text that is set flush, or justified, on the right margin. Also known as right justified or *flush right*.

ragged right Text that is set flush, or justified, on the left margin. Also known as left justified or *flush left*.

raised cap See *elevated cap*.

rasterization The conversion of a digitized image into a format that can be rendered on screen, or printed from an output device.

reference mark A symbol used in text to point to a footnote or other relevant piece of information.

relative unit A fractional unit of an em space, proportional to the type size.

rendering The placement of rasterized pixels on screen. Also referred to as *screen rasterization*.

resolution (1) The measurement of image sharpness and clarity on screen, typically measured in pixels per inch. (2) The sharpness and clarity of text and graphics imaged on an output device; normally measured in dots per inch.

reversing Setting white or light-colored text against a black or dark background.

right justified See *flush right, ragged left*.

roman (1) Refers to an upright, regular weight of a typeface. (2) capitalized: *Old Style* or Modern designs. The classical Roman letter style was conceived around AD 114 and was typified by the letterforms chiseled into Trajan's Column in Rome.

Rotunda A class of Blackletter types. Also known as Rotonda.

Round Hand Types with broad, rounded letters, modeled after the handwriting style of the same name. See also *Copperplate*.

run-in quotation A quotation, typically enclosed in quotation marks, indented in the main body of text.

Sans Serif From the Latin, meaning "without serifs." Faces designed without serifs are also referred to as in the Lineale style. Categories of Sans Serif types include Grotesk/Grotesque/Gothic, Geometric, Neo-Grotesque, and Humanist. Also known as unserifed.

scalable font Describes the fonts generated by a computer's mathematical algorithm, which allows the size to be varied proportionally on the fly while retaining the integrity of the design.

screen font See *bitmap font*.

Script Script letters are typically joined. The earliest script types were modeled on formal cursive handwriting in the sixteenth century. Classes of Script fonts include Casual, Calligraphic, Blackletter and Lombardic, and Formal styles.

Serif (1) A small finishing stroke drawn diagonally or horizontally across the arm, stem, and tail of letterforms. (2) The term, often capitalized, is used to describe a class of typefaces drawn with serifs. Major categories in the Serif class include Old Style/Old Face, Transitional (Réale), Modern (Didone), and Slab/Square/Egyptian styles.

set-width The actual width of a character and its surrounding space, or the amount of space needed to set a line of text in a particular typeface. Also known as advance width.

side bearing The space between the origin of a character and its leftmost point (the left side bearing), or the space between the rightmost point and width line (right side bearing).

Slab Serif A class of Serif types with square-ended serifs. Examples include Clarendon and Rockwell. Also known as Square Serif or Egyptian.

slanted See *oblique*.

slope The angle of inclination of the ascenders, descenders, and stems of letterforms.

small cap figures A set of numerals designed for use with the small cap alphabet of a given typeface.

small caps An alternate alphabet of capital letters that are approximately the same height as the *x-height* of a typeface. Small caps are common in *Roman* types. Although many graphics applications can generate faux small caps, true small caps are correctly drawn with regard to proportion and weights, and are usually found in PostScript and TrueType expert sets or in some OpenType fonts.

spacing The space, or the way space is arranged, between characters, words, and lines of type.

spur A type of finishing stroke found on some letterforms in certain typefaces, such as **G** and **b**.

Square Serif See *Slab Serif*.

stem The main vertical stroke or the main oblique stroke of a character. **L** and **V** are examples of letterforms with stems. An **O** has no stem, while the letter **l** is made up of a stem and serifs only.

stress The emphasis on the stroke of a letter; typically vertical, stresses may also be horizontal or diagonal.

stroke The main line or curve that makes up a character.

style The variations of a given typeface. A wide range of variants are available to type designers, including bold, condensed, italic, extended, oblique, roman, and many others.

swash capitals Uppercase letters that take up extra space or contain added flourishes. Swash caps are usually cursive, and are generally designed to complement italic types.

tabular figures Numerals designed with a uniform set-width, intended for aligning tabular data.

tail A character's downward projection, such as that found in the letter **Q**, or the short diagonal stroke that rests on the baseline in letters such as **K** and **R**.

teardrop terminal A teardrop-shaped swelling at the end of the arm in characters such as **a**, **c**, **f**, and **y**, often given decorative treatment. Typically used in typefaces from the late Renaissance, baroque, and neoclassical periods, examples of which include Caslon and Baskerville.

terminal The free-hanging stroke of letters such as **a**, **c**, **f**, and **y**, often given decorative treatment. See also *ball terminal, beak terminal, half-serif terminal, teardrop terminal*, and *finial*.

text face Typefaces specifically designed for readability, text faces are typically Serif types set between 9 and 12 points. Times and Goudy Old Style are examples of classic text faces.

text figures See *Old Style figures*.

Textura A class of Blackletter types.

thick space A unit of measurement equaling one-third of an em.

thin space A unit of measurement equaling one-fifth of an em.

tied letters See *ligated* and *ligature*.

tracking See *letterspacing*.

Transitional Serif A class of Serif types introduced in the late eighteenth century by John Baskerville combining features from both *Old Style* and *Modern* faces. Baskerville and Times are examples of Transitional Serifs. Also known as Réale or Realist.

tricameral An alphabet with three forms. A typical roman font can be considered tricameral, having an uppercase, a lowercase, and small caps. See also *bicameral* and *unicameral*.

TrueType An outline font format developed by Apple Computer in the late 1980s for its operating system, designed to compete with Adobe's then-closed PostScript Type 1 font format. TrueType was eventually adopted by Microsoft Corporation for use with Windows and became the font format of choice on that OS. TrueType fonts can be used for both screen display and printing, eliminating the need for separate screen and printer fonts.

type foundry A foundry is a place where metal is cast. Historically, a type foundry was a place for the manufacture of metal type. A type founder may have designed type, cut punches, made matrices, and cast metal type. Eventually, each of these operations became separate crafts performed by specialists. Although punchcutting and the casting of metal type may no longer be involved, in modern terminology, a designer or company that creates and/or distributes digital typefaces is often called a type foundry.

typeface Sometimes named after its designer, a typeface is a collection of all the characters of a single design, regardless of style or size. A typeface typically consists of letters and figures (the alphanumerics), punctuation, and commonly used accents and symbols.

typographic color See *color*.

typography The study and process of producing typefaces, and how to select, arrange, and use type in general. Traditionally, typography referred to the use of metal types used in letterpress. In modern terminology, typography includes the arrangement of type on screen and in printed output.

u&lc Denotes upper- and lowercase. This is the traditional form for setting text in the bicameral Latin, Greek, and Cyrillic alphabets.

uncial A calligraphic typestyle with large rounded letterforms combining elements of both upper- and lowercase letters. The term is derived from the Latin *uncus*, or *crooked*.

unicameral An alphabet having only one case, such as the Hebrew alphabet and some Roman titling faces. See also *bicameral* and *tricameral*.

uppercase Originally called *majuscules*, these are the large letters of a typeface. Majuscules were traditionally stored in the upper section of a printer's typecase, and it eventually became common practice to use this term to describe these characters. Also referred to as *caps* or *capitals*.

upright Standing vertically or straight upward; in typography, the term typically refers to a roman face or regular Sans Serif type.

Venetian See *Old Style*.

versal A large initial cap which is typically elevated or dropped in text.

vertex Where the stems of a character meet at its lowest joint.

weight The darkness or blackness of a typeface, not relating to its size; the measurement of a stroke's width. There are many weight variants available, including thin, light, demibold, and ultrabold. Many typeface families, especially in the text range, have multiple weights.

white space The blank sections of a page where text and graphics are not printed.

Whiteletter The typographical counterpart to Romanesque in architecture, Whiteletter describes the light roman and italic letterforms typically favored by scribes and typographers in fifteenth- and sixteenth-century Italy. Compare with the generally darker Blackletter styles in use in Northern Europe at the time.

wood type A form of type used in printing and popularized during the nineteenth century. The use of wood as a material for letterforms and illustrations dates back to the first known Chinese woodblock print from the ninth century. Darius Wells introduced the means for mass-producing wood type letters circa 1827. This was an important development, as wood letters could be cost-effectively cut at extremely large point sizes, whereas it was largely impractical to cast fonts of oversized display type in heavy metal.

word spacing In a line of text, the amount of space between words. When type is set unjustified, the word space is typically of a fixed size. When setting justified text, the word space must fluctuate, enabling the text to align at both margins.

x-height The distance between the baseline and the midline of an alphabet, approximately the height of the lowercase **x**. The measurement is based on the **x** because typically, it rests squarely on the baseline and has no ascenders or descenders.

CONTRIBUTORS

Contributing Type Foundries

Adobe Systems Inc.
345 Park Avenue
San Jose, California 95110-2704 USA
www.adobe.com

Bauer Types, SL (Neufville Digital)
C/ Dr. Ferran 6-8 Entlo 2°A
08034 Barcelona, Spain
www.bauertypes.com

The H. Berthold Foundry
Berthold Types Limited
47 West Polk Street #100-340
Chicago, Illinois 60605 USA
www.bertholdtypes.com

Bitstream Inc.
245 First Street, 17th Floor
Cambridge, Massachusetts 02142 USA
www.bitstream.com

Elsner+Flake
Winterstraße 4
22765 Hamburg, Germany
www.elsner-flake.com

The Font Bureau, Inc.
50 Melcher Street
Suite #2
Boston, Massachusetts 02210 USA
www.fontbureau.com

FSI FontShop International GmbH (FontFont)
Bergmannstraße 102
10961 Berlin, Germany
www.fontshop.com

International Typeface Corporation (ITC)
500 Unicorn Park Drive
Woburn, Massachusetts 01801 USA
www.itcfonts.com

Linotype GmbH
Werner-Reimers-Straße 2-4
61352 Bad Homburg, Germany
www.linotype.com

Monotype Imaging
500 Unicorn Park Drive
Woburn, Massachusetts 01801 USA
www.monotypeimaging.com

P22 type foundry
PO Box 770
Buffalo, New York 14213 USA
www.p22.com

URW ++
Poppenbütteler Bogen 36
D-22399 Hamburg, Germany
www.urw.de

Visualogik Technology & Design (Neufville Digital)
Kerkpad 16A
NL-4818 PK Breda, the Netherlands
www.visualogik.com

Submitting Designers and Studios

160over90
Philadelphia, Pennsylvania, USA
www.160over90.com

Ryan Adair
Brooklyn, New York, USA
www.theryanadair.com
also with **Mattias Mackler**
www.mattiasmackler.com

Brent Barson
Springville, Utah, USA
www.brentbarson.com

Marianne Beck (missbeck)
Paris, France
www.missbeck.com

Ben the Illustrator
Helston, Cornwall, England
www.bentheillustrator.com

Chris Bolton
Helsinki, Finland
www.chrisbolton.org

Bradbury Branding & Design
Regina, Saskatchewan, Canada
www.bradburydesign.com

Braley Design
Brooklyn, New York, USA
www.braleydesign.com

Roy Burns (TEN)
Birmingham, Alabama, USA
www.tenonefive.com

Susanne Cerha (Silo Design Inc.)
Brooklyn, New York, USA
www.silo-design.com
also with **JRVisuals LLC**
Buffalo, New York, USA
www.jrvisuals.com

Aurore Chassé
Lyon, France
aurorechasse.free.fr

Chen Design Associates
San Francisco, California, USA
www.chendesign.com

Jack Chung
Alameda, California, USA

Nancy Sharon Collins, Stationer
Covington, Louisiana, USA
www.nancysharoncollinsstationer.com

Ricardo Córdoba
Brooklyn, New York, USA
www.coroflot.com/halftone_dots

Jacob Covey (Unflown Dsn)
Seattle, Washington, USA
www.unflown.com

Crave, Inc.
Boca Raton, Florida, USA
www.cravebrands.com

Nils Davey (Jawa and Midwich)
London, England
www.jawa-midwich.com

desres design studio
Frankfurt am Main, Germany
www.desres.de

DHNN (Design has No Name)
Buenos Aires, Argentina
www.dhnn.com.ar

DISTINC
Los Angeles, California, USA
www.distinc.net

Jeanine Donofrio (Emblem)
Austin, Texas, USA
www.emblemcreative.com

Simon Dovar (Jawa and Midwich)
London, England
www.jawa-midwich.com

David Drummond (Salamander Hill Design)
Elgin, Quebec, Canada
www.salamanderhill.com

Ben van Dyke
Buffalo, New York, USA
www.benjaminvandyke.com

Elapse
Brooklyn, New York, USA
www.elapse.se

elbow
San Francisco, California, USA
www.elbow.com

Elizabeth Resnick Design
Chestnut Hill, Massachusetts, USA

End Communications
Chicago, Illinois, USA
www.endcommunications.com

Germans Ermičs (Design Academy Eindhoven)
Eindhoven, the Netherlands

Estudio Wonksite
Bogotá, Colombia
www.wonksite.com

Evenson Design Group
Culver City, California, USA
www.evensondesign.com

Ferroconcrete
Los Angeles, California, USA
www.ferro-concrete.com

Martin Fewell (Yolo)
Manchester, England
www.yolo.info

Jessica Fleischmann (still room)
Los Angeles, California, USA
www.still-room.com

From Keetra
New York, New York, USA
www.fromkeetra.com

Alisha Fund (Academy of Art University)
San Francisco, California, USA
www.academyart.edu

Mara Garcia
Alameda, California, USA

Glossy.tv
Ghent, Belgium
www.glossy.tv

James Grieshaber (Typeco)
Chicago, Illinois, USA
www.typeco.com

groovisions
Tokyo, Japan
www.groovisions.com

Florent Guerlain
Paris, France
www.zukunft.fr

HADDEN 3
Draper, Utah, USA
www.hadden3.com

Joey Hannaford (Hannaford Design)
Atlanta, Georgia, USA
www.joeyhannaford.com

Florian Hardwig
Berlin, Germany
kaune.hardwig.com

Helena Seo Design
San Jose, California, USA
www.helenaseo.com

Hero Design Studio
Buffalo, New York, USA
www.heroandsound.com

**José Ignacio Zárate Huizar
(huizar 1984)**
Oaxaca de Juárez, Mexico
www.huizar1984.com

**Claire Hyde
(University of West Georgia)**
Carrollton, Georgia, USA
www.westga.edu/~artdept

Jeff Fisher LogoMotives
Portland, Oregon, USA
www.jfisherlogomotives.com

Bart Kiggen
Antwerp, Belgium
www.kiggen.be

Sarah King
London, England
www.sarahaking.com

**Justin Knopp
(TYPORETUM)**
Colchester, England
www.typoretum.co.uk

konnectDesign
Santa Monica, California, USA
www.konnectdesign.com

**Tom Lane
(Ginger Monkey)**
Bristol, England
www.gingermonkeydesign.com

Lippincott
New York, New York, USA
www.lippincott.com

**Jonathan Lo
(SHoP Architects)**
New York, New York, USA
www.shoparc.com

**Chris Lozos
(Dezcom)**
Falls Church, Virginia, USA
www.dezcom.com

**Andrew and Matt McCracken
(Doublenaut)**
Toronto, Ontario, Canada
www.doublenaut.com

MacFadden & Thorpe
San Francisco, California, USA
www.macfaddenandthorpe.com

Shaz Madani
London, England
www.smadani.com

Sam Mallett
Cardiff, Wales
www.sammallett.com

Ana Sofia Mariz
Rio de Janeiro, Brazil
www.anasofia.net

Mark Simonson Studio
St. Paul, Minnesota, USA
www.marksimonson.com

Michael Renaud Design
Chicago, Illinois, USA
www.michaelrenaud.com

Rune Mortenson
Oslo, Norway
www.runemortensen.no

**Joachim Müller-Lancé
(Kame Design)**
San Francisco, California, USA
www.kamedesign.com

**Jason Munn
(The Small Stakes)**
Oakland, California, USA
www.thesmallstakes.com

Neue Design Studio
Oslo, Norway
www.neue.no

**Sébastien Nikolaou
(sebdesign.eu)**
Athens, Greece
www.sebdesign.eu

**Jérémie Nuel
(atelier aquarium)**
Lyon, France
www.atelieraquarium.com

Timothy O'Donnell
Bloomfield, New Jersey, USA
www.timothy-odonnell.com
also with **v23**
London, England
www.v23.biz

P22
Buffalo, New York, USA
www.p22:com

**Tom Pappalardo
(Standard Design)**
Northampton, Massachusetts, USA
www.standard-design.com

Nicolas Portnoï
Paris, France
www.nicolasportnoi.fr

Nicolas Queffélec
Pantin, France
www.queffelec.fr
also with **Malte MartinNicolas**
www.atelier-malte-martin.net

**Robynne Raye
(Modern Dog Design Co.)**
Seattle, Washington, USA
www.moderndog.com

**Simon Renaud
(atelier aquarium)**
Lyon, France
www.atelieraquarium.com

**Chris Ro
(ADearFriend)**
New York, New York, USA
www.adearfriend.com

**Ashley Saleeba
(University of Washington Press)**
Seattle, Washington, USA
u.washington.edu

Sarah Rainwater Design
Providence, Rhode Island, USA
www.srainwater.com

Sarah Ridgley Letterpress
Fort Smith, Arkansas, USA
www.sarahridgley.com

**Lindsey Selden
(Academy of Art University)**
San Francisco, California, USA
www.academyart.edu

**Michael Strassburger
(Modern Dog Design Co.)**
Seattle, Washington, USA
www.moderndog.com

**A. Micah Smith
(My Associate Cornelius)**
Gardner, Kansas, USA
www.kamedesign.com

strawberryluna
Pittsburgh, Pennsylvania, USA
www.strawberryluna.com

Studio Chris Allen
Vancouver, British Columbia, Canada
www.christopherallen.ca

Studio Lisa Maione
Brooklyn, New York, USA
www.lisamaione.com

StudioMakgill
Brighton, England
www.studiomakgill.com

Peter Sunna
Brooklyn, New York, USA
www.petersunna.com
also with **JDK Design**
Burlington, Vermont, USA
www.jdk.com

Think Studio
New York, New York, USA
www.thinkstudionyc.com

Natalia Tomaszewska
Sunnyside, New York, USA

toormix
Barcelona, Spain
www.toormix.com

Turnstyle
Seattle, Washington, USA
www.turnstylestudio.com

Robin Uleman
Amsterdam, the Netherlands
www.robinuleman.nl

Olivier Umecker
Lyon, France
graphistetypographe.free.fr

**Craig Ward
(Words are Pictures)**
London, England
www.wordsarepictures.co.uk

Stefan Weyer
Trier, Germany
www.stefan-weyer.com

**Søren Wibroe
(Design Academy Eindhoven)**
Eindhoven, the Netherlands

Samantha Wiley
Brooklyn, New York, USA
www.samwileydesign.com
also with **Cannonball
Advertising and Productions**
St. Louis, Missouri, USA
www.cannonballagency.com

**Chuck Williams
(Seedoubleyou Design)**
South Ogden, Utah, USA
www.design-cw.com

**Randy Yeo
(SMEEK)**
Singapore
www.smeek.net

REFERENCES

Bibliography

Agfa Typography
Type Reference Book for Postscript Users
Dublin: Agfa Typography, Ltd., 1994

Altsys Corporation
Type Terminology on the Desktop
Richardson, Texas: Altsys Corporation, 1991

Bringhurst, Robert
The Elements of Typographic Style
3rd edition
Point Roberts, Washington: Hartley & Marks, 2004

Kegler, Richard, James Grieshaber, and Tamye Riggs, eds.
Indie Fonts
Buffalo, New York: P-Type Publications, 2002

Lawson, Alexander
Anatomy of a Typeface
London: Hamish Hamilton, 1992

Nesbitt, Alexander
The History and Technique of Lettering
revised 1st edition
New York: Dover Publications, Inc., 1957

Romano, Frank J., and Richard M. Romano
The GATF Encyclopedia of Graphic Communications
Pittsburgh: Graphic Arts Technical Foundation Press, 1998

Ruffa, Gregory
The Art of Wood Type
Plainfield, New Jersey: GRA Publishing, LLC, 2008

Spiekermann, Erik, and E. M. Ginger
Stop Stealing Sheep and Find Out How Type Works
1st edition
Mountain View, California: Adobe Press, 1993

Further Reading

Carter, Rob, and Phillip B. Meggs (contributor)
Typographic Specimens: The Great Typefaces
New York: John Wiley & Sons, 1993

Felici, James
The Complete Manual of Typography
Mountain View, California: Adobe Press, 2002

Gill, Eric
An Essay on Typography
Boston: David R. Godine, Publisher, 1993

Haley, Allen
Typographic Milestones
New York: John Wiley & Sons, 1997

Kegler, Richard, James Grieshaber, and Tamye Riggs, eds.
Indie Fonts 2
Buffalo, New York: P-Type Publications, 2002

Kegler, Richard, James Grieshaber, and Tamye Riggs, eds.
Indie Fonts 3
Beverly, Massachussetts: Rockport Publishers, 2007

McGrew, Mac
American Metal Typefaces of the Twentieth Century
2nd edition
New Castle, Delaware: Oak Knoll Press, 1993

McLean, Ruari
The Thames & Hudson Manual of Typography
reprint edition
London: Thames & Hudson, 1992

Stone, Sumner
On Stone: The Art & Use of Typography on the Personal Computer
San Francisco: Bedford Arts, 1991

Tschichold, Jan
The New Typography: A Handbook for Modern Designers
Berkeley, California: University of California Press, 1995

Organizations and Institutions

American Printing History Association (APHA)
www.printinghistory.org

Association Typographique Internationale (ATypI)
www.atypi.org

The Hamilton Wood Type Museum
www.woodtype.org

Museum of Printing
www.museumofprinting.org

Museum Plantin-Moretus
museum.antwerpen.be

St. Bride Library
www.stbride.org

The Society of Typographic Aficionados (SOTA)
www.typesociety.org

The Type Directors Club (TDC)
www.tdc.org

Typography Information Online

Identifont
www.identifont.com

Microsoft Typography
www.microsoft.com/typography

MyFonts and WhatTheFont
www.myfonts.com

Typographica
www.typographica.org

Typophile
www.typophile.com

CREDITS

INDEX

THE AUTHORS

Tamye Riggs is a writer, designer, editor, and event planner specializing in typography and the related arts. She is the executive director of The Society of Typographic Aficionados (SOTA), a volunteer-driven nonprofit organization which presents the TypeCon conference annually in North America.

Riggs studied journalism at the University of Oregon with the intent of becoming an investigative print journalist. An ever-increasing fascination with type led her into the graphic arts, and she embarked on a career in advertising and design in Dallas, Texas. Riggs later headed creative and management areas for Phil's Fonts/ GarageFonts near Washington, D.C., and FontShop San Francisco. Riggs now consults on a variety of projects for a number of type foundries and distributors.

She is co-editor of SOTA's *Interrobang* magazine and is a regular contributor to design publications such as *HOW*, *STEP Inside Design*, *Creative Pro*, *Font*, and *Computer Arts*. Riggs has edited six other books on type and design, including the three-volume Indie Fonts series. She lives and works on the island of Alameda just across the bay from San Francisco.

WWW.TYPELIFE.COM | WWW.TYPESOCIETY.ORG | WWW.TYPECON.COM

Contributing author James Grieshaber is a graduate of the graphic design program at New York's Rochester Institute of Technology (RIT). His early career was spent as an art director for advertising agencies and newspapers. In the late 1990s he joined the design staff at P22 type foundry in Buffalo, where he helped establish the company's International House of Fonts label. In 2001, Grieshaber opened his own type design studio, Typeco, to showcase his typographic vision and provide custom typographic services.

Grieshaber has been honored for his type design with awards from the Association Typographique International (ATypI), the Tokyo Type Directors Club, and Moscow's TypeArt'05 (for one of his Cyrillic faces). Grieshaber serves as chairman of the board of directors of SOTA, and lives and works in Chicago.

WWW.TYPECO.COM | WWW.TYPESOCIETY.ORG | WWW.TYPECON.COM

COLOPHON

When contemplating the primary typography for this book, the authors considered many possibilities. Since the book contains so many type specimens at different sizes, and hundreds of photos and illustrations, it was paramount to choose text faces that would blend harmoniously with the visual material. It was also essential that the text be highly legible and form a solid foundation to anchor the greatly varied content.

Staying true to the concept of the book, Riggs and Grieshaber opted for two well-executed updates of classic typeface designs. The serif seen throughout is Sabon Next, Parisian designer Jean François Porchez's modern revival of the Garamond model (released by Linotype in 2002). The sans is Linotype's Avenir Next, an expanded and refined version of the original 1988 masterwork by Swiss legend Adrian Frutiger. The Avenir update was a collaboration between Frutiger and Linotype Type Director Akira Kobayashi, and was published in 2004.

The OpenType Pro versions of both families were perfectly suited to extensive book typography, featuring multiple weights and styles as well as beautifully crafted small caps, ligatures, and diacritics. Although a clean, legible Geometric sans, Avenir Next carries the mark of Frutiger's hand, and mates companionably with the warm Old Style Garalde forms of Sabon Next.

Most of the body copy in this book was set in the regular and italic styles of Sabon Next. Heads, subtitles, labels, diagrams, and some of the back matter employ the standard widths of Avenir Next in several weights. For economy of space, captions were set using Avenir Next's condensed variants.